BOUNDARY REPRESENTATION IS NOT NECESSARILY AUTHORITATIVE
Panama and the Caribbean
U.S.
Miami
Atlantic Ocean
Gulf of Mexico
Nassau
The Bahamas
Havana
Cuba
Cienfuegos
Camagüey
Mérida
Mexico
Santiago de Cuba
Haiti
Dom. Rep.
San Juan
Jamaica
Port-au-Prince
Santo Domingo
Puerto Rico
Kingston
Belize City
Belmopan
Belize
Guat.
Guatemala
Honduras
Caribbean Sea
San Salvador
Tegucigalpa
El Salvador
Nicaragua
Managua
Netherlands Antilles
Maracaibo
Baranquilla
Caracas
Costa Rica
San José
Canal Zone
Panama
Panama
Venezuela
Pacific Ocean
Colombia
Bogotá
0 250 500 Miles
0 250 500 Kilometers
Brazil
Ecuador

503790 5-78

The Fractured Continent

President Dwight D. Eisenhower visits Argentina (February 1960). *From left to right:* the president; Argentine President Arturo Frondizi; the author, Willard L. Beaulac (then US ambassador to Argentina); and an Argentine diplomat, Ambassador Carlos Leguizamón.

The Fractured Continent

LATIN AMERICA IN CLOSE-UP

Willard L. Beaulac

HOOVER INSTITUTION PRESS
Stanford University, Stanford, California

Illustrations Credits

Frontispiece is from United States Information Service.

Photographs 2, 3, 7, and 8 are from Inter-American Development Bank.

Photographs 5 and 10 are from United States Agency for International Development.

Photograph 6 is from United States Information Service.

Hoover Institution Publication 225

International Standard Book Number: 0–8179–7251–X
Library of Congress Catalog Card Number: 78–70885
Printed in the United States of America

Designed by Elizabeth Gehman

For
Caroll, Noel, Joanie, Ana, and Lee

Contents

PART IV LATIN AMERICA AND THE UNITED STATES

Preface

When the fledgling Carter administration decided to reduce or withhold economic and military assistance to foreign governments that it accused of violating human rights, it announced that it would exempt from such treatment countries that were strategically important to the United States. While many notorious rights violators thus went unpunished, sanctions were freely imposed on a number of friendly Latin American countries. The implication that those countries were not strategically important to the United States surprised many persons who were familiar with Latin America, and with good reason.

A critical international problem in the late 1970s derived from the near-monopoly that OPEC, the Organization of Petroleum Exporting Countries, had on the supply of petroleum to much of the free world. OPEC had succeeded in raising prices of the product by some 700 percent. Importing countries, including the United States, found themselves hard pressed to pay for the petroleum on which their economies and their societies had come to depend. Furthermore, OPEC members demonstrated an awesome ability to cut off petroleum supplies to any country, also including the United States. The organization brought about a dramatic redistribution of wealth and power within the free world. Venezuela, a Latin American country, was a principal architect of OPEC.

And recent discoveries indicate that Mexico, which is not a member of OPEC, has petroleum reserves that rival those of some leading OPEC countries. With the oil-producing countries of the Persian Gulf and North Africa vulnerable to Soviet influence and possibly to Soviet aggression, those reserves may become indispensable to the security and prosperity not only of the United States and other American republics, but also of the rest of the free world.

In 1962 three Latin American countries, Chile, Ecuador, and Peru, braving international censure and retaliation, extended the territorial waters over which they claimed jurisdiction to 200 miles from their coastlines. The United States and many other countries protested the change but most of them, again including the United States, decided to travel the same route. Control of the seas, protection and exploitation of the immense wealth of the seas, are among the most important subjects the nations of the world are now debating. Latin Americans have had an important role in promoting the debate and in helping to determine its directions.

The first and, it is to be hoped, the last nuclear confrontation in history occurred in 1962 after the United States discovered that Soviet Russia had placed nuclear missiles in Cuba, a Latin American country. In 1975 Cuban troops, using arms supplied by Russia, placed a Marxist faction in power in Angola, a strategically important country in southwest Africa. They have continued to maintain the faction in power. And Cuba, also in cooperation with Russia, has intervened in Ethiopia and other African countries. It supported the effort that overthrew Nicaragua's Somoza regime in 1979. Cuba, which was lost to freedom while the United States was obsessed with distant Viet Nam, has been a willing instrument of Soviet imperialism. Nor has Castro abandoned his designs in Latin America. On June 18, 1979, a day after President Carter had signed a strategic arms limitation treaty (SALT II) with Soviet president Leonid Brezhnev, he informed the US Congress that he had made clear to Brezhnev that the growing Cuban involvement in the problems of Central America and the Caribbean could only have a negative impact on US-Soviet relations.

In 1970 a Marxist was elected president of Chile with slightly more than one-third of the popular vote. He was the first Marxist to reach the presidency in free elections anywhere. After his government had engaged in gross violations of the civil rights of citizens and foreigners and had destroyed the country's economy, the military, with powerful civilian encouragement and support, overthrew it. Soviet Russia has never forgiven Chileans for their action. When Portugal's Communists were trying to seize power in 1975, Radio Moscow announced repeatedly, "A new slogan has been born in the broad movement of solidarity with the Portuguese democrats, a slogan that rings with grave concern: *Portugal must not be another Chile!*" Moscow's determination to make up for the defeat Marxism suffered in Chile remains strong.

Karl Marx said that religion was the opium of the people. More recently Raymond Aron has said that Marxism is the opium of the intellectuals. One might add that today it is also the opium of some churchmen. We have come full circle. The Church in Latin America remains anti-Marxist but many of the clergy, including some bishops and archbishops, have been making their peace with Marxism. Some have actually identified themselves with it. The possible gains for Marxism from such an association are clear.

Fidel Castro is undoubtedly the Latin American who is most widely known throughout the world, but Raúl Prebisch, an Argentine who is little known outside official and academic circles, may have influenced the world much more than Castro has, and more than most world leaders have. Prebisch, a modest, soft-spoken banker and economist, evolved an ideology that has prompted not only Latin America but the entire Third World to bring pressure to bear on the United States and other more-developed countries to share their wealth and their opportunities with the less-developed countries.

We all know about the Chinese sage who, when he was invited to prepare a code of laws for another country, said he would not think of drawing up laws for a people he did not know. We all know the story but we too often forget it.

The United States has frequently been charged with "neglecting" Latin America, and the charge is justified, but not in the terms it is usually made. Most persons who make the charge allege that we have not "done enough" for Latin America; in particular that we have not given it enough economic aid. What is more probable is that we have done too much for Latin America—in wrong ways.

The United States has carried out in Latin America the most massive program of economic aid ever extended by a country to any area of the world, but our aid has not achieved the results we and the Latin Americans hoped for. Under the Alliance for Progress we told people whom we did not know how to solve problems that we did not understand. We aroused expectations that could not be met. We accepted blame for failures that were not ours, and we never came to grips with our own failures. Meanwhile our relations with the Latin American countries deteriorated.

Deterioration of relations with Latin America was part of a larger phenomenon—the deterioration of United States diplomacy in general. As the new importance of foreign affairs was impressed not only upon government but also upon the mass of citizens, as relations with other countries became an increasingly important factor in national elections, diplomacy became more and more a continuation of domestic politics by other means. Increasingly, rhetoric and media exposure, gag men and gimmicks, became a part of diplomacy. When Richard Nixon received Russia's Chairman Brezhnev on the White House lawn he sounded, at times, less like an American president than another Bob Hope, while Brezhnev happily played the role of George Burns. President Carter received China's Vice Premier Teng Hsiao-ping with humor and effusion, and Americans saw Teng as a lovable Foxy grandpa with whom their government should cooperate closely.

Powerful tyrants with bloodied hands clearly find it useful, in certain circumstances, to be viewed as engaging comics or cuddly teddy bears, and it is conceivably useful to Americans, at times, for them to be viewed in that light. But while Teng was winning popularity in the United States more than one Latin American president, though striving against great odds to eliminate terrorism and establish a base for political and economic freedom in his country, was cast in the role of a bloody tyrant, and his people were deprived of United States cooperation that they sorely needed. So far as public approval and, frequently, official approval in the United States was concerned, the scales were heavily weighted against Latin America.

Latin America's interests and influence embrace the globe. For most of us, however, it remains a land of stereotypes. How can we replace stereotypes with reality, rhetoric with reason? What is this area which is so important to the United States and yet in so many ways is unfamiliar? Who are the Latin Americans? What are they really like? And what do they mean to the United States?

Acknowledgments

I wish to express appreciation to Southern Illinois University Press which has authorized me to borrow liberally from my earlier volume, *A Diplomat Looks at Aid to Latin America* (I have done this especially in Chapter 14). I have also had the cooperation of many Latin American friends and of officials of the Department of State. I am grateful to them. I am grateful, as well, to Dr. Bryce Wood; to my colleague at Southern Illinois University, Dr. Charles T. Goodsell; to Ambassadors Milton Barall and Harold M. Randall; and to my associates in the Foreign Service, Dr. Jacob Canter, Dr. Edward A. Jamison, and Joseph A. Silberstein, who combine long experience in Latin America with academic accomplishment. All those friends have given me valuable assistance. Responsibility for the final text is, of course, my own.

PHOTOGRAPHS

1. Secret city of the Incas: the cloud-capped ruins of Machu Picchu, Peru. Latin American governments are taking more interest than they used to in the Indian past, but most Indians continue to resist integration.

2. This new highway between Chile and Argentina cuts through mountains that, for many years, made the two neighbor countries less accessible to each other than to England, with which they traded by sea.

3. Wheat harvest on the Argentine *pampa*, one of the richest grain-growing areas in the world.

4. Six thousand feet above sea level, the Chuquicamata open-pit copper mine is the world's largest. It is situated in territory won by Chile from Bolivia during the War of the Pacific (1879–1883).

5. Brazil, a huge country with a promising future, still exhibits the extremes of wealth and poverty to be found in most of Latin America. Here, a *favela* (shanty town) overlooks the chic residential area of south Rio de Janeiro.

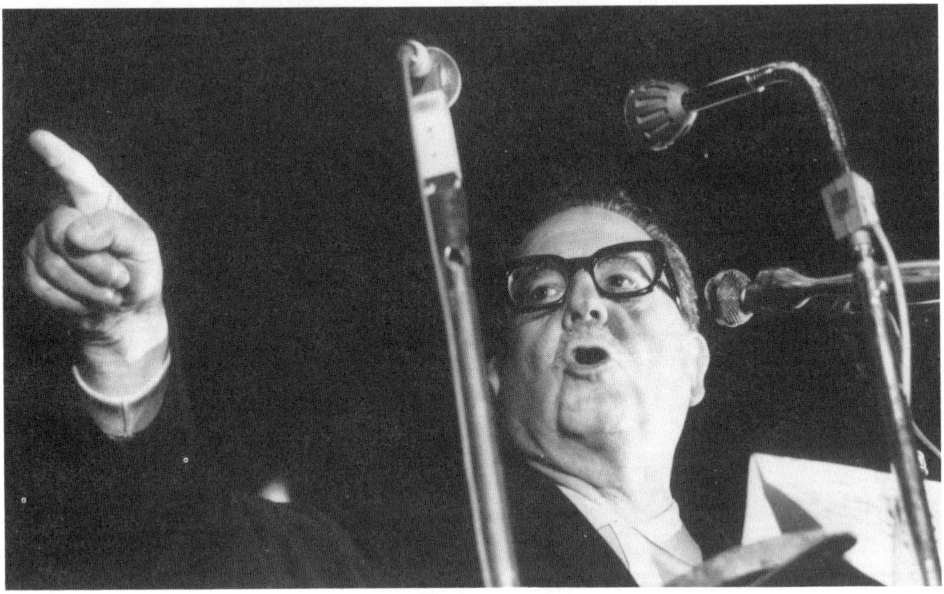

6. "I am not the president of all the Chileans. . . ." Salvador Allende, head of Chile's short-lived Socialist-Communist government, was elected president by a plurality, not a majority, but proceeded to dismantle the Chilean economy and constitution while making pronouncements like this one. He and his private army of leftists were overthrown by the Chilean military in 1973, after the Chilean Chamber of Deputies had declared his regime illegal (see chapter 17).

7 and 8. The two frontiers: the scientific-technological frontier will have to be pushed back further if Latin Americans are to exploit their geographical frontier successfully. *Above:* A science building opened in 1972 is the scene of this physics lecture at the Paraguayan National University of Asunción. Jobs for scientists remain scarce in Latin America. *Below:* A hydroelectric works under construction on El Salvador's Lempa River. Such projects offer hope for the future but do not assure political stability in the short run.

9. The author (left) presents his credentials as US ambassador to President Pedro Eugenio Aramburu of Argentina (June 1956). President Aramburu, one of the generals who combined to overthrow the Perón regime, survived his term of office only to be kidnapped and killed by terrorists.

10. Self-help in Bolivia: this housing project, financed by the US Agency for International Development and the "sweat equity" of Bolivians, indicates that foreign aid works best when it relies on genuine cooperation between donor and recipient.

I

THE ROOTS OF UNDERDEVELOPMENT

1
THE LATIN AMERICANS

NOT LONG AGO one of the longest nonstop commercial flights anyone could take was between Rio de Janeiro, Brazil, and Lima, Peru. It is well worth retracing today. Portuguese-speaking "Rio," which looks out upon the Atlantic, is one of Latin America's most modern cities, and probably its most beautiful. Shortly after takeoff the traveler flies over another Brazilian city, São Paulo, which is even more modern and in many ways more impressive than Rio de Janeiro. São Paulo is one of the largest and fastest-growing cities in the world: skyscrapers spring out of its concrete like mushrooms out of a farmer's field. New York is middle-aged and stodgy in comparison.

From São Paulo the plane continues northwestward over Brazil's sparsely settled Mato Grosso and over the northern tip of the Bolivian Chaco. Above the heart of South America now, it soars over the city of Santa Cruz, in the Andean foothills, where descendants of early Spanish settlers live and from where they direct their large cattle farms. Activity of United States oil companies and a United States government–financed highway up the Andes to Cochabamba have helped to rescue Santa Cruz from the isolation that used to characterize it and that some of its inhabitants recall with nostalgia.

Beyond Santa Cruz the Andes rise swiftly. Rocky areas alternate with cultivated fields. Looking down the traveler sees horses and cattle grazing, and another animal which at first he does not recognize. It is the llama, indigenous to the Andes and a source of meat, wool and transport. He searches eagerly for the wool-capped Indian he has seen in countless photographs, and there he is. Indian and llama . . . the traveler has the sensation of flying into an earlier period of time. Then he is over the *altiplano*, the high plain, perhaps a thousand feet above it.

Suddenly an immense crater comes into view. At the bottom of the crater, some 12,000 feet above sea level, is Bolivia's capital, La Paz.

The traveler barely has time to take in the drama when La Paz is lost behind and the plane is skimming over the plateau, flying an irregular pattern among the peaks that rise above it. Here villages, fields and people all have the brown color of the earth. He flies over the pre-Inca metropolis Tiahuanaco and its massive and mysterious stone figures; over Lake Titicaca, the highest large body of water in the world, where fishermen maneuver their traditional sailboats made of reeds; and over the great desert that lies beyond. At last he sights the blue Pacific on his left, and minutes later he lands in Spanish-speaking Lima, one-time City of Kings and capital of the Viceroyalty of Peru. He has spanned a continent of enormous diversity and peered into its history, a history that sometimes appears to hold it as in a vise.

THE INDIANS

Quite a few years ago I lived in the tiny port of Arica, Chile. Arica is an oasis in the Pacific desert. One day I left town and drove up a twisting and rising course which once had been a riverbed. When it was not possible to drive further I left my car and climbed a hill in order to determine what lay ahead. Beyond that hill rose another hill, and beyond that another and still another. After an hour or two of climbing I reached a broad plateau some thousands of feet above the sea.

The plateau stretched level in all directions. It was covered with coarse sand. Not a tree nor bush nor blade of grass grew on it. Except for the dim outline of the high Andes, far to the east, I could see nothing but an immense expanse; nothing, that is, except a line of stones that faded into the horizon. They clearly marked a route that connected places where people could live. But along that part of the route there was no living thing, nothing that moved or was capable of moving, nothing that protruded above the level of the earth except the stones, nothing but the stones to remind a person that he was not alone on the earth.

There is no doubt that people once traveled that route. When Christopher Columbus "discovered" the New World it was already known to millions of human beings. People had been living in what is now known as Latin America for many thousands of years—in desert oases, in the great rain forests, in the salubrious climates of the temperate zone and of the tropical highlands. Some of those people were still living a primitive existence. Others were highly civilized. Their civilizations were destroyed by the European invaders, and only fragments of their culture have survived.

The Maya. The most brilliant of the Indian civilizations was the Maya, which extended from southern Mexico to the western fringe of Honduras. The Maya excelled in mathematics, astronomy, and chronology. In fact few peoples anywhere could equal them in those fields. During the fifth and sixth centuries A.D. their astronomy may have been superior even to that of the Egyptians. Until the Gregorian calendar was reformed, their calendar was the most accurate ever devised.

More than one hundred Maya cities have been identified. Tikal, Copán, Chichén Itzá, Uxmal and Mayapán may have had as many as two hundred thousand inhabitants each. Tikal, the largest, had a mile-square religious-civic center that was filled with handsome monuments, ball courts, and meeting places, all dominated by five pyramid temples, the highest about 250 feet. Visitors from all over the world wonder at the beauty and the grandeur of the Maya cities.

The Aztecs. The Maya civilization had nearly disappeared when the Spaniard, Hernán Cortés, and his few followers reached Mexico in 1519. In contrast the Aztecs, whom the Spaniards found there, were near the apogee of their power. The Aztecs, too, were builders—of cities, of temples, and of monuments. When Cortés, after dismantling his ships in Veracruz, had made his way to Tenochtitlán, the Aztec capital on the site of today's Mexico City, he found Moctezuma presiding over an empire that extended south into Oaxaca, west into Michoacán, and east to the Gulf of Mexico. Tenochtitlán was built upon islands in Lake Texcoco. The Spaniards were impressed, and even awed, by its splendor, its luxury, and its sophisticated planning.

Agriculture was the principal occupation of the Aztecs, as it was of other Indian groups, and as in the case of the others it was based on communal ownership of land. Land was synonymous with life. It was a gift of the gods to the community, and it was reserved for community use. A man who married was allotted land for his own use, but only the produce belonged to him. To have permitted the land to be divided up among a few, or even among the many, would have seemed unnatural.

Government among the Aztecs was, in theory, democratic. First loyalty was to the family; families joined to form clans; clans joined to form tribes; and tribal representatives elected a chief or emperor. But in the real Aztec world, as in the Indian world in general, power was concentrated in the hands of a few. Not democracy but rather absolutism characterized the Aztec system, although absolutism was never institutionalized as it was among the Incas, in South America.

The Incas. Francisco Pizarro and Diego de Almagro, two Spanish adventurers, led the conquest of the Inca empire, which had many parallels to the Mexican episode. The Inca civilization was, in some ways, even more impressive than the Maya or the Aztec. The Incas were a ruling class, a preferred people, who governed over an estimated 3.5 million or more persons. Centered in Cuzco, in the highlands of today's Peru, their empire extended southward to the River Maule, in Chile, throughout Bolivia into the eastern portion of the Amazon Basin, and as far north as Ecuador where a second capital had been built at Quito. It was the most highly organized empire of pre-Columbian America. Indeed, it was one of the great empires of the world.

Numerous monuments and cities have revealed a great deal not only about the Incas but also about pre-Inca peoples whom the Incas conquered and absorbed and who themselves were highly accomplished in agriculture and the arts. Some of these peoples built intricate systems of irrigation. They were expert in the use of fertilizers. The Incas themselves were expert engineers. They diverted streams by cutting tunnels through the mountains, sometimes starting at both ends and meeting in the middle, precisely as calculated. Roads and bridges connected Cuzco with the farthest reaches of the empire, and a system of signals permitted messages to be sent a thousand miles in a few hours. The Incas, and also some of the pre-Incas, were skilled in medicine and surgery. They were familiar with the use of quinine. They trepanned skulls without infection.

The descendants of the Incas, and of the Maya and the Aztecs, show little evidence of the exceptional capabilities their ancestors had, but they surely possess them in latent form. Of the considerable number who have abandoned tribal life some have had great success. For many years, however, Latin American governments, and Latin Americans in general, showed little interest in the Indian past. There is a different attitude today. In Peru the eminent political leader, Víctor Raúl Haya de la Torre, has spoken of Indo-America rather than of Latin America or

Ibero-America. Brazilians have romanticized the Tupi-Guaraní contribution to their race. Mexico has made a cult of its Indian background.

But in general Indians, in those countries where they constitute a large sector of the population, have resisted integration. They are a withdrawn, taciturn, backward-looking people. Although they have adopted, or in some cases adapted, the religion of the Europeans, they have rejected the culture the Europeans tried to impose upon them. Their separateness has been an obstacle to national unity and a challenge that governments are increasingly trying to meet, not only by returning a portion of the lands that were wrested from them but in other ways as well. The task is not an easy one. We can be sure that in the legends that today's Indians repeat to one another on the cold Peruvian and Bolivian *altiplano,* in large areas of Mexico, Guatemala and Ecuador, and in other parts of Latin America where they outnumber whites, justice and mercy were meted out fairly in pre-Colombian America. The Indians are not convinced that either is available to them today.

THE SPANIARDS

Isabella, the Spanish queen, sponsored Columbus's voyages, and Spanish arms conquered most of what today is known as Latin America. There were many reasons for the tremendous, sometimes explosive, effort that went into the discovery and the conquest. For some the objective was the greater glory of the Spanish Crown. For others it was to spread the Catholic faith—to save souls. Columbus, of course, was looking for a westward sea route to Asia. He, and Isabella as well, were interested in trade. By trade they hoped to enrich themselves and also raise Spain above the poverty that enveloped it.

Spain's Miguel de Unamuno wrote:

> The land that fed Don Quixote is a poor land, so wasted by the downpours of centuries that its granite bones crop out everywhere. . . . Its rivers in winter run squeezed into cuts, gorges, and canyons, carrying to the sea in their muddy waters the rich coating that would have given the earth its verdure. This poverty of its soil made wanderers of its people, for they had either to go to distant parts in search of bread or to drive from pasture to pasture the sheep on which they lived.[1]

Thousands of Spaniards were willing to go to distant parts, to face the unknown dangers of America, in the hope of escaping poverty.

Many of them were members of the lesser nobility. Others were shepherds, tired of driving their sheep from pasture to pasture, and nearly starving in the process. Still others, including young Pizarro, were swineherds.

Spain's geography is no more conducive to unity than to prosperity. Its rivers and mountains have divided it into distinct regions. Regionalism is a product of Spanish geography, and separatism is imbedded in the Spanish character.

Racial differences also have fostered separatism. "Spain is a world," the Spaniards say, and it is. It is a world of diverse races and cultures. The Gallegos are of Celtic origin. The Catalans are Celtic and Frankish. No one knows where the Basques came from or whom they are related to. Civilization was brought to Spain by the Phoenicians, the Greeks, the Carthaginians and the Romans. Spain was for several centuries a part of the Roman Empire. In the sixth century Germanic tribes invaded the peninsula and the Visigoths set up a kingdom. They continued to rule Spain until shortly after the Arab invasion.

Arabs and Jews. It is probable that North Africans began to infiltrate into Spain five thousand years ago. In the year 711 Tarick, the Arab governor of Tangier, crossed the narrow Strait of Gibraltar with an invading Arab and Berber army. The Arabs succeeded in occupying all except the northern tip of the peninsula. They remained in Spain until 1492, the year Columbus discovered America. Some of them intermarried with Spaniards and profoundly influenced Spanish character. In Morocco people are fond of saying of the Spaniards, "They are Moors who wear hats." That is a caricature, of course, but like all good caricatures it has an element of truth. Arabs have what seems to many persons to be an exaggerated sense of personal dignity. They sometimes give as much importance to the word as to the deed. Spanish Quixotism, and many of the other characteristics that make Spaniards such interesting people, remind us strongly of the Arabs.

But in general Christians and Arabs, and Jews as well, lived separate lives in Spain. Basically, Christian society was made up of two layers. At the top were the great lords and the *caballeros* who supported them. At the bottom was the mass of serfs who were tied to the land and depended on the lords and *caballeros* for protection and sustenance. Industry and commerce were left to Arabs and Jews.

The Arabs were lovers of learning. Through Spain they gave the world arabic numerals, algebra, and geometry. They taught Spaniards astronomy, alchemy, and mechanics. They had learned from the Chinese how to manufacture paper, and the art flourished in Spain some three centuries before it was common north of the Pyrenees. Córdoba, the Arab capital, was one of the world's richest cities and one of its great centers of learning. Arab, Christian, and Jewish scholars worked there side by side. The Arabs were excellent agriculturists who planted new crops. They built industries and stimulated trade.

But Arabs also quarreled among themselves and, in any case, the Spaniards were unhappy with Arab predominance. From strongholds in the mountains of Asturias they undertook the task of reconquering Spain. The effort took centuries. It was not continuous, and the motives of the Spanish princes were mixed. Profit—that is, the acquisition of lands—probably moved them as much as anything else. And they were far from being united. Christians frequently found themselves fighting beside Arabs against other Christians. There were long periods of détente. Nevertheless the result was a gradual destruction of Arab power until the last stronghold, Granada, fell in 1492. Bitterness and hatred marked the final years of the war. Christian intolerance was matched by Arab intolerance. The reconquest had become a crusade. In the end it wrecked the economy, both Arab and Christian. It also severely diminished freedom in Spain.

Following the surrender at Granada many Arabs departed Spain of their own free will. Those who remained were granted liberal rights to practice their religion. But the efforts of Christian missionaries to convert them stirred them to revolt. In Castile they were ordered to choose between accepting Christian baptism and going into exile. Many chose exile.

Like the Arabs, the Jews also had acquired wealth and power during many centuries of living in Spain, and like the Arabs they were strongly resented. Soon after the fall of Granada they were told to accept Christian baptism or leave Spain. Some 165,000 chose to leave. By the middle of the twentieth century their more than two million descendants, many speaking the Spanish of fifteenth-century Castile, were widely spread over two hemispheres.[2]

Spain in the New World. While Spain's economy suffered grievously from the reconquest and the expulsion of Arabs and Jews, individual Spaniards, and the nobility in particular, profited from them.

In Andalusia the nobility acquired large estates where wheat, olives and grapes were grown. The landed estate, with a largely immobile labor force, had become a status symbol in Spain; it was to become a pattern for the *latifundio,* or large estate, in America.[3]

Eighteen of today's Latin American countries formed part of Spain's colonial empire. What qualities, what traditions, did Spain carry to the New World? They were in some cases contradictory. There was a tradition of centralism, of authoritarianism, in government. Someone has suggested that the colonial system was so planned that not a leaf should move in the vast American forest without the Spanish sovereign's consent. It did not work that way, of course, but it is not a great exaggeration to say that such was the intent. One reason centralism did not always work was Spanish individualism, a belief in the dignity and uniqueness of every man. Regionalism and separatism were by-products of individualism as they were of geography and race.

Spain left a distinctly military imprint on Latin America. Its golden age was an age of military conquest; its heroes in America were the *conquistadores,* not the *colonizadores.* Following the conquest in America, the Crown engaged in grandiose military campaigns in Europe and Africa. The results impoverished the nation, but today the campaigns are among the proudest pages in Spanish history.

THE PORTUGUESE

Portugal shares a peninsula with Spain, and for many years its history paralleled Spain's. From the twelfth to the fourteenth century it found itself fighting two wars: to expel the Arabs and to gain independence from Spain. In 1249 the Arabs yielded their lands in southern Portugal, and in 1385 a Portuguese army, reinforced by English soldiers, defeated the armies of Castile. John I (reigned 1385–1433) defended the new country against Spain's attempts to reimpose its authority, organized it as a cohesive political unit, and even attacked the Arabs in their stronghold, North Africa.

John's son, Henry the Navigator (1394–1460), was a man ahead of his time. He had a curiosity about the world that was insatiable and an energy that was inexhaustible. He assembled near his court a coterie of geographers, mapmakers, navigators and shipbuilders; under his eager direction, Portugal proceeded to explore the seas to the south. While Spain was still absorbed in its effort to expel the Arabs, Portugal colonized the Azores, which lie one-third of the distance to the Americas, discovered the Cape Verde Islands, and set up trading posts on the West African coast as far south as the Gulf of Guinea.

Henry never fulfilled his hope of finding a sea route to the East, but his interest and enthusiasm survived him. In 1497, only five years after Columbus had landed in America, Vasco da Gama rounded the Cape of Good Hope, explored Africa's east coast, and reached India. Portugal gave great importance to da Gama's discovery, much greater than it gave to Columbus's. While it was generally assumed that Columbus had reached the East, there was no good evidence that he had. In any case, he had returned to Spain empty-handed, while da Gama had brought spices and precious stones from India and tales of great wealth that Portugal was confident it could share.

Following Vasco da Gama's return a second fleet was quickly prepared under the command of Pedro Alvares Cabral. Cabral touched the Brazilian coast, possibly by inadvertence, and claimed it for Portugal. But America offered no immediate gain. On the other hand, the spice lands of the East were now within reach, and Portugal exploited its opportunities there with great skill. It soon dominated the Indian Ocean's maritime routes, and had a virtual monopoly of trade between China and Japan in spices, silks, porcelains and other luxury goods.[4]

After Pope Alexander VI had granted Spain control over all pagan lands to the west of a line 100 leagues west of the Azores and the Cape Verde Islands, he awarded a protesting Portugal the lands to the east of that line. Not content with the award Portugal induced Spain to sign the Treaty of Tordesillas (1495) which moved the line of demarcation 270 leagues to the west. The new line was to give Portugal a part of what is now Brazil.

But Portugal's resources were too limited to permit it to exploit much of its new possession. As it was, its halfhearted efforts to consolidate control of the seaboard were aimed principally at preventing other Europeans from developing supplies of dyewood there. A handful of Portuguese did carve out sugar estates in the area and enslaved Indians to work them. When Indian slaves proved to be scarce and unsatisfactory they imported blacks from their African colonies, the first large-scale importation of slave labor into America.

THE BLACKS

Portuguese and Spaniards in America were few in number and had spread themselves over an area that dwarfed their homelands. Little disposed to engage in manual labor themselves, they could prosper only if they were able to find a sufficient supply of workers. In some circumstances Spaniards as well as Portuguese turned to Africa, where slaves were readily available.

The slave trade was carried out under conditions of great cruelty. Nevertheless the lot of slaves in some ways (although not by any means in all) appears to have been less cruel in Spanish and Portuguese America than it was in the British colonies. The fact that neither Spaniards nor Portuguese brought many women to America tended to give slaves a different status. In Brazil, particularly, planters often bought female slaves because of their comeliness and their gentleness. Lighter-skinned females were frequently installed as mistresses of the household; their progeny were accepted as members of the planter's family. As a result of these and other circumstances the attitude toward blacks in Latin America is different from the attitude that was formed in the United States. In the United States a few drops of black blood make a person black. In Latin America, on the other hand, a few drops of white blood may make a person white. And wealth also may confer status on blacks. The Brazilians have a saying, *Negro rico e branco, e branco pobre e negro* ("A rich black is white, and a poor white is black").

Racism and Integration. That is not to say that there is no prejudice against blacks in Latin America, and no discrimination against them. There are both. Discrimination against blacks is more subtle in Latin America than it has been in the United States but it exists. And frequently it is not subtle. Many Brazilians take pride in the fact that they are a mixed, "universal" race. But the 1951 Alfonso Arinos law, which provides penalties for discrimination against persons in public accommodations on account of color or race, was sparked when Katherine Dunham, a famous black American dancer who in Brazil would be described as *mulata* (she is in fact light-skinned), protested after a hotel in São Paulo had refused her accommodation.[5]

For many years the Brazilian government had an overt policy of "whitening" the population by attracting immigrants from Europe.

More recently, since the Brazilian government has chosen to identify with the Third World, and has given special attention to its relations with Africa, it no longer espouses "whitening," but the Brazilian elites, and also the mass of Brazilian whites, continue to favor it.[6]

Prejudice and discrimination against blacks are common in the Spanish American countries as well as in Brazil. There has been nothing in Latin America to compare with the tremendous and largely successful effort made in the United States to improve the condition of blacks and other minorities. Living standards of blacks in Latin America (and of Indians and most whites of course) are far below those of American blacks. There are no black mayors of large cities as there are in the United States. The effort to place blacks on the level they occupy in the United States will take many years, and it has hardly begun.

How many blacks came to Latin America? No one knows. It is easier to point to the incidence of blacks in the various countries today. Substantially all Haitians are black or mulatto. Brazil, Cuba, and the Dominican Republic have a high percentage of blacks, and in the three countries miscegenation has been common. In the coastal areas of most mainland countries that touch the Caribbean there is a high incidence of blacks. On the other hand in landlocked Bolivia one rarely sees a black. And in countries such as Chile, Argentina, and Uruguay, where slaves were few in number, they have been absorbed into the population.

The black is an integral part of Latin America and has been from its beginning. It is possible that the first black to come to Latin America accompanied Columbus. At any rate blacks followed closely after him and in rapidly increasing numbers for many years. They helped to make nations and to free them. Many served in the armies of Bolívar and San Martín. Haitian volunteers fought on the side of American revolutionists at the Battle of Savannah. One of them was Henri Christophe (1767–1820), who became the fabled king of northern Haiti. Years later blacks were to constitute the bulk of the Cuban forces which, with help from the United States, won independence from Spain.

It has been estimated that more than one-half the population of "Latin" America is of mixed ancestry, "representing the largest mixture of Mongoloid, Caucasoid, and Negroid to be found anywhere in the world."[7] And of the less than half who are not of mixed ancestry, a very large number are pure Indians or pure blacks.

The black brought his labor to Latin America. He also brought technical skills (the Sudanese had invented iron smelting) that were useful in mining and agriculture.[8] What other contributions did the black make? For one thing he brought a sense of rhythm and melody in dance and song that permeated Latin American culture. Individual blacks have been outstanding in the arts, in architecture, in painting, and in sculpture. The Spanish and Portuguese imprint on Latin America is as plain to see as the Indian. So, too, is the blacks'.

2
FROM CONQUEST TO INDEPENDENCE

THERE WERE MARKED differences between the English and Spanish enterprises in the New World. "Colonization" aptly describes the English enterprise. The English came with their families—to build homes, to grow crops, to remain, to colonize in other words. Many Spaniards also came to colonize, but many others wanted to "make a pile" and return to Spain to live in leisure, as befitted Spanish gentlemen of the period.

THE SPANISH LEGACY

The Spaniards wanted to discover quickly the richest mines; to concentrate on projects that would bring prompt results and large returns. They rapidly spread out over an area more than twice the size of Europe. The English, on the other hand, found no Mexico or Peru, no great civilizations that could be despoiled or rich deposits of precious minerals that could be worked. They built their homes and cultivated their lands on a narrow fringe of the Atlantic coast. It was years before they ventured beyond the nearby Alleghenies. It would be two hundred years before they began to settle in California. By that time Spain's empire in America had broken up into separate states.

There was a difference, too, in attitude toward the Indians. The English set out to displace the few Indians they found. War with the Indians, and among the Indians, and the diseases that Europeans brought with them, went far toward accomplishing that purpose. The situation of the Spaniards was quite different. They needed the Indians. They could never have exploited a continent without their help.

Since few of the early Spaniards had brought women to America, most of them bred with Indians. While North America became white, Spanish America became mestizo. And just as Castilians differed from Andalusians, so Aztecs differed from Chibchas, and Quechuas from Araucanians. Latin America became mestizo but the racial mixture was far from being uniform. Nations were being formed that would be distinct from one another.

Government. Government of the Spanish colonies was characteristically authoritarian. Immigration was carefully controlled. Whereas the English did not seem to care much who emigrated to their colonies Spain excluded non-Catholics and, in most cases, non-Spaniards. The intention was to keep out heretics and to preserve for Spaniards the wealth of the New World. One adverse effect was to limit the talent that was available for promoting political, economic, and social development.

The principal agency for directing colonial affairs was the Royal and Supreme Council of the Indies (Consejo de Indias), created in 1521. The Council had virtually absolute authority and enjoyed nearly complete freedom in making laws, in administering justice, in controlling finance and trade, and even in supervising the Church and directing armies. The Council acquired a large bureaucracy whose task it was to regulate and control the activities of government and governed in the colonies. A flood of laws and edicts prescribed the conduct of colonists down to minute details of their daily lives (many of them were cheerfully ignored by the colonists).

The Spaniards were great city builders and city dwellers. Under Castilian law the municipality was under the direct protection of the king. Government was exercised by a *cabildo,* or municipal council, which had great power in local matters. Cortés declared his independence from Governor Diego Velasquez, in Cuba, by creating the municipality of Veracruz in Mexico. The *cabildo* which he appointed responded by naming him Governor and Commander of New Spain.

Since the *cabildo* was so powerful in local affairs, appointment to it was eagerly sought. In general colonial officials were named by the king, and were *peninsulares,* that is, persons born in peninsular Spain. In 1523 Charles I, in an unusual effort to liberalize government, decreed that a few *cabildos* should be elected by local landholders. But when wars in Europe impoverished the court, kings undertook to sell offices in many *cabildos*. In some cases purchasers were permitted to bequeath the office as part of their estate. The *cabildo* did make it possible for creoles, persons of Spanish blood born in America, to make their voices heard in local affairs. The *cabildo abierto,* or local town meeting, at which selected citizens occasionally were permitted to express themselves, played a notable role in the movement to bring about independence from Spain. But as a training school for democratic nationhood the *cabildo* had little if any utility.

The Society. Society was highly stratified, as it was in Spain itself, but the elements that made it up were different. The *peninsulares* were at the top. They had the highest offices in the state and in the Church, and received the highest salaries. Creoles were just below them. They included wealthy landowners, business and professional men, and artisans. Next were the mestizos. Neither white nor Indian, they were looked upon with suspicion by both. They were a new breed, landless, restless, forced to fend for themselves in a world that did not fully accept them. Below the mestizos were the Indians, who clung to old habits, old traditions, old values, and old manners of speech. They tried also to cling to the lands they had long occupied, but in that they had less success. And at the bottom were the blacks, unwilling intruders in an already divided world, cut off even from their historic past.

The social organization was of course not as rigid as it sounds. Not all *peninsulares* were affluent. Many lived at the poverty level. Some wealthy creoles outranked most *peninsulares.* Money was a great equalizer. A mestizo who had managed to raise himself economically had little difficulty in being accepted as white. In general, however, the several groups had little in common. Their purposes were not the same. Often they were in conflict. The *peninsular* wanted wealth. He wanted land, lots of it, and Indians or blacks to work it. The creole wanted to share the privileges of the *peninsular.* The mestizo wanted to acquire an identity of his own. The Indian wanted to regain his identity. The black wanted to survive, and to be free.

Forced Labor. The Spaniard obtained his land and, usually, Indians to work it. A device that helped him achieve his ends was the *encomienda. Encomienda* derives from *encomendar,* which means "to entrust." The recipient of an *encomienda* was entrusted with a specified number of Indians toward whom he acquired certain obligations in return for their labor. The *encomienda* was designed to replace the infamous *repartimiento* which permitted Spaniards to seize Indians at random and compel them to labor in mines and on the land. The aims of the *encomienda* system were humane, but they were not achieved. The system permitted the Spaniards to possess the Indians and frequently their land as well. Thus Cortés was entrusted with 100,000 Indians on 25,000 square miles of land. Other leaders received comparable rewards; even foot soldiers were given *encomiendas.* The *encomienda* provoked more than one revolt on the part of the Indians, but it was not finally abolished until the end of the eighteenth century. By that time the Indians had become serfs and many of their lands were in the possession of the great estate owners and of the Church.

The Church. The Church accompanied the conquerors to the New World and was better received than they were. The Indians already had many gods, but the idea of one Supreme Being also was widely accepted, or at least widely suggested. Many rites and practices of the Church were already familiar. Some Indians had a form of baptism with water. Others practiced confession and penance. Fast days and feast days were common. So the shift to Christianity was easy, even natural, especially since the Church early assumed the role of the Indians' protector, and since it was patient and tolerant when, instead of substituting Christianity for their old religions, many Indians merely added it to them. Even today the tourist who visits Chichicastenango, in Guatemala, can see Indians practising their ancient rites on the very steps of the church as they prepare to engage in Christian worship inside.

One institution the Church devised was the mission village where Indians, frequently numbering into the thousands, could be isolated not only from Europeans but also from other Indians. The missions represented an effort to save the Indians from enslavement, to teach them the true faith, and also to train them in agriculture and the simple crafts. At the same time they were a lucrative source of revenue for the Church, which sold much of the cotton, the hides, the tobacco and other products of the Indians' labor in competition with private producers. Ruled over by dedicated priests, the missions were benevolent concentration camps where the Indians were safer and possibly happier than they would have been in the larger world outside. But when they were broken up the Indians found themselves ill prepared to live in that larger world.

Among the most successful protectors of the Indians were the Jesuits, who not only conducted missions with verve and devotion but also became leaders in education, and even in banking and commerce. The Jesuits were intelligent, hardworking, progressive, incorruptible—and powerful. The combination of power and virtue was too much for laymen, who found it difficult to compete with them in the material world, and also for other churchmen, who could not match their religious zeal. Both groups rose up against them. In 1767 they were expelled, not only from the colonies but from peninsular Spain as well. The Jesuits went the way of the Arabs and the Jews, victims of their own accomplishments, which were quickly dissipated after their departure. And as in the case of Arabs and Jews, many of their lands and other possessions fell into the hands of those who already were wealthy and privileged. The *latifundio* as an economic and social phenomenon was reinforced.

By that time the Jesuits and the Church as a whole had become too rich and powerful for their own good. In some countries church buildings had proliferated beyond need or reason. More and more lands had become church property through bequests, and remained so because of the Church's tax-exempt status. Furthermore the Church had remained foreign. It still was the king's agent. It was the Spanish Church rather than the Church of Rome that had come to the New World, and in the Spanish kingdoms Church and throne were indissoluble. The king had the power of decision over the appointment of clergy, including the most lowly. Some creoles and indeed a few mestizos had been permitted to enter the clergy but the Church still was Spanish rather than colonial—or universal.

The Economy. Spaniards were committed mercantilists: they wanted to sell more than they bought and to pile up the surplus in the form of bullion. The colonies were to furnish precious metals and raw materials that Spain required, and Spain was to return manufactured products. The Crown's chief instrument for controlling trade was the Casa de Contratación (Board of Trade), which was established in Seville only eleven years after Columbus reached America. The Board controlled both exports and imports. It was price fixer, tax collector, court of appeals, and, above all, defender of the interest of the Crown.

Spain early designated monopoly ports for the colonial trade. On the peninsula, Seville was the monopoly port until it was replaced, in 1717, by Cadiz. In America the monopoly ports were Cartagena in what is now Colombia, Nombre de Dios and later Portobello on the Isthmus of Panama, and Veracruz in Mexico. Trade between the colonies and other powers, and of course trade among the colonies themselves, was prohibited.

Encouraged by the teachings of liberal economists (and by the very high percentage of contraband that was reaching the colonies), Charles III (reigned 1759–88) started to change all this. In 1765 he opened the Caribbean islands to almost unlimited trade, not with foreign countries to be sure, but with nine of Spain's principal ports. The same privilege was extended eventually to all Spanish America except New Spain (Mexico) and Venezuela. Trade among the colonies was also opened and taxes were sharply reduced.

The result for the colonies was a swift increase not only in trade but in all kinds of economic activity. By 1800 they were prospering at last. Their industrial system was more extensive than that of Spain itself, although it was still primitive compared with that of northern Europe and the United States.

Spaniards who came to America sought land as well as gold, but it was gold and silver that impelled them to explore the greater part of the continent in fifty years and to settle and develop large areas of it. It was precious metals the Crown was principally interested in (one-fifth of all precious metals mined went directly to the Crown), and it was the same metals that made it possible for the more enterprising and more fortunate entrepreneurs to become millionaires. As it turned out, silver produced more profits than gold. Guided by reports of Indians, impelled by a lusty spirit of adventure and a desire for gain, and aided by superb physical resistance and indomitable courage, the Spaniards quickly uncovered most of the major gold and silver deposits in their new empire.

The land of course ultimately provided much more than the mines. The farmer and livestock raiser, rather than the miner, forged Spain's empire in America. But they did so in the face of formidable obstacles. Mountains, jungle, and desert made it impossible to employ much of the land. There was a chronic shortage of labor. Indians were not willing or dependable workers. And most of the usable land was concentrated in the hands of a few persons who were under no great need to work it.

THE PORTUGUESE IN BRAZIL

Much of what has been said concerning Spain's empire in America could also be said of Portugal's. But there were differences too. Portugal eventually achieved an empire that covered nearly half of South America. Nevertheless her interest in the New World developed more slowly, as we have seen. Aside from the dyewood that the Portuguese discovered and that they named *brazil,* after a similar product that had long been imported from the Far East, there was nothing in Brazil, as the new colony came to be called, to match the silks, spices, and jewels that India provided.

Several developments awakened Portuguese interest. For one thing, as Europe's textile industry expanded the market for brazilwood became brisk and lucrative. Also, the French, who had refused to recognize the claims of Spain and Portugal to monopoly in America, began to cut brazilwood and to raid Portuguese shipping. Portugal retaliated by establishing a garrison in Pernambuco. In 1530 the French destroyed it, but that only increased Portugal's determination to control Brazil.[1]

Furthermore, despite the guarantees of the Treaty of Tordesillas, Spain was a source of concern. The Spanish empire in the New World had grown with astonishing rapidity, and navigators carrying the Spanish flag had already sailed close to the Brazilian coast. Portugal was not at all sure that, treaty or no treaty, Spain did not have its eye on Brazil. Finally, trade with India fell off. Europe was surfeited with spices and other Indian products. The Far Eastern bonanza came to an end. Brazil was now the promised land.

Government. The initial instrument of Portuguese penetration of Brazil was the captaincy, a grant of land to an individual who by accepting it acquired broad privileges and responsibilities. The grant corresponding to a single captaincy was a strip of land measuring 25 to more than 60 leagues along the coast and extending inward to the line fixed by the Treaty of Tordesillas.

The *donatario,* the person accepting the grant, had to depend on his own resources to carry out his responsibilities and to exercise his authority. He even had to conquer his empire before he could rule it. Nevertheless a captaincy was not a private domain. Only a part of it belonged to the *donatario.* Most of it was reserved for settlers. Some persons have referred to the captaincy as an example of rugged private enterprise. In contrast with the Spanish system, certainly, the role of the Portuguese Crown was minimal. In reality, however, the captaincy reflected Portugal's poverty and its tiny population, and the government's consequent inability to administer Brazil with its own resources.

Two events in the middle sixteenth century were important to Brazil's future. One was the appointment of a captain-general whose power was superior to that of the *donatarios.* The other was the arrival of six Jesuit priests. In the opinion of some historians the new captain-general and the Jesuit fathers were the founders of Brazil. The Jesuits tried to protect the Indians from oppression and exploitation, and they instructed them in mission villages, as they did in the Spanish colonies. But they antagonized fellow churchmen who thought them too efficient and too virtuous. Most of their enemies agreed that they were too powerful. In 1750 the Jesuits were expelled from Portugal and Brazil, as they would later be expelled from Spain and its colonies.

The Society. The Portuguese were not city builders as the Spaniards were. Rio de Janeiro was a modest place compared with Mexico City or Lima. Sugar, rather than precious metals, determined the early pattern of Brazilian society. The plantation, the *fazenda,* was the all-important economic and social, and even political unit. Here the *fazendeiro* lived, rarely visiting the city except for religious ceremonies and *festas.* Here also lived the slaves. By 1700 blacks outnumbered whites two to one.

The *fazenda* was apt to cover an immense area. If the *donatario* was an emperor the *fazendeiro* was a king, and his authority was more real and more complete than a king's. He was lord of his domain, the person with most authority in all Brazil. He was slave owner, employer, banker, merchant, and judge, and he had his own private army. He paid little attention to the viceroy whom Lisbon eventually sent out.

Colonial society was not static or sedentary. During the sixteenth and seventeenth centuries missionaries and farmers explored the interior and many settled there. From São Paulo groups of fearless men known as *bandeirantes* ("flag carriers on the march" from *bandeira,* meaning "flag") penetrated far to the west in search of Indians to enslave. One result of their activities, probably not intended, was to push Brazil's frontier beyond the line set in the Treaty of Tordesilla into areas claimed by Spain.

The Economy. Unlike the Spaniards the early Portuguese had found no great Indian civilizations. Nor had they found any precious metals. It was not until the end of the seventeenth century that the discovery of gold and diamonds aroused the colony, and the mother country too, and set off a round of feverish activity that uprooted homes, caused plantations to be abandoned, and brought slaves by the thousand to the vast areas north of Rio de Janeiro—Minas Gerais, Mato Grosso, and Goiás. Like the Spaniards before them many of these treasure seekers earned fortunes for themselves and for the Crown, which collected the usual royal fifth and spent it on foolish vanities and luxuries. As in the case of the Spaniards, too, the new wealth produced inflation in colony and motherland, ruined industries that were more important and more helpful than gold and diamonds, and caused suffering to a majority of the people.

Lisbon had a monopoly of trade with Brazil, but only in theory. In practice, competition from the Dutch, the English, and the French was very great. Portugal's device for meeting it was the monopoly company. The Company of Brazil, for example, had a monopoly in wine, oil, codfish, and flour. The Maranhão Company had a monopoly of the slave trade. But the companies were not entirely Portuguese. The English also had an interest in them. In the economic field England, rather than Portugal, was the imperial country.

THE UNDERDEVELOPED IMPERIAL COUNTRIES

England, the great colonial rival of Spain and Portugal, underwent a radical transformation of its economic and political structures during the two centuries that followed the discovery of America. A powerful aristocracy still presided over large landed estates. But it was not a stagnant aristocracy; it was ready and anxious to cooperate with enterprising groups of merchants, miners, and shipowners in exploiting the opportunities that the New World offered. The monied classes in England were willing to risk their capital in corporate ventures overseas.

An elite merchant class, together with others who supported trade, acquired a majority in Parliament. London was not only the seat of government and a locus of political power; it was also an administrative and commercial center that encouraged and protected free enterprise in colonial development. Obstructions to development—privileges of all kinds, monopolies, tolls, and controls—were reduced or removed. The Bank of England, the joint stock company, and the growth of religious tolerance all added to the climate for improvement. England brought in artisans from the continent and developed a flourishing textile industry. It imported Merino wool and dyestuffs from Spain and Portugal and returned them in the form of finished goods, for local consumption as well as export to the colonies. "By 1700," the Steins note, "England had made a breakthrough into what we now call the modern world."[2]

The French, too, and Holland as well, became suppliers of manufactured goods to Iberia. When Frenchmen complained that France had no Indies to enrich it, a noted commentator suggested that Spain, itself, was France's Indies. Louis XIV (reigned 1643–1715), in his instructions to the French ambassador to Spain, said that "the greater the merchandise carried to the Spaniards, the more ingots and piasters from the Indies are returned to us. . . ."[3]

Ingots and piasters were indeed returned, not only to France but also to England and Holland. Gold and silver stayed in Spain long enough to enrich the privileged few and to encourage the Crown to engage in costly wars in Europe (they also produced inflation and stifled the growth of Spanish industry). Most of the wealth, however, flowed to the more developed countries of Europe to compensate for the deficit in Spain's balance of trade.

During the seventeenth century Spain declined from first to third rank among European powers. It was a weakened colonial country when independence came to America. By that time Portugal was an economic colony of England. The Steins have said: "This anomalous status as colony and empire shaped the history of the Iberian countries and their colonial possessions. It conditioned colonial society, economy, and politics, and indeed the course of Latin American history to modern times."[4]

INDEPENDENCE

It was the Indians who had most grievances against the Spaniards, and it was they who staged the first major revolt. Their leader was Tupac

Amaru, descendant of a great Inca of that name whom the Spaniards had executed in 1571. Tupac Amaru had been carefully educated by Jesuits and given the title of Marquis de Oropesa by the Crown. Honored by Spaniards in high places, and with abundant wealth at his disposal, he nevertheless made himself defender and spokesman of the Indian masses who were toiling as virtual slaves in mines and factories and on lands that were no longer theirs. But he was unable to induce the authorities to relieve their plight.

In 1780 Tupac Amaru assembled some seventy to eighty thousand poorly armed followers and, while proclaiming his loyalty to Crown and Church, quickly gained control of an area extending from what is now southern Peru, through most of Bolivia, to northern Argentina. But the Spaniards brought in reinforcements and captured him. After forcing him to witness the execution of his wife, his sons, and his close aides, they cut out his tongue and tied his arms and legs to four horses which proceeded to tear him apart. When the news of his death was spread additional thousands of Indians rebelled, but to no avail. The rebellion failed after taking an estimated eighty thousand lives on both sides. It was not repeated. Blacks, rather than Indians, were to take the lead in ridding Latin America of its European masters.

Haiti. The first colony to win its independence was France's Saint Domingue, which occupied the western third of the island of Hispaniola. Saint Domingue was one of the richest colonies in the world. It supplied half of Europe's sugar, and accounted for half of France's colonial trade. But it was a bitterly divided colony, with slaves outnumbering whites by fifteen to one.

The French Revolution, which abolished slavery in France, had immediate repercussions in Saint Domingue. The mulattoes rose up first, and soon all groups were involved. Toussaint L'Ouverture (?1744–1803), a brilliant ex-slave who was grandson of an African king, led the black masses against the French and the mulattoes (after first assuring the safety of his former masters), and later against the English and Spanish when they intervened. He gained control of the colony but was betrayed and captured by forces sent out by Napoleon, and died in prison. On New Year's Day, 1804, the illiterate black General Jean Dessalines declared the colony's independence. He named the new country Haiti, which in the Indian language meant "place of mountains." Meanwhile the French, after losing some thirty-five thousand of their forty-three thousand men (mostly from yellow fever), had been expelled and those white residents who had not been massacred had fled. Haiti was black and was to remain black.

The Spanish Americans. By the beginning of the nineteenth century Spanish colonists may have already felt greater loyalty toward America than to Europe. And in Europe itself the winds of freedom were blowing strongly. Voltaire, Montesquieu, and Rousseau had written of the rights of man, of people's right to determine the laws they would be governed by, to forge their own destinies. Subversive, un-Spanish literature of that kind was of course banned from the colonies, which only increased its attractiveness; it was circulated clandestinely and read avidly. In addition many young, affluent creoles traveled to Paris, which they considered the intellectual capital of the world, and read the new works freely. Nevertheless the Spanish colonists were probably influenced more by the American Revolution than by European thought. The United States and Spanish America shared a continent. American leaders had not only talked of freedom and written about it, they had achieved it. In contrast, the French Revolution, and especially its aftermath, the Terror and the rise of Napoleon Bonaparte, had a sobering influence on the colonists. Clearly not all revolutions had the results that had been hoped for.

Spanish America's grievances were more economic than political. There was no great loyalty to the Spanish Court but neither was there any strong urge to break away from it. The colonists did not want to cease being Spaniards. They wanted to be Spaniards in fact and to be treated as Spaniards. They were tired of being second-class subjects, of seeing the highest honors and the best jobs go to *peninsulares.* They also wanted freedom to trade and other freedoms they believed Spaniards were entitled to. Nevertheless by no means all were prepared to fight for these aims. The creoles, who were to lead the revolt, had little wish to abolish the existing political system. The landed proprietors among them, who lived in luxury and independence and hardly bothered to learn the names of the Spaniards who in theory governed them, were not anxious for freedom from Spain if freedom meant the loss of their privileges. But Spain's weakness made revolt inevitable.

By 1800 the Spanish Court was corrupt and impotent. It was the victim of easy wealth, of foolish wars, and of self-indulgence by effete kings and nobles. But even those circumstances would not have impelled the colonists to revolt when they did had Spain not become enmeshed in Europe's dynastic wars. In 1808 Ferdinand VII was tricked into renouncing the Spanish throne in favor of Joseph, Napoleon's brother, and Spain was occupied by French forces. The movement for independence, for independence from France that is, began in Spain itself. In 1810 a "free" Spanish government was set up in Cadiz under the protection of English guns. Colonists who happened to be in the city aided in drawing up a constitution that provided, among other things, that sovereignty resided in the nation; that the nation included Spaniards of both hemispheres; and that Spain was not the patrimony of any family or person.

The colonists supported the rebellion with enthusiasm. But most of them insisted on their loyalty to Ferdinand VII, whom Napoleon was holding prisoner, even though many knew that for ineptness, immorality, and stupidity Ferdinand had few if any equals in Spanish history. This caricature of a king had become to Spaniards on both sides of the Atlantic *el deseado* ("the desired one"). What was most desired, of course, was an end to French intervention in Spain.

Ferdinand, freed by the French and apparently secure on the throne, quickly repudiated the liberal constitution of Cadiz and proceeded to govern Spain with ruthless tyranny. Furthermore when revolt again broke out in Cadiz he called in French forces to help subdue it. For the colonies the die was cast. The war for independence from France became a war for independence from Spain. The uprisings in the various colonies occurred independently but the causes were the same. The time for Spanish Americans to cast off the chains that bound them to Europe had come. By 1825, after fifteen years of war, Spain's enormous American empire, which had lasted more than three centuries, had broken up into sixteen independent states. Only Cuba and Puerto Rico remained in Spanish hands.

The wars of independence had been costly in property as well as life; more than one patriot had contributed his entire fortune to the cause. The new nations faced appalling economic problems. But their economies were weak principally because Spain had kept them weak. The colonies had not been something to nourish and make strong, but something to feed upon. They had been suppliers of primary products and importers of manufactures because the Crown had decreed that they should be.

The United States and the Spanish American countries had quite different colonial legacies. When independence came to it the United

States, like England, was part of the modern world. Americans were a homogeneous people, occupying a territory that was rich in resources and compact enough to be manageable. They possessed a merchant marine that kept them in touch with one another and with overseas peoples. Trade and English investment insured continued rapid development. By 1870 they were probably the second industrial nation in the world.

In contrast neither the Spanish colonies nor Spain itself had been part of the modern world. There was little that underdeveloped Spain could offer in the way of trade and investment, and if there had been more the new countries might have been slow to accept it. Feeling against the mother country had become strong. Nor was cooperation with other countries, or among the new countries themselves, easy to achieve. Spanish policy had hindered the development of local shipping industries, and distance and topography added to the difficulties of communication. Whites constituted only a small minority of the population, and many of the nonwhites lived outside the market economy. Spanish Americans continued to be exporters of primary products after independence not because others decreed it but because they had neither the will nor, perhaps, the capacity to be anything else. It would be many years before most of the countries made any serious effort to industrialize.[5]

No social revolution took place in the former colonies. To the masses the wars had brought little but misery. Indians had been pressed into military service against their will—those Indians who could be found, that is. Whole villages had moved in efforts to escape induction. The gap between the creole and the Indian had widened, if that was possible, and freedom for the Indian probably had lessened; at least there was no longer a Court to go through the motions of protecting him. Whereas in France the revolution had brought an end to feudalism, in Spanish America it confirmed the *latifundio,* on which Indians worked in virtual serfdom, as the dominant economic and social unit.

Political change, in contrast, appeared to be drastic. New constitutions on the American and French models were adopted amid popular acclaim. But legislating democracy was not the same as achieving it. Unlike the people of the United States, Spanish Americans had almost no background in self-government. They had had little opportunity to develop the qualities that democracy requires.

The new republics needed a period of peace but instead they got war. Creoles in the cities fought each other for positions of power; rural creoles fought to wrest power from the cities. As in Spain following the final defeat of the Arabs, military leaders sought a new role for themselves and found it in politics. The military *caudillo* ("boss" or natural leader) and the military coup d'état became institutionalized, and the masses had little more influence on events than they had had under the Spaniards. Their role, when they were called upon to have one, was to follow one or another political leader, frequently with little understanding of what he stood for or what his aims might be. Argentina's José de San Martín and Venezuela's Simón Bolívar had led South America to freedom. San Martín, his task completed and finding himself without honor even in his own country, quietly embarked for Europe where he died alone in poverty. Bolívar had come to symbolize freedom to Latin Americans and to many persons outside Latin America. But he died an ostracized dictator, believing that Latin Americans were ungovernable, that his life had been a failure, that he had done little more than (in his own words) "plow the sea."

Independent Brazil. Portuguese America took a different course.

> The clipping of the ties that bound Brazil to Portugal was a gentle operation, almost bloodless. There were no heroic liberators, no forced marches over high passes; with simply a declaration of independence, a few mild skirmishes, Brazil emerged a sovereign empire. In Spanish America, independence was won in defiance of kings; in Portuguese America, the heir apparent to the Braganza throne himself raised the cry of freedom.[6]

At the beginning of the nineteenth century the days of Portugal's glory were long past. That small, weak country had been crushed under the burdens of empire and under its bounties. It had acquired the same easy wealth and suffered the same destructive inflation as Spain. It had become an economic colony and, in a sense, a political colony, of England.

Brazilians, like Spanish Americans, had no uncontrollable urge to be free from Europe. Two-thirds of them were slaves. Probably not more than one-tenth were politically conscious. The very size of the country, and its *fazenda* culture, made it difficult for its people to think and act in national terms. Yet Brazil had more vigor than the mother country. Isolated from Europe, and neglected by Portugal, Brazilians had learned to do things on their own. *Bandeirantes* and gold seekers had extended the colony's frontiers and instilled a forward-looking spirit in its people.

In addition, of course, the Brazilians had the same kinds of grievances against Portugal as Spanish Americans had against Spain. Portugal was impoverished and decadent, unable to fulfill its obligations as mother country. The child had outgrown the parent.

As in the case of Spain, the mother country's weakness probably made independence inevitable. Here, too, it was Napoleon's ambition that sparked the movement toward independence. In November 1807, as a French army bent on overthrowing the Braganza dynasty approached Lisbon, the royal court, a thousand persons in all, together with the crown jewels and the royal treasury, were loaded into ships and, escorted by the British, set sail for Brazil. It was the first royal visit to America.

Prince Regent John was well received by the Brazilians, and he responded to the attentions that were shown him. Shocked by evidence of past royal neglect he repaired streets and highways, built schools, and set up a printing press, a national library, and an art museum. He invited immigration and encouraged industry. And, wonder of wonders, he opened Brazilian ports to the trade of the world! The English had a hand in that, of course, and they received special privileges.

In December 1815 John gave Brazil dominion status within the empire. The following year he was crowned "John VI of the United Kingdom of Portugal, Brazil, and the Algarves." Rio de Janeiro took on the appearance of a royal capital. Palaces were built, titles were conferred on Brazilians, *fazendeiros* were drawn into the city. The *fazenda* gradually lost its place as the center of Brazilian society. The king of tired old Portugal had helped bring youthful Brazil into the modern age.

Nevertheless, events in Portugal continued to determine events in Brazil. A new government in Lisbon condemned the opening of Brazilian ports, countermanded many of John's decrees, and urged the colonists to ignore the king. Again acting under English advice, John collected his court and his royal treasury and sailed back to Lisbon, leaving his twenty-three-year-old son Pedro to rule as regent. Before departing he said to Pedro, "If Brazil demands independence, grant it, but put the crown upon your own head." Pedro followed his father's advice. When the Lisbon parliament began to make demands of him, he rebelled. On September 7, 1822, while standing near the Ypiranga River in São Paulo, he tore the Portuguese colors from his uniform and shouted, "Independence or death!" His Grito ("cry") do Ypiranga was Brazil's declaration of independence. In 1889 Brazil became a republic.

II

TODAY'S LATIN AMERICA: POLITICS AND THE 'ISMS

3
CONSTITUTIONS AND PARTIES

> *Many nations, ancient and modern, have shaken off the juggernaut of oppression, but few indeed have been able to enjoy even a few happy hours of their new-won freedom; they promptly fall back into their old political vices; for tyranny is bred by Peoples, and not by Governments . . . . The more I admire the excellence of the Federal Constitution of Venezuela, the more I am convinced that it cannot be applied to this country.*
>
> Simon Bolivar
> speech before the Venezuelan Congress
> February 15, 1819

WHILE I WAS ambassador to Paraguay I said, in one of my dispatches to Washington:

> Our Saviour Himself, if given the task of governing this country, would have to have recourse to all his undoubted talents, human and divine. He would be hard pressed to furnish an answer, in the case of Paraguay, to Abraham Lincoln's question, "Must a government, of necessity, be too strong for the liberties of its own people, or too weak to maintain its own existence?"

The constitutions of all the Latin American countries except Castro's Cuba provide for the practice of democracy. Democracy is much on the lips of Latin American orators and in the pages of international agreements to which Latin American countries are parties. The Charter of the Organization of American States (OAS) asserts that "the solidarity of the American States and the high aims which are sought through it require the political organization of those states on the basis of the effective exercise of representative democracy." The Alliance for Progress, the US-led program of economic cooperation that was agreed to in Punta del Este, Uruguay, in 1961, presupposed that Latin Americans were devoted to democracy. "This Alliance is established on the basic principle that free men working through the institutions of representative democracy can best satisfy Man's aspirations," the governments said in the Declaration to the People of America that accompanied the Alliance. And they added: "No system can guarantee true progress unless it affirms the dignity of the individual which is the foundation of our civilization." The declaration was signed by representatives of countries with democratically elected governments and, with equally good grace, by representatives of governments that were frank dictatorships.

In theory Latin American countries are democratic. But practice is something else. Violence and instability, rather than democracy, characterize Latin America's politics.

> The popular image of Latin America as an area of endemic revolution is warranted. The resolution of succession problems by methods not authorized by constitutional prescription is a recurring phenomenon, and the replacement of leading personnel, notably presidents, by acts of violence is common. Between January 1, 1950 and January 1, 1965, . . . at least forty successful revolutions occurred. . . . Revolutions took place in sixteen of the twenty Latin American republics. Only in Mexico, Uruguay, Chile and Costa Rica was the period marked by the absence of revolution.[1]

Uruguay and Chile have since joined the revolutionary countries of course.

Instability is so common in Latin America's politics that some scholars have raised it to the institutional level. That is to say, the very absence of institutions has been institutionalized. Kalman H. Silvert has said:

> "Unpredictable" and "unstable" are the two adjectives most often applied to Latin American politics. The implications of both pejoratives are partially erroneous. First, to be "unstable" is not necessarily to be "unpredictable." As a matter of fact, one of the easiest things to predict is instability itself. And second, some types of revolutionary disturbance do not indicate instability. If the normal way of rotating the executive in a given country is by revolution, and there have been a hundred such changes in a century, then it is not facetious to remark

> that revolutions are a sign of stability—that events are marching along as they always have.[2]

Learned statements such as these are capable of confusing as well as instructing. If it is not facetious to suggest that revolutions are a sign of stability, neither is it irrelevant to observe that a government that is apt to be thrown out of office tomorrow is an unstable government, and that if throwing out governments is characteristic of a country's politics then that country is politically unstable. Political instability, whether it is so labeled or whether it is called stability, and whether it is cause or effect of economic and social problems, is basic to any consideration of Latin America.

Why are political instability, and the violence that attends it, so common in Latin America? Eliseo Vivas maintains that the Spanish character has had a great deal to do with the low state of Latin America's politics as well as of its economics. Recalling that Spaniards came to America as *conquistadores* rather than *colonizadores,* Vivas says that when those who first tried to settle Buenos Aires and Asunción faced starvation, "it never occurred to them that with small effort they could eke a living out of the land. . . . Their solution when out of supplies was to undertake raiding expeditions to steal food from the aborigines; that failing they simply sat down and waited for help or died of starvation."

> The attitudes brought with them by the *conquistadores* were transmitted to their heirs, who have since then kept themselves fairly distinct as a social class, even if they have not kept themselves as ethnically "pure" as they would like to believe. Increased by subsequent immigrations from Spain and by mixture with aboriginals and slaves, this class has remained, nevertheless, small in number relatively to the masses over which it rules, but it has managed successfully to retain political preeminence and economic control in every Spanish-American country except Mexico. Possessed of superior knowledge, wealth and military power, it does not mean to give up its place easily.[3]

Some observers, one might add, believe that despite the Mexican Revolution the class Vivas refers to has managed to retain, or possibly regain, political and economic power in Mexico as well.

Many students of Latin America place the blame for the state of the area's politics on the poor start the countries got—on the effort the new republics made to practice democracy, or in some cases the pretense they made of practicing it, when the conditions essential to democracy did not exist. Those persons consider that the gap between ideology and reality, between what people profess and what they practice, has deepened in the case of many countries, that it has become a characteristic of the political system.

Other persons suggest that instability and violence result from low levels of economic development; that the pie that is cut is so small that the struggle to obtain portions of it is inordinately intense. Still others point out that low national income means low levels of education, that low levels of education preclude the development of qualities that democracy requires, and that in the absence of democracy violence and instability are inevitable.

There are also those who point to what they call the colonial nature of Latin America's economy. They note that, in most countries, land ownership has been concentrated in the hands of a few families who manage to hold on to it, while mineral exploitation has been largely in the hands of foreign corporations. Since the countries have failed to industrialize, or to industrialize sufficiently, land and minerals remain the principal sources of wealth. Both are beyond the reach of the masses and even of most of the educated. As a consequence, such persons say, the most readily accessible source of wealth is government. Government offers jobs. It also offers power—the power to tax, to regulate, to influence owners of wealth, and sometimes to seize wealth or at least to share it. In these circumstances competition for control of government is extreme, and violence is a principal instrument.

THE ELEMENT OF TRUST

Whatever the origins of Latin America's political inadequacies, they reflect a lack of trust among citizens. Argentina is a striking example. Its people are of European origin and highly literate. Its humid *pampa* (prairie) is one of the richest agricultural areas of the world. Its living standards have been higher than those of some European countries. It should be well on its way to becoming one of the world's great nations. And yet it has not been able to achieve democracy—or stability. In the world of business Argentines are trustworthy and trusted. In the world of politics, on the other hand, they have little confidence in one another.

Paraguay, which is just north of Argentina, has a history of dictatorship that is longer and more flagrant than Argentina's. In Paraguay there are two principal parties, the Liberales and the Colorados. Characteristically, the Liberales have been in power until they were forcibly expelled by the Colorados, and the Colorados then have been in power until they were expelled by the Liberales. "What a way to run a country!" we might say. But we might also try putting ourselves in the place of Paraguayans. Why has neither party in Paraguay been willing to risk relinquishing power to the other in free elections? Because each fears and believes that if it does so it will never be given the opportunity to regain power in free elections. And its fears are solidly justified by history.

As ambassador to Paraguay from 1944 to 1946 I developed a close friendship with the country's dictator, General Higinio Morinigo. Even before the American republics had agreed, in 1933, not to intervene in each other's affairs, I had been opposed to United States intervention, largely as a result of my own experiences in Central American and Caribbean countries. Nevertheless, during a casual conversation with President Morinigo I suggested that Americans would feel better about the economic aid they were giving Paraguay if some steps were taken to lay the political basis for the establishment of democratic institutions in the country. To my surprise and gratification the president quickly fell in line. He made what appeared to be a courageous effort to introduce a measure of political freedom in the country. But he failed.

The first meeting of the political opposition that was freely held adjourned to the street in front of the presidential palace where it quickly became a mob. Participants threatened to climb to the second floor, where the president was working, and throw him out the window. They had to be restrained by police. The political group that had talked loudest of freedom was the first to use violence against its opponents.[4] Freedom in the sense of freedom to elect governments in a democratic fashion could not be achieved overnight, nor will it soon be achieved in Paraguay.

Political trust, of course, is a fragile quality in any part of the world: difficult to achieve, it is no less difficult to retain. McCarthyism, in the 1950s, brought about a sharp lessening in political trust among Americans. In 1960, after John F. Kennedy had been elected president, Republicans charged that he owed his election to fraud in Cook County, Illinois. When the charge was finally dropped, possibly because there were reasons to suspect fraud on the Republican side in other parts of Illinois, more than one observer breathed a sigh of relief. The charge that a president of the United States had attained office by fraud, if it had been pressed, was capable of lowering trust between the two great political parties below the level required for democracy to function effectively. The sensational Watergate scandal of 1972 and 1973 also lowered confidence between the parties, as well as in US government institutions, but the thorough manner in which it was investigated and perpetrators tried tended to restore confidence. Such accountability to the public is little known in most Latin American countries.

There have been tragic examples of despotism and oppression in Latin America. The infamous Rafael Leonidas Trujillo who, in and out of the presidency, governed the Dominican Republic from 1930 until he was assassinated in 1961, was one of them, and he merited the opprobrium that was attached to his name. But Trujillo and his numerous supporters were products of Dominican society. A society that is capable of democracy may achieve it. What has not been demonstrated is that a society that does not possess the requisite qualities can achieve democracy. For such a nation the alternative to today's tyrant is likely to be not democracy but a new tyrant.

Governments that are well inclined can help to create conditions that are favorable to democracy. The process may be a long one, however, and the prospect of success may not be good. People change only slowly and not always for the better. Of the twenty Latin American countries only four—Colombia, Costa Rica, the Dominican Republic and Venezuela—had freely elected governments in the mid-1970s, and in the Dominican Republic and Venezuela democracy had been tested only briefly. Democracies, in short, are as rare in Latin America as they are in the rest of the world.

MADE-TO-ORDER CONSTITUTIONS

No Latin American country has, today, the constitution it originally adopted after it became independent. In a few countries—in Argentina, Chile, and Mexico, for example—constitutions have been relatively long-lived. In others, adopting new constitutions has not been much more difficult than adopting new laws. More than one regime that has achieved power by violence has proceeded quickly to promulgate a new constitution in order to "legitimize" itself. Bolivia adopted two constitutions in one year, 1939. During the eight-year period 1874–81, the Dominican Republic adopted seven.

An issue that, during the early days of the republics, gave rise to controversy and to more than one bloody civil war, was whether governments should be unitary or federal in structure. Unitarians argued that a strong central government was required in order to combat regionalism and insure that the laws would be administered with justice. Their opponents, on the other hand, contended that federalism would encourage the development of grass-roots democracy, and that it would permit governments to adjust to local circumstances and local needs. Countries such as Chile and Colombia experimented with federalism for brief periods but concluded that it encouraged dissension and disunity. Argentina, Brazil, and Mexico are, in theory, federal republics today. In Brazil the states do, in fact, have considerable autonomy, and state governors are politically powerful persons. But the circumstance that in most countries national governments appoint and remove state governors, decree and collect nearly all taxes, and control the administration of justice, deprives the states of real authority. Even governments that are federal in form are apt to be unitary in fact.

All Latin American constitutions provide for a legislative body and an equitable system of justice, but since most governments are authoritarian such provisions usually have little meaning. Some dictators abolish or suspend the legislature and proceed to legislate by decree. They usually justify this as being more "efficient" and as better meeting the needs of "the people," in whose name dictators invariably govern. Other dictators permit the legislature to function so long as it does what it is told; any show of independence involves the risk of closure. Similarly the courts (including the highest ones) are traditionally packed with unconditional supporters of the dictatorship, while the police system is closely attuned to the dictator's wishes. Justice tends to be what the dictator says it is.

Most constitutions contain a provision that prohibits a president from succeeding himself in office. But a president who has convinced himself that continuing in power is vital to the country's "peace and prosperity" is not apt to be deterred by such provisions. He may discard the offending constitution and decree another, or instruct the legislature or a friendly constituent assembly to decree one. Power, rather than constitutional provision, is the determining factor. A president in Latin

America does not "take office" as he does in the United States, he "assumes power." Assuming power frequently means what it says. When it does, constitutionalism may well go by the board.

THE DEMOCRATIC PARTIES

If most Latin American countries have not achieved the democracy their constitutions proclaim or the stability they seek it has not been for lack of political parties. During the early years of independence party politics was a monopoly of the aristocracy, who divided more or less naturally into two groups: conservatives and liberals. Conservatives tended to ally themselves with the Church; they favored centralism in government and tariff protection for domestic industry. Liberals, most of whom were as Catholic as the conservatives, nevertheless tended to be anticlerical; they wanted to divest the Church of its secular influence, its control of such matters as registration of births, marriages, and deaths, and much of its landed wealth. They favored federalism in government and laissez-faire in economics.

Latin Americans may still be classified in a rough way as conservatives and liberals. In most countries, however, political parties have grown in number and variety even when we exclude the hundreds of groups that have sprung up overnight around the personalities of individual leaders and quickly disappeared. And, as in the case of the United States, conservatives and liberals have tended to exchange roles. Latin American liberals have come to favor a strong central government with power to direct the economy, while conservatives advocate limiting the power of the state and preserving economic freedoms.

Among the newer democratic parties are some that were imported from Europe. There are socialist parties, for example, in more than half the countries. Organized, in most cases, by European immigrants, they have met with little success, with the notable exception of the Socialist party of Chile, of which Salvador Allende Gossens was a leader. Chilean Socialists, however, became radicalized and in 1970, when Allende became president, they were well to the left of the Communist party with which they shared power. In some countries socialist programs, or certain features of them, were adopted by other parties. In Venezuela, for example, Acción Democratica largely preempted the Socialists' program and became the country's leading party.

Another European-inspired group is the Christian Democrats, principally Catholics who owe their ideological inspiration to the social encyclicals of the popes. An offshoot of the old conservative parties, they are a middle-class, leftist-oriented group who compete with the more extreme leftists for the vote of the masses. Their most spectacular success came in Chile, in 1964, when Eduardo Frei Montalva won the presidency. Although the party was comparatively new, Frei obtained the largest majority in Chile's modern history. In 1968 the Christian Democratic candidate, Rafael Caldera, was elected president of Venezuela, and in 1979 a second Christian Democrat, Luis Herrerra Campins, became president. In the seven other Latin American countries where they are organized, however, the Christian Democrats have had little success. Nevertheless they remain potentially strong contenders in a number of countries.

Socialists and Christian Democrats imported their ideologies from Europe, but most other democratic parties were "made in Latin America." Among the best known are the so-called "national revolutionary" parties such as the Alianza Popular Revolucionaria Americana in Peru, the Acción Democratica in Venezuela, the Movimiento Nacionalista Revolucionario in Bolivia and, before Castro, the Autentico and Ortodoxo parties in Cuba. The Partido Revolucionario Institucional, in Mexico, is sometimes included in the group but despite its name it was organized not by persons in the political opposition, as the other revolutionary parties were, but from within the government and at a time when the Mexican Revolution was already advanced. It has remained a government party, and its candidate is always elected president. Mexico is essentially a one-party state.

Although the national revolutionary parties arose separately in the various countries, the purposes they claim to have are, in general, the same, and in that sense the Partido Revolucionario Institucional, in Mexico, may properly be included among them. All of them direct special appeals to city workers and peasants, although they also aspire to represent the growing middle sector. They sponsor agrarian reform. They seek to elevate the status of the Indian and to incorporate him into the nation. They are nationalistic but less anti-American than the Marxists. In general they recognize that foreign as well as domestic private capital can make important contributions to the ends they proclaim.

Of the many extremist parties of the Left that have been formed around the personality of a dominant leader none has had any lasting prominence except the Justicialista party of Argentina, which was organized by Juan Domingo Perón. Perón's reelection to the presidency in 1973, after eighteen years of exile, was dramatic evidence of the persistence of the Peronist myth. To what extent *justicialismo* constituted a party, a labor movement, or a personal vehicle of Perón, however, was never clear during Perón's lifetime. Even before his death it had begun to break up into opposing factions.

THE TOTALITARIANS

Latin America has had its share of totalitarian parties, and some of them have left imprints on society, but in general they have not prospered. Fascism had adherents in some countries when nazism in Germany and fascism in Italy seemed to many persons to represent the wave of the future. But it never had any success. In November 1937 Getulio Vargas established what many called a fascist state in Brazil, but it had only a superficial resemblance to fascist regimes in Europe and Vargas promptly outlawed the Integralista party, which aspired to establish authentic fascism in the country. In Mexico, Bolivia, and Chile fascist-type parties unsuccessfully vied for power. In Bolivia, nevertheless, the Falange Socialista Boliviana, modeled originally after the Spanish Falange, joined with the leftist Movimiento Nacionalista Revolucionario to support the conservative government of Colonel Hugo Banzer in 1971. At that time, however, it could hardly be called a fascist party.

The most persistent of the totalitarian groups have been the Communists. There is no country that does not have a Communist party functioning openly or clandestinely. And communism has had its successes. Cuba became a Communist state following Fidel Castro's takeover of the country, although the Communists had only a minor role in that success. Cuba was Castro's gift to communism. In Chile, on the other hand, the Communists, in cooperation with the even more leftist Socialists, won their own victory within the democratic process when they placed Allende in the presidency. The two groups, plus the once powerful Radical party and three smaller groups, received slightly more than a third of the total vote. Success was short-lived however. After the Socialist-Communist government had led the country into political and economic chaos the Chilean armed forces, despite a long record of supporting elected governments, intervened and overthrew it.

The Communists claim to be the vanguard of the proletariat but in Latin America they have had to work long and hard to interest the proletariat in their cause. Many young persons enter the party but most leave it out of boredom, or because they are unwilling to submit to the discipline required of party members, or because they cannot tolerate the party's subservience to Soviet Russia, or because they disagree with what they understand to be the party's ideology, or for several or all of these reasons. Nevertheless a high percentage of Communist leaders have entered the party during their student days.

As might be expected, Communists have been a disruptive force. In many countries they have achieved leadership in labor unions, and their ability to bring about damaging strikes has given them strong leverage with governments. If an industry is not only basic to a country's economy but also foreign-owned, the power to disrupt is even greater.

Communist leaders are professionals. They have survived repression by governments and purges by the party. A good number have served in the international communist bureaucracy. Nearly all have visited Russia, and many have lived there. They enjoy Russian support, and Russia is a refuge for them in time of need. They are skillful in interpreting and exploiting the zigs and zags of Russian foreign policy and making them acceptable to the rank and file of the party. Most of them are fully identified with the Soviet government's aims and purposes in the world. Through them Russia intervenes systematically in the internal affairs of all the Latin American countries.

4
CAUDILLISMO AND MILITARISM

IT IS COMMON, in discussions such as this, to speak of "interest groups"—of landowners, industrialists, businessmen, farmers, labor unions, and others who influence a country's politics. Latin America of course has many such groups. In most countries professional politicians and the military constitute the most powerful interest groups, but their importance naturally varies from country to country.

In addition to interest groups there are certain forces that strongly influence events. Among them are what I shall call the "'isms"—*caudillismo* (bossism) and militarism, anti-imperialism, nationalism, and Marxism. The 'isms are both cause and product of circumstances that are common to all the countries. *Caudillismo* and militarism are as old as the republics themselves; nationalism on the other hand is a relatively new phenomenon. Anti-imperialism is largely a state of mind; it and Marxism feed on people's frustrations. All the 'isms also feed on one another. Together they exercise a powerful and often a dominant influence on the politics and the economics of most of the Latin American countries.

If democracy is lacking in a country that is theoretically democratic, what takes its place? Nations have to have some kind of government, if not democratic then some other kind. Chaos is not an alternative to institutional government. Someone steps in to prevent chaos or to reduce chaos to order. In Latin America the common substitute for democracy has been *caudillismo,* or government by the *caudillo,* the natural leader. The *caudillo* may be elected president, he may become president without the formality of elections, or he may dominate a country's politics without occupying the presidency. Fidel Castro is a *caudillo* who has utilized communism, support by the Soviet Union, and anti-Americanism as tools for retaining power over Cubans. *Caudillismo* has a respectable tradition in Latin America, as it has in the mother countries, Spain and Portugal. Generalisimo Francisco Franco Bahamonde was not only chief of the Spanish state; he also was *El Caudillo.*

The *caudillo* is not necessarily a military man. José Gaspar Rodriguez Francia, *El Supremo,* who forged Paraguay's independence, was a doctor of sacred theology. He ruled his country with cruel absolutism for twenty-four years. Getulio Vargas, Brazil's president-dictator for fifteen years, was a mild-mannered lawyer. Neither a uniform nor a military title can make a *caudillo.* Nevertheless most *caudillos* have been military men.

Latin Americans, in general, are still far from achieving institutional government, but in most countries there is one institution that has managed to gain in stability and power: the military. Except in Costa Rica, which has no military establishment, the military are important in the politics of all the countries and they dominate the politics of more than half of them. At the same time they rarely act alone. More often than not it is civilians who take the lead in urging military intervention. Many civilian politicians prefer victory with military support to defeat without it, especially if they have reason to fear that the alternative is military support of the opposition. In any event the military seldom intervene without first gaining substantial civilian support.* The military were subjected to overwhelming civilian pressure before they intervened in Chile (1973) and in Argentina (1975).

Latin America's military establishments have changed a great deal in recent years. Today's military leaders are professionals. Beginning in the late nineteenth century German, French, and British instructors were brought in to train the armies and navies of several of the larger countries. Later, Americans filled the role. Some Latin American officers helped to train the armed forces of other countries. Instead of riding a horse at the head of an ill-clothed, undisciplined troop many of

*The military's need for the good opinion of citizens can be a powerful brake on political adventures (it might be decisive if civilians were less divided than they usually are). Near the end of the first Perón regime many Argentines began to exert subtle pressure on the military to withdraw their support from the regime. They had ways of embarrassing the military—by the way they looked at them, the way they spoke to them, the words they used when the military were within hearing, the way they ignored the military in shops, restaurants, and other public places, and their attitude toward the families of the military. Officers became uncomfortable and defensive in the presence of civilians.

today's military leaders command tank units. Some are skilled in anti-submarine warfare; others fly supersonic fighter planes. In countries that have moved toward socialism, military men are managers of steel mills and of petroleum companies. And of course some serve as cabinet officers and as presidents of their countries, as military men have done since the earliest days of independence.

But the general who reaches the presidency today is apt to have different purposes from those of earlier military presidents. Until recently, for example, the general who retired from the presidency without having amassed a fortune was a rarity. Trujillo in the Dominican Republic, Perón in Argentina, Batista in Cuba, and Pérez Jiménez in Venezuela became multimillionaires in office. There are still generals who become rich in office but if they are not yet a rarity neither are those who leave office as poor as they went in. The new military president tends to be quite a different person from the old-fashioned *caudillo.* He is apt to be placed in office by the military institution or, perhaps more accurately, by the leaders of the military institution, and to remain in office only so long as he carries out the will of those leaders.

THE MONITORING ROLE

Today's military see themselves not as vulgar seekers after power but as monitors of the government's performance. Interestingly enough, this monitoring role is sanctioned by tradition and even by law. Some fifteen of the Latin American constitutions designate the military as guardians of the constitution, and the military are apt to take the provision seriously—more seriously than the drafters of the constitutions probably intended them to.* The armed forces are alert to government acts that might be in violation of the constitution or that might endanger national security or internal peace. The monitoring role gives them an informal veto power over decisions of civilian agencies, including those of the presidency itself. In most countries they have ways of communicating their apprehension or displeasure at steps the executive power, or even the legislature, may be contemplating, and prudent

*This does not mean that when the military themselves take over the government they are necessarily respectful of the constitution. In fact the contrary is apt to be the case.

political leaders take such warnings seriously. Although politically ambitious military leaders are never lacking, as a rule the military hope that the veto power will serve their purposes. In general their aim is not to place a military man in the presidency but to control or strongly influence events. If they can do that without violence, without the necessity of a coup d' etat or a revolution, they prefer it that way.

One development that is apt to bring on military intervention is a threat to the military institution. While the armed forces' role in politics is often accepted it is also resented, and many efforts have been made to reduce it. Political leaders would like to free themselves from military constraint. One possible way to do that is by reducing the armed forces' appropriations. Reducing appropriations would not only curtail the armed forces' political power (at least the political leaders hope it would); it would also release funds that are needed for other purposes, or that could be used for purposes that are more politically attractive. But except in the case of Mexico and Costa Rica efforts to lower military appropriations have met with little success. In many countries there is an understanding that a certain percentage of the national budget will go to the military. The understanding is rarely violated. A president who refused to respect it might find himself replaced in office.*

The Military as Builders. More recently the military have broadened their concept of what constitutes a threat to their institution. They now regard poverty, discontent, protest by citizens, and the failure of government to solve the economic and social problems that give rise to protest as threats not only to domestic tranquility, which the military have the duty of safeguarding, but to the military institution itself. They are quite aware that when Fidel Castro undertook to subvert Cuba's society he first destroyed the armed forces and rebuilt them on his own pattern and with his own men, and they are determined to prevent the rise of new Castros. And more and more of them have come to believe that the way to do that—perhaps the only way—is for the military institution to become the instrument of economic and social change.

*In comparison with expenditures in other less-developed areas of the world military expenditures in Latin America are moderate. In most of the countries they do not exceed 25 percent of budgetary expenditures. In Mexico they are as low as 10 percent. What concerns many Latin Americans and many of Latin America's friends is that the countries are spending more than they need to spend and much more than they can afford.

The US government had a role, although an unwitting one, in encouraging the Latin American military in this belief. In its military assistance program it stressed what its officials called "civic action"—activities such as road building, bridge building, and furnishing medical care to persons in rural areas, all of which the military are capable of carrying out although the activities do not have primarily military purposes. The Americans had a number of reasons for urging and supporting civic action. There were charges that United States assistance was helping to build up the armed forces in Latin America at the expense of the civilian economies and, in some cases, at the expense of the political freedoms of citizens. The Americans hoped that civic action would improve their image in Latin America and the image of the Latin American military. They also hoped, of course, that it would contribute to economic and social improvement. Some of it undoubtedly did. But much of it was little more than blowing in the wind.

A sample of civic action "in action" was revealed during a Senate "Hearing on Defense Department Sponsored Foreign Affairs Research" on May 9, 1968. I shall let the record speak for itself.

> The CHAIRMAN (Senator FULBRIGHT). Senator Mundt, you raised exactly the question I raised in the beginning. The question is not that some of these activities are not interesting to everybody, but whether or not this is the responsibility of the Defense Department.
>
> There are a great many of these. Another is called "Resettlement in Latin America, an Analysis of 35 Cases."
>
> The summary gives an indication of what it is about. I will read a paragraph . . . "The analysis indicated that physical characteristics of the settlements, namely, the quality of the soils, favorable terrain and accessability are significantly correlated with success. The resettlements consisting of parcels over 25 hectares, about 50 acres in size, were most likely to be successful. All settlements with a homogeneous population succeeded, while about one-third of the settlements with heterogeneous composition failed. . . . The selection of crops should be made on the basis of soils, climate and marketability. Parcel sizes should be based on scientific assessments of soils, terrain, crops and family size."

Senator Fulbright, obviously perplexed by what he had read, continued: "It is difficult for me to see what interest this is to the Army. These are settlements of agricultural people, I suppose, out of the northeast section of Brazil. . . . If anybody is going to do research in this area I would think it would be Agriculture or AID."[1]

The Defense Department, presumably with a straight face, later furnished the committee the followng explanation of the material Senator Fulbright had read at the hearing.

> One of the missions of the United States Army is to advise, on their request, the armies of developing nations on their missions within their countries. In many developing nations, the indigenous armies are actively engaged in civic action programs such as resettlement. Generally, the local government desires to resettle people in an area offering greater potential and stability for their future existence. In many cases the indigenous army is given the assignment to carry out the program. If US military officers are to be successful in advising their counterparts on such matters, then it is important to estimate the effectiveness of the planned programs. To illustrate: in comparing the effectiveness of several resettlement operations, it is important to know whether, for example, the quality of the soil in one area was the primary factor in the success of one project as compared to another.[2]

Paraphrasing Wellington's comment on the low quality of the troops London had just sent him, this American–Latin American military invasion of the field of agriculture may not have scared the Brazilian farmers but it certainly scared the hell out of me.*

Civic action was not new, by any means, although the name was probably new. The Corps of Engineers of the US Army had a long and impressive record of civic action, if by this we understand nonmilitary action presumed useful to the nation's economy. Its support in the Congress, especially among representatives of states that wanted dams and other public works constructed at federal expense, was so great that it was sometimes beyond the power of the president himself to defy or alter it. The Paraguayan army, which furnishes most of the country's presidents, had engaged in civic action for longer than could be remembered. Batista, in Cuba, had practiced civic action with elán. Other leaders, similarly, had engaged in civic action without attaching a label to it. The difference in the civic action of the 1960s was that it had United States moral and material support and a made-in-the-United States mystique. The Latin American military began to take their nonmilitary role more seriously. They saw themselves as nation builders.

---

*In its aid programs the Department of Defense long ago lost interest in such nonmilitary fields as agriculture.

THE WAR COLLEGES

During most of Latin America's history, the common procedure when the military took over a government, at least in the larger countries, was to form a military junta whose principal function was to find a way to turn the government back to an acceptable civilian group. Since 1964, however, the pattern has been modified in some countries. In Brazil, Peru, Bolivia, Chile, and Argentina, for example, the military decided not only to run the government for a prolonged period of time but to restructure it, ideologically and functionally. Their hope, and the hope of their civilian supporters, was that after ten or twenty or more years of "disciplined" and "well-managed" government, and after needed economic and social reforms, past errors would have been corrected and rapid and permanent improvement brought about.

In the late 1970s one was bound to be impressed by the number of military governments in Latin America. More than half the countries had military presidents. One was impressed also with their differing ideologies. Although military government had been common in Latin America, leftist military governments had not been. They were beginning to appear, however. And there was another phenomenon that was new and that had little to do with either Right or Left (though perhaps it had to do with both): military leadership in government—civic action on a grand scale—was being institutionalized, to a degree, under the leadership of the war colleges. Again the US government had a rolc in the process.

The National War College, in Washington, is at the pinnacle of the US armed forces' institutions of learning. In it selected military officers, and some civilian officials as well, study national security policy and national security strategy. But the stress is on the nonmilitary aspects of national security—on politics, economics, and social problems. A growing number of Latin American countries have set up institutions patterned after the National War College. Some of them were set up with the college's assistance.

At Fort Lesley J. McNair, in Washington, only a few hundred yards from the National War College, there is still another war college, the Inter-American Defense College, to which the American republics, the United States among them, send students. The commandant is an American; its deputy commandants are Latin Americans. Here military men from nearly all the Latin American countries gather and listen to the same kinds of lectures that are heard at the National War College, but frequently with much greater interest and no little expectation that the lessons learned can be put to good use when the officers return to their countries.

The general idea of the National War College was that the military in the United States needed to be "civilianized"—to be instructed at high levels in nonmilitary matters related to national security. Increasingly, Latin American war colleges have had a different objective: to "militarize" civilians. A substantial number of their students are civilian officials, university professors, and professional men, and the military's purpose is to indoctrinate them with the military's view of how the countries' problems should be met. It is not a coincidence that a high percentage of the leaders of Latin America's recent revolutions have been associated with the war colleges. War colleges in Latin America, by their very nature, spark revolution.[3]

PLUSES AND MINUSES

The military role in Latin America's politics is traditional. In its origins it was unavoidable. Few countries have been able to suppress it, or even to modify it very much. But granted that it is important, is it also useful? There is no easy or single answer to that question. If one assumes that military intervention is the most acceptable alternative to chaos, which it sometimes seems to be, he is apt to think that without it things might be worse (the overthrow, in Chile, of the Socialist-Communist government of Salvador Allende Gossens, in 1973, and its replacement by the military government of Augusto Pinochet, rescued Chile from anarchy and possibly saved it from communization). On the other hand if he believes that civilians would get along better with one another, and meet problems more successfully, if they were denied the option of bringing the military into their quarrels, he may take the view that military intervention has been harmful (the overthrow, in Peru, of the democratic government of Fernando Belaúnde Terry, in 1968, and its replacement by the military government of Juan Velasco Alvarado, had disastrous effects on Peru's politics and economy).

The problem is a human one, of course, and the human factor varies from country to country. Costa Rica and Nicaragua are neighboring countries in Central America. Costa Rica has no army and is close to being a classic democracy. Nicaragua has a well-trained army. The army's commander became the country's dictator. Does that mean that if Costa Rica had an army it would be governed by a dictator, and that if Nicaragua had no army it would be a democracy? Probably not. Costa Ricans are different people from Nicaraguans. Similarly, in Brazil the military aspire, one day, to return the government to civilians, while in next-door Paraguay the military are a privileged caste who probably have no intention of giving up political power.

What the military usually bring to a country, at least for a period, is "order." They usually take office with high hopes that "orderly," that is to say dictatorial, government will permit people to forget disorderly and disruptive politics and concentrate on solving urgent economic and social problems. But problems may prove to be more difficult to solve than the military had assumed. And the presence of the military in power creates new problems. All those problems together may be less grave than chaos but they still can be very grave. As a rule the military, after early euphoria has disappeared and cracks have developed in their ranks, have opted to return the government to civilians. It remains to be seen whether the institutionalization of military leadership that appears to be taking place will change that. Will the military assume the responsibilities of government in more and more countries and for longer and longer periods? There are some indications that they will, or at least that they will try to.

But great hazards attend the effort. When the military take over the political function they become politicized, subject to the same divisions, the same conflicts, and the same temptations that exist among civilians in political life. The discipline the military wish to impose on civilians may be lacking in their own ranks. Military effectiveness may be seriously lowered. Nor is political success assured.

Latin Americans have a long history of living under dictatorship. They also have a history of getting rid of dictators, or at least of changing dictators. They are quite likely to take for granted whatever improvement the military may bring them (which in any case may be insufficient to meet their expectations) while resenting their loss of freedom as much as ever or even more. In those circumstances the military may have to choose between turning the government back to civilians or resorting increasingly to repression. Either course involves risks for the military as well as for the nation.

5
ANTI-IMPERIALISM

IMPERIALISM IS as old as civilization. It reached a peak when the discoveries of the fifteenth and sixteenth centuries led to the creation of great empires in America. But by 1825 most of the New World had gained its freedom. Imperialism seemed to be on the wane. Nevertheless before the century was over it had taken on new life. Almost overnight Britain, France, Germany, the Netherlands, Belgium, and Italy had carved out new empires in Africa and Asia.

The motives of the earlier imperialists were various. Bernal Díaz, the doughty Spanish soldier and chronicler who fought with Cortés in Mexico, said that the Spaniards had come to America "to serve God and the King and also to get rich." Similarly, there were a number of motives behind the later imperialism. Power rivalries among the imperial countries certainly provided some. But whatever the motives it was technology that principally accounted for it. Technology had made the early empires possible; arrows and spears were no match for blazing guns and coats of armor. Technology also was responsible for imperialism's revival.

Geoffrey Barraclough has reminded us that the industrial revolution, which ushered in the age of coal and iron, was followed by the technological and scientific revolution, which brought into being the age of steel and electricity, of oil and chemicals. The economies of the industrialized countries expanded with explosive force. Steel, which had been considered almost a semiprecious metal, suddenly became inexpensive and common. The Krupp Works, in Germany, which in 1846 had employed 122 men, was employing 16,000 by 1873 and almost 70,000 by 1913. Similar changes were taking place in England and France, and of course in the United States as well.

Not only industry but agriculture, too, was revolutionized. Sterilization and pasteurization provided new means of preserving food. Bulk conservation and transportation of food became practicable for the first time. Completion of great railroad systems, construction of large ships, and new techniques of refrigeration made it possible to ship foods over long distances. By 1877 Argentine chilled beef was reaching England. About the same time Brazilian coffee began to arrive in Europe and the United States in bulk. All this constituted a revolution in feeding industrialized and urbanized populations, and it brought a revolution in world trading patterns.

The new activities required new sources of raw materials. As Barraclough has well said, "the voracious appetite of the new industrialism, unable of its very nature to draw sufficient sustenance from local resources, rapidly swallowed up the whole wide world. . . . Industry now went out into the world in search of the basic materials without which, in its new forms, it could not exist."[1] One effect of the new forces was a revival of mercantilist doctrines. The neomercantilists argued that, since no nation now could expect to be self-sufficient, each industrial country should develop a colonial empire that would constitute a self-sufficient trading world, with the home country supplying manufactures in return for foodstuffs and raw materials. "The day of small nations," said Joseph Chamberlain, England's great Liberal political leader, "has long passed away; the day of Empire has come."[2]

The new imperialism lasted only three-quarters of a century. It came crashing down after World War II when demography, in the form of colonial population growth, and technology, the transfer to the colonial peoples of the very technological and scientific skills that had brought imperialism about, made it no longer possible. The former imperial countries joined together in a European Common Market. Integration, not empire, had become Europe's device for assuring prosperity.

The industrialized nations found that they did not need colonies in order to gain access to raw materials. Economic progress had taken place quite independently of imperialism—perhaps despite it. Belgium and the Netherlands, and France and Germany as well, found themselves more prosperous without colonies than they had been with them. The new imperialism died because colonies were no longer willing to remain colonies. It died also because it was unprofitable to the imperial countries.[3]

THE MONROE DOCTRINE

The United States was never a convinced imperialist, but it was certainly expansionist, and it is difficult to criticize those who saw little difference between the two. Before the nineteenth century ended, the small nation that had not earlier ventured far from the Atlantic seaboard had extended its domain over a large part of the North American continent. It had also acquired overseas territories that, if they did not compare with those of England, or even of Portugal, were still extensive and gave an impression of burgeoning ambition and power.

At the very time the United States itself was busy acquiring land, it was warning Europe against any new territorial adventures in the Americas, and with ample reason. Europe continued to consider itself the power center of the world. Spain was not entirely reconciled to the loss of its American colonies, and European monarchs probably were no more pleased at the expansion of republicanism in the Western Hemisphere than the United States and Western Europe were at communism's expansion throughout the world a century later. Not all European monarchs were content to leave things as they were.

The first warning against any meddling with the new status quo in the Americas came from the Congress, in 1811. There were rumors that Spain was planning to transfer the Floridas to England. A joint congressional resolution declared that "the United States cannot without serious inquietude see any part of the said territory pass into the hands of any foreign power." According to other rumors the Holy Alliance was planning to support Spain in an effort to recover its American colonies. In a message to Congress on December 2, 1823, President James Monroe said:

> The American continents, by the free and independent condition which they have assumed and maintain, are henceforth not to be considered as subjects for future colonization by any European powers. . . . With the existing colonies or dependencies of any European power we have not interfered and shall not interfere. But with the governments who have declared their independence and maintained it, and whose independence we have, on great consideration and on just principles, acknowledged, we could not view any interposition for the purpose of oppressing them, or controlling in any other manner their destiny, by

any European power, in any other light than as the manifestation of an unfriendly disposition toward the United States. . . .

The Monroe Doctrine, as it came to be known, is regarded by many as one of the most important utterances in the history of American diplomacy, but reaction to it at the time was less than sensational. Austria's Metternich spoke of "indecent declarations." The Russian czar considered that the document merited "only the most profound contempt."[4] Metternich and the czar would doubtless have agreed that the United States itself merited profound contempt. It was still far from being a member of the Great Powers' "club."

Despite the brave words of the Monroe Doctrine, Europe continued to intervene in Latin America. Spain landed forces in Mexico in 1829, reoccupied Santo Domingo in 1861, and fought a brief war against Peru and Chile in 1864. France occupied Veracruz in 1838 and intervened in Argentina and Uruguay. It invaded Mexico in 1862 and left Austria's Archduke Maximilian there as emperor. Britain intervened in Argentina and helped in the creation of Uruguay as a buffer state between Argentina and Brazil. In 1833 it occupied the Falkland Islands, off Argentina's coast just east of the Straits of Magellan (it has continued to hold them in the face of Argentine protest). And there were numerous other European incursions into Latin America. The United States was too weak to defend the continent. Latin Americans could be forgiven for not attaching excessive importance to the Monroe Doctrine or to any protection they might expect from it, especially since Americans were making their own incursions into Latin America and acquiring their own reputation as "imperialists."

MANIFEST DESTINY

In 1845 the United States annexed Texas, which had once been a part of Mexico. As a result of its war with Mexico (1846–48), and by later purchase, it acquired an additional large area of land from that country.

In 1855 William Walker, an American soldier of fortune who weighed all of 100 pounds, accepted the invitation of Nicaragua's Liberals to support them in their civil war against the Conservatives, and succeeded in having himself "elected" president of Nicaragua. His government was promptly recognized by the United States. Walker was a vociferous exponent of "manifest destiny," the emotional conviction shared by many Americans in the 1840s and 1850s that the United States was destined by Providence to extend its republican institutions over much of the Americas. Walker had the support of a number of southern states that hoped Nicaragua would be added to the Union as a slave state. The British, who were interested in controlling a possible future Nicaraguan canal, covertly opposed him.

Walker made the mistake of seizing a vessel belonging to Cornelius Vanderbilt, a rising American entrepreneur who ran a transit system across Nicaragua. Many Americans involved in the gold rush to California were using it in preference to the long and dangerous overland route across the United States. With Vanderbilt, the British, and most of Central America against him, Walker was soon driven out of the presidency and out of Nicaragua. On his third expedition to Central America he surrendered to a British naval officer who turned him over to Nicaragua's neighbors, the Hondurans. They shot him.

After the Civil War was ended, and the United States was free to turn its attention outward, it began to take more seriously what it considered to be its obligations under the Monroe Doctrine. The country was growing in strength and confidence. The new mood became evident at the time of the Venezuela–British Guiana boundary dispute in 1895. Britain had gradually extended its colony's boundary until it nearly reached the delta of Venezuela's Orinoco River. When Venezuela, invoking "the immortal Monroe," appealed to the United States to intervene, President Cleveland decided it was time to give the doctrine some teeth. Richard Olney, his secretary of state, informed the British government in a burst of euphoria:

> Today, the United States is practically sovereign on this continent, and its fiat is law upon the subjects to which it confines its interposition. Why?. . . . It is because, in addition to all other grounds, its infinite resources combined with its isolated position render it master of the situation and practically invulnerable as against any or all other powers.[5]

The young nation went wild. The Congress cheered the president on. Theodore Roosevelt and Henry Cabot Lodge were exuberant. Britain, faced with serious problems with the Boers in South Africa, and a growing threat from Germany, agreed to submit the dispute to arbitration. In the end it divided the disputed territory with Venezuela. Political leaders in the United States took advantage of the new public mood. McKinley was elected in 1896 on a platform calling not only for "the eventual withdrawal of European powers from the hemisphere" but, more specifically, for American help in freeing Cuba from Spain.

The Spanish-American War, which brought Puerto Rico and the Philippines under the American flag and made Cuba an American protectorate, was popular in the United States. John Hay, McKinley's secretary of state, referred to it, in an unguarded moment, as a "splendid little war." Roosevelt, as leader of the Rough Riders in Cuba, became a much-publicized national hero; he had no trouble reaching the vice-presidency and, later, the presidency. "Our rightful supremacy in the Western Hemisphere cannot be relinquished," said Henry Cabot Lodge. Albert J. Beveridge, an ebullient senator from Indiana, said, "God has marked the American people as his Chosen Nation to finally lead to the regeneration of the World." Latin Americans read these and other similar statements with interest. Few liked them.

THE PANAMA CANAL

The United States built the Panama Canal, which has performed notable service to international commerce, and probably to international peace, but Latin Americans objected to the way the matter was handled. Panama, a province of Colombia, had much more in common with readily accessible New Orleans and New York than it had with remote Bogotá. On several occasions it had tried, without success, to free itself from Colombian domination. Colombia had authorized a French group to build a canal across the Isthmus of Panama; the French had tried to build one but had failed. Now Colombia wanted the United States to do the job, and the Americans were anxious to comply. And Panamanians wanted the United States to do the job even more than their rulers in Bogotá did.

In August 1903, to the dismay of Panamanians, the Colombian Congress rejected the Hay-Herrán Treaty (already approved by the United States Senate), which authorized the United States to build a canal. On November 3 rebellious Panamanians declared their independence. A contingent of some 400 Colombian soldiers, probably enough to prevent or put down the rebellion, tried to reach the provincial capital, but was unable to obtain transport across the isthmus. A small United States naval force, under instructions from Washington, had prohibited transit in any direction and, in any case, the American-operated Panama

Railroad was unable to find cars with which to transport the soldiers. The revolution was unopposed. On November 6 the United States recognized the Republic of Panama; on November 19 it signed a treaty with a representative of the new government in which it guaranteed Panama's independence and obtained authorization to construct a canal. The treaty was agreed to in Washington before authorities in Panama had read the text (it was ratified later by both parties). Among other provisions it granted the United States perpetual control over a ten-mile strip across the isthmus, with all the rights, power, and authority it would possess if it were sovereign, as well as the right to take any additional lands it might need for canal purposes.

President Roosevelt was directly involved in these events. He always maintained that his acts were proper, that he had never encouraged the Panamanians to revolt, but Dana G. Munro, an eminent authority, considers that the revolution would never have occurred if Roosevelt had tried to discourage it. He further considers that by receiving Philippe Bunau-Varilla, the French engineer who was one of the conspirators (and who was to sign the treaty on behalf of Panama), and permitting him to discuss his plans, Roosevelt "tacitly encouraged" the revolution. And it was difficult even for good friends of the United States to justify its use of force to prevent Colombia from putting down the revolution.[6]

The canal proved a boon to Panama and to the rest of the world, but its terms and the manner of its signing fueled increasing protest on the part of Panamanians. Revision of the treaty became an inflammatory banner in Panama's politics. Successive administrations in the United States, Republican and Democratic, undertook to negotiate an agreement more acceptable to Panama. Despite prolonged and vociferous opposition in the United States, two treaties, one providing that ownership and operation of the canal would be fully assumed by Panama at noon on December 31, 1999, and another providing for the permanent neutrality of the canal, were signed on September 7, 1977, and later ratified by both countries.

THE ROOSEVELT COROLLARY

Despite emotional claims to hegemony by some US politicians, European countries continued to intervene in Latin America when they were unable to obtain peaceful redress for their grievances. In 1902, after Cipriano Castro, Venezuela's dictator, had dealt with foreign creditors in a high-handed manner, Germany and Great Britain bombarded two Venezuelan forts, seized several Venezuelan warships, and instituted a naval blockade of the country.* The blockade was lifted when Venezuela agreed to submit the matters in dispute to arbitration. But the incident showed that steps would have to be taken immediately to prevent recurrences. The matter was all the more urgent because Europeans insisted that, Monroe Doctrine or no Monroe Doctrine, the Latin American states should not be permitted to evade their international obligations with impunity. In his message to Congress of December 6, 1904, President Roosevelt said:

> If a nation shows that it knows how to act with reasonable efficiency and decency in social and political matters, if it keeps order and pays its obligations, it need fear no interference from the United States. Chronic wrongdoing, or an impotence which results in a general loosening of the ties of civilized society, may in America, as elsewhere, ultimately require intervention by some civilized nation, and in the Western Hemisphere the adherence of the United States to the Monroe Doctrine may force the United States, however reluctantly, in flagrant cases of such wrongdoing or impotence, to the exercise of an international police power. . . . We would interfere with them only in the last resort, and then only if it became evident that their inability or unwillingness to do justice at home and abroad had violated the rights of the United States or had invited foreign aggression to the detriment of the entire body of American nations. . . .

President Roosevelt was expressing what came to be known as the Roosevelt Corollary to the Monroe Doctrine. In a letter to Elihu Root he had said: "If we are willing to let Germany or England act as the policemen of the Caribbean, then we can afford not to interfere when gross wrongdoing occurs. But if we intend to say 'Hands Off' to the powers of Europe, then sooner or later we must keep order ourselves."[7]

The Dominican Republic, at the time, had outstanding debts owing

*Roosevelt engaged in some effective gunboat diplomacy by informally warning Germany that he would send the American fleet, then assembled in the Caribbean, to the Venezuelan coast if agreement amont the countries was not reached within a period of time. (Dana G. Munro, *Intervention and Dollar Diplomacy in the Caribbean, 1900–1921* [Princeton, NJ: Princeton University Press, 1964], pp. 72–73.)

to nationals of France, Belgium, Germany, Italy, and Spain, as well as to nationals of the United States. Some of the European governments were threatening to occupy the country or take over its customhouses if the debts were not paid. In 1905, after conditions in the country had continued to deteriorate, the United States, in agreement with the Dominican government, appointed an American to take over all the country's customhouses. He was instructed to distribute 55 percent of customs revenues to the foreign creditors and the remaining 45 percent to the country's treasury. Ironically, the Dominican government received more from its 45 percent than it had formerly received from 100 percent—a sad commentary on the efficiency and honesty of Dominican customs officials.[8]

The language that President Roosevelt used in his message to Congress was not as diplomatic as it might have been. When he seemed to imply that some Latin American nations might not be civilized, more than one felt alluded to. When he talked of the United States exercising an international police power, the United States became a colossus to be feared.

The Roosevelt Corollary led to prolonged military interventions in the Dominican Republic, Haiti, and Nicaragua. Ironically, it was President Woodrow Wilson, apostle of self-determination, who intervened most.

The Roosevelt Corollary, in turn, led more or less naturally to President William Howard Taft's "dollar diplomacy," which came to have a bad name although the idea behind it was rational, if a little ahead of its time. The idea, in simple terms, was that those Latin American countries that were politically unstable and economically backward needed, and presumably wanted, new investment in the private sector and fiscal stability in the public sector. As it happened, the United States thought that its investors and its bankers could help to supply both.

Dollar diplomacy anticipated the later aid programs, which reached a peak in the Alliance for Progress. Like the Alliance it aimed at economic and political improvement in Latin America; like the Alliance it was condemned by some Latin Americans, and by some Americans, as an example of United States "imperialism."

Looking back from today's vantage point, it is easy to criticize the Monroe Doctrine and especially the Roosevelt Corollary. But phenomena should also be examined in the context of their times. The Theodore Roosevelt period was not exactly one of international permissiveness. Thus for a country to confiscate oil refineries and sugar properties belonging to citizens of more powerful countries, as Castro's Cuba did in 1960, or to confiscate the properties of large foreign mining companies, as Allende's Chile did in 1971, without forcible retaliation from the country or countries whose interests were affected, would have been inconceivable.

Nevertheless the considerations behind United States interventions were less economic than strategic. They reflected the nation's concern with its own security, especially with the security of the Panama Canal, one of the most important and at the same time most militarily vulnerable waterways of the world. The chronically unstable politics of the Central American and Caribbean countries, and the frequent interventions of those countries in one another's affairs, offered tempting opportunities to nations interested in obtaining footholds in the area. Evidence is not lacking that, were it not for the vigilance of the United States, some nations would have taken advantage of their opportunities. Great Britain had tried for years to insure that it would have at least partial control of whatever transcontinental canal might be built. Not until 1901 did it agree, in the Hay-Pauncefote Treaty, that the United States might build, control and, by implication, defend such a canal.[9] And both France and Germany landed forces in Haiti just prior to United States intervention there in 1915.

What would have happened if Roosevelt and later presidents had not followed the policies they did? We cannot tell, of course. History does not reveal its alternatives, it has been said. And yet only by considering possible alternatives can we properly evaluate a course of action. Would it have been better to permit European countries to continue to collect debts by force or the threat of force, as they had been doing? Should the United States have refrained from intervening in Latin America and risked war by trying to prevent Europeans from intervening? If European countries that were frankly imperialist had occupied lands in America, would they have withdrawn later, as the United States did? Would there have been fewer interventions in Latin America if the United States had followed a different policy, or more? It is possible that there would have been more. But of course no one knows.

The Philippines have long since been delivered to the Filipinos; the United States has agreed to turn the Panama Canal over to the Panamanians; and Puerto Rico has been offered, and has declined, its independence. Despite the oratory of the times the United States was never truly imperialistic. Many Latin Americans favored annexation by the United States. The Dominican Republic, El Salvador, and Yucatan requested it. On one occasion Theodore Roosevelt said, "As for annexing [the Dominican Republic] I have about the same desire . . . as a gorged boa constrictor might have to swallow a porcupine wrong-end-to." The United States joined the imperialist world briefly but was never happy in it. It had, itself, been under imperialist domination. It opposed imperialism. It continued to regard itself as freedom's guardian in the world.

"ECONOMIC IMPERIALISM"

The Roosevelt Corollary led to three interventions in depth, but most interventions were minor and short-lived. Revolution was the most common device for changing governments in many Caribbean and Central American countries, and contrary to popular impression the United States frequently was invited to intervene in order to limit loss of lives and destruction of property. A Special Service Squadron of small naval vessels was based on the Panama Canal Zone. One of the "special services" it performed was to respond to such invitations. Characteristically, if a belligerent force was approaching a coastal city where its opponents maintained a garrison, government officials and inhabitants, often in agreement with one or the other contending groups, and sometimes in agreement with both, would appeal to the nearest American consul to call a warship. It was almost a pattern in such cases for the commander of the warship to set up a neutral zone where noncombatants might assemble in safety, and to require the opposing sides either to negotiate for control of the city or to fight it out beyond the city's limits. United States neutrality was generally accepted, and US forces, few in numbers, were rarely fired upon.

Sometimes hostilities were avoided without the necessity of setting up a neutral zone or indeed without the opposing forces even coming close to each other. In a book written some years ago I described one such incident in which an American businessman and I played the role of peacemakers. From 1923 to 1925 I served as consul at Puerto Castilla,

Honduras, a United Fruit Company town. During the final days of the Tiburcio Carías revolution I received a radiogram from the revolutionary leader on the north coast asking me to arrange for the government commander in Trujillo, across the bay from Puerto Castilla, to turn over the city peaceably. The sequel was straight out of O. Henry.

> After a number of telephone conversations with Trujillo it became evident that the government followers had little intention of resisting if they could obtain guarantees for their persons. The fruit company officials were old hands at this game. One of them, George Bennett, was given authority to represent the company and to utilize its resources and facilities in helping to keep violence down. Trujillo was the vital point, since it was the capital of the department and the headquarters of the military commander. It was the only place in the district where there was any sizable concentration of government troops. Once Trujillo was turned over, the risk of disorder in other parts of the district would be reduced to a minimum.
>
> As soon as news reached Trujillo that the revolutionists had won out in La Ceiba and other places on the north coast, the adherents of the revolution came out in the open. They were joined by deserters from the government side and by the usual hangers-on who hoped to profit by disorder. Government adherents, on the other hand, barricaded themselves inside the old fort, and closed the heavy doors and shuttered the windows of their houses to await developments, while praying for peace.
>
> One of my first acts was to send a radiogram to Comsperon (Commander Special Service Squadron), requesting that a warship proceed immediately to Trujillo. Then Bennett and I boarded a rail motorcar and started out for that port. We arrived to find the streets nearly deserted. Sporadic gunfire indicated that there was some disorder. We proceeded on foot and by a devious route to the home of the Melhados, a Portuguese-British family who for generations had been the leading merchants of the area. One or another Melhado usually acted as honorary British consul. A Melhado, I was told, was British consul in Trujillo, in 1860, when William Walker was turned over to the Hondurans and executed by them after his last futile excursion into Central American politics. No Melhado had the title in 1924; it was vested in one of the Melhado clerks, a Bay Islander of British origin and Honduran nationality. However the Melhados represented the merchant class, and it was quite in accordance with local tradition for Bennett and me to enlist their aid in bringing about what all of us desired: a peaceable turnover in Trujillo.

The Melhado home was tightly shuttered and heavily barred. The family was expecting us, however, and we were quickly admitted. After a few minutes' discussion we decided to invite the military commander in for a parley. The telephone was still working, indicating that no organized revolutionary force was yet operating in the city. The commander agreed to meet with us, and soon appeared at the door escorted by a dozen or so loyal officers and soldiers. Thus were represented the governments of the United States and of Great Britain, as well as the government of Honduras, the fruit company, and the local merchants. There was lacking a representative of the revolution. The military commander promptly agreed to release from prison the outstanding revolutionary leader in the district, who had been placed in protective custody some weeks before. He was brought in and the "armistice commission" went into session. Bennett and I gave a straightforward story of what we knew concerning the success of the revolution along the remainder of the north coast. The government commander had no illusions and expressed his readiness to surrender the fort if guarantees were given to his officers and men.

After some discussion, in which everyone took a remarkably accommodating attitude, a protocol for the turnover was agreed upon. The government commander was to turn over command to the revolutionary leader. All government officers were to be given safe conduct to Puerto Castilla and out of the country if they so desired. Bennett immediately ordered a train to come from Puerto Castilla for the purpose. The soldiery were to stack their arms, and those opting for the revolutionary cause would be free to join up. The others were to be released from service. All political prisoners were to be freed. The American warship that I had called, and that we all earnestly hoped would arrive, would guarantee the faithful carrying out of the protocol by all parties.

Nothing, meanwhile, had been heard from the warship, and at this inopportune time the telephone system went dead. The military commander and his successor left for the *cuartel* to carry out their part of the pact. The rest of us waited at the Melhados'. We of course anticipated that the turnover would not be accomplished without difficulty, and we were not wrong. The government commander returned accompanied by his loyal officers, all disarmed, and reported that a considerable group of soldiers had declined to lay down their arms, and were even then in the process of looting the town. They had first broken into a cantina and got themselves properly "liquored up." The sound of rifle fire and the yells of the rebellious soldiery reached us as we sat and pondered the situation. It was clear that only the opportune arrival of the warship would prevent major looting and disorder.

We were effectively incommunicado and had no way of knowing whether the warship had arrived or was even on its way, since we had no view of the harbor from where we were; it was possible, of course, that the warship was already in port, with its commander not knowing what to do next. There was clearly only one thing to do, and that was to go down to the waterfront and see whether or not the warship had arrived. It was clear, too, that I was the person who should go, as no one else had authority to treat with the vessel's commander. Bennett, always helpful and capable, volunteered to accompany me. We left the house as quietly as we could. The sight that met our eyes was not reassuring. The revolutionary commander had evidently had little success in controlling his own followers, let alone those soldiers who had declined to give up their arms and the other disorderly elements who had been awaiting their opportunity to loot. Groups of armed men, in various stages of inebriation, were pillaging stores and occasionally firing at one another in a disorganized way. The waterfront was several hundred yards away, and there was no way to reach it without coming into contact with the groups. Bennett and I quickly decided that nonchalance would be our best protection. We walked through the streets as though nothing unusual were happening. No one paid the slightest attention to us. No stray bullet even came close to us.

When we finally came to the street that leads straight to the bay, we saw the finest sight that I for one have ever been privileged to see. There was an American destroyer, with the Stars and Stripes gallantly waving from its stern, edging its way toward shore. Bennett and I, resisting the temptation to run, walked out to the end of the rickety pier and waved our hats. The destroyer sent a boat and we went aboard. It took us only a few minutes to explain the situation. The commander agreed to accompany us back to town. We went ashore and started for the Melhados'. The news of the warship's arrival had spread like magic. The new military commander had patrols in the street, looting had stopped, and it was evident that the crisis had passed.*

The possibility that US forces would be sent to a trouble spot increased sharply if there were large US investments and a large group

*Willard L. Beaulac, *Career Ambassador* (New York: The Macmillan Company, 1951), pp. 81–84. Copyright, 1951, by Willard L. Beaulac. Copyright renewed 1979 by Willard L. Beaulac. Reproduced by permission of Macmillan Publishing Co., Inc.

of Americans there. When possible neutral zones were set up on land owned by US companies. Newspapers around the world often reported that they were there to protect US investments, as in part they were. The events were usually more sensational as reported in New York and Buenos Aires than as they actually occurred in Central America. Such reporting encouraged charges of economic imperialism, of a United States whose armed forces were at the beck and call of its investors abroad. The fact that US investments in the Dominican Republic, Haiti, and Nicaragua, where prolonged interventions took place, were almost negligible did not modify the views of those who saw intervention as an instrument of US economic imperialism. Nor were they modified by the circumstance that President Wilson, who intervened most, was almost hostile to United States investment abroad.

A Lowered Profile. While I was still at Puerto Castilla, Secretary of State Charles Evans Hughes decided that it was time the United States got out of the business of refereeing revolutions in Latin America. He instructed consuls and naval commanders not to take any action that might favor one side in a revolution as against the other. Within a short time La Ceiba, one of Honduras' most important cities, was threatened by a revolutionary group. The American consul, in a more or less routine way, called a warship. But the routine had changed. Under the new orders the ship's commander was compelled to let the two forces fight it out as they saw fit, with the result that La Ceiba became a battlefield and was burned to the ground. It was a loss that poverty-stricken Honduras could ill afford. Happily, the number of revolutions in Central America decreased for a time. Perhaps the loss of La Ceiba, together with the continued refusal of the United States to referee revolutions, helped to bring about that result.*

Nevertheless there was resistance to change. It came less from the United States than it did from Latin America. Just as Latin Americans in political life had often found (and still find) it convenient to seek support

*The American consul in La Ceiba at the time was George Platt Waller. During earlier troubles he had seen to it that many noncombatants, most of them Hondurans, were given protection. Denied the opportunity to do that again, Waller, despite the fact that the consulate was in the line of fire between the contending forces, radioed the State Department a blow-by-blow report of the battle. In Puerto Castilla, a hundred miles down the coast, I was deciphering his reports and picturing him diving into the bathtub when firing became heavy. He

from their own armed forces, so in Central America and the Caribbean area many such persons had gotten into the habit of involving the United States in their internal problems. The habit was hard to break.

In December 1925 President Miguel Paz Barahona of Honduras asked the United States to send marines to his country to preserve order in the event he should venture to remove certain persons from public office. The State Department denied his request and instructed its representative in Tegucigalpa to "make use of every opportunity to impress upon the members of the Government and others in Honduras that the responsibility for the Government rests upon them; that the center of Honduran political activities is in Honduras and not in Washington."[10] But pressure for intervention continued.

In the autumn of 1934, after General Anastasio Somoza, commander of Nicaragua's Guardia Nacional, had developed presidential ambitions, the incumbent president, Juan Bautista Sacasa, sent his brother, don Federico Sacasa, to Washington to discuss the problem with the Department of State. I had spent four years in Nicaragua, had had friendly relations with all the persons involved, and was handling Central American affairs in the department. Don Federico, for whom I had especially high regard, sought my counsel concerning the course the president should take. Under the department's policy I had to decline to advise him. At the end of a long conversation don Federico told me that he regretted that I had hesitated to give him advice. I replied (gently I hope) that there was no hesitation on my part; that I was determined not to give him advice.[11] President Sacasa's concern was justified: Somoza later overthrew him.

There were many other instances in which the United States resisted pressure from Latin Americans in and out of government to become involved in their countries' internal affairs.

Using warships to protect American (and other foreign and national) lives and property always created news stories, but it happened only

---

later confirmed that he did that until he was forced to abandon the consulate. During World War II Waller was our ranking representative in Luxembourg. The United States was still neutral when the Germans invaded that small country, and Waller took it upon himself to extend protection to its inhabitants. He did that with great success. Following the war's end the grandduchess of Luxembourg journeyed to the United States and conferred a high decoration on Waller. His experiences in Honduras had served him and Luxembourgers well.

occasionally. It was the State Department, not the Navy, that was responsible for protecting Americans and their investments on a day-to-day basis, and the Department took its responsibility seriously. A large part of a diplomat's or a consul's time was taken up in protecting private interests, that is, in trying to assure that private investors would receive fair treatment from foreign governments. Of course all state departments and foreign offices try to protect their investors abroad.* But that did not make the practice more palatable to Latin American governments.

Nevertheless the State Department was not the harsh defender of private capital that it sometimes appeared to be. When I was serving in Managua, in the 1930s, a severe earthquake destroyed most of the city. Several days later, while the legation was housed in a tent furnished with a table and two chairs, and most of the Nicaraguan government was similarly housed, we received a radiogram from the department instructing the minister to inquire of the government concerning a bill it owed to an American company for merchandise delivered to it. The department (as well as the legation) was busy arranging relief for the earthquake's victims at the time. Although it was plainly a case of the right hand not knowing what the left was doing, the minister sent the department a curt reply. "This legation is not in the business of collecting bills for private firms," he said. The department never communicated with us again about that bill or any other bill. I have always felt that Secretary of State Henry L. Stimson approved of the minister's reply. In fact I am certain he chuckled when he read it. Nor do I remember ever having been asked to collect a bill at any of my later posts. So far as my own experience is concerned the minister's telegram marked the end of an era.

The behavior of some of the large American companies lent credence to the charge of economic imperialism. The businessman's idea of social responsibility, in the United States and elsewhere, was not then

---

*The Communist countries are exceptions of course. Following the example of the free industrialized countries they extend economic aid to some less-developed countries (and make every effort to obtain reimbursement for credits they may extend to those countries). But their aid represents only a small percentage of the aid extended by the free countries. More importantly, in the absence of a private sector with funds to invest abroad their total contribution to development is minuscule compared with the contribution the free countries make. The Communist role is rather to criticize and encourage criticism of those countries as "imperialistic." This they do with considerable effectiveness.

what it became later. Many companies had a public-be-damned attitude, and they carried that attitude abroad. The oil companies in Mexico sometimes acted in ways that could only be termed arbitrary. To be sure, working in Mexico in the early 1900s was not easy for foreigners. It was not easy for Mexicans either. The Mexican Revolution had uprooted old institutions, and new ones had not been firmly established. The government could not count on the loyalty or the honesty of all persons who represented it. When I was serving as vice-consul in Tampico, for example, the general in charge of maintaining order in the bandit-infested oil fields told me that the government in Mexico City was denying him the munitions his troops required to act. In these circumstances the companies often had to provide their own protection. Many government officials felt the companies were fair prey. Nevertheless the companies might have done better than they did, and when the Mexican government later expropriated their properties it had the support of public opinion in the country.

The large American fruit companies in Central America had little more success in protecting the reputation of American capital. They paid a tax on every stem of bananas exported. The tax was one of the government's principal sources of revenue and a tempting prize for political groups. Political leaders sought fruit company support with promises of more favorable treatment and also by threatening the companies if support were withheld. Sometimes they got what they wanted. Whether the companies could have stayed clear of politics if they had tried harder is doubtful. In any event the fact that they were sometimes involved in politics was resented by Central Americans.

American companies were by no means the only ones whose practices offended some Latin Americans; in many areas they were not even the principal offenders. Not all the oil companies were American, and not all the companies that offended were oil companies or fruit companies. Argentines (and one British ambassador as well) have told of the arrogance the directors of the British-owned railroads displayed during their occasional visits to Argentina. Their behavior, as described, differed from that of royalty chiefly in the scant attention they paid to the officials and people of the country, who were made to feel like true colonials. Nor did Latin Americans behave any better, or were they any more popular when the shoe was on the other foot. In Paraguay the "exploiters" were not the British or the Americans but Paraguay's neighbors, the Argentines—the same Argentines who so keenly resented British dominance of the railroad industry in their country.

Neither were foreign corporations as arbitrary as some domestic corporations or, indeed, as some Latin American governments. Víctor Alba reports tersely:

> Many years ago, Bolivia had little Anglo-Saxon capital. The owners of the tin mines were Bolivian. (There was also some Chilean capital.) On the average, the miners, victims of tuberculosis or pneumoconiosis, seldom lived beyond the age of twenty-seven. In 1923, miners in the Uncía workings, owned by Simón Patiño . . . , demanded an increase in pay. The president of Bolivia, Juan Batista Saavedra . . . , promptly ordered a massacre of the workers.[12]

All those things were products of the times, but times have a habit of changing. Latin American governments eventually learned that they could exercise a high degree of control over foreign corporations and also heavily tax them; that the power of government, in even the smallest country, was greater than the power of a company, even the largest. And President Franklin D. Roosevelt's Good Neighbor Policy brought about a great change in the United States attitude toward its investors in Latin America. Eduardo Santos, then president of Colombia, described the new situation accurately when he noted that, during an earlier period, it had been the American companies that threatened to take their case against the Colombian government to Washington, whereas now it was the Colombian government that threatened to appeal to Washington against the companies.[13]

I recall the occasion when our change of policy with respect to American investments abroad was brought strikingly to my attention. It was the year 1933 and I was serving in the State Department. An American firm was in trouble with the Dominican government and was trying to induce the department to take up the cudgel in its behalf. However the department declined to intervene. The company looked around for someone who might bring pressure to bear on the department and found a likely helper in the person of a well-known member of the Democratic National Committee. The national committeeman called on Secretary Hull and explained his business. The secretary listened gravely. Then he looked at the department's organizational chart and saw that I was handling Dominican affairs. He referred the committeeman to me.

The committeeman came into my office, which I shared with three colleagues as junior as myself, and stated his case. I was quite familiar with the problem. I told him the State Department could not intervene and explained why. He picked up his hat and walked out, and we never heard from him again with reference to the case, nor did the company try to bring further pressure to bear on us. Cordell Hull, in his austere way, had indicated, unmistakably, that politics was not going to influence decisions in such matters, and that the Department of State was as much concerned with the rights of foreign countries as it was with the rights of American investors.

Times have a habit of changing but the myth of American imperialism persists among Latin American intellectuals and persons in political life. The anti-imperialists maintain that large-scale foreign investment continues to be an instrument of imperialism. Their countries, they claim, are serving the very function that early imperialists had for their colonies, supplying raw materials at low prices and serving as markets for high-priced industrial products. And the United States, which leads all the others in investments in Latin America, imports from Latin America, and exports to Latin America (as well as aid to Latin America), is the anti-imperialists' principal target.

By no means all Latin Americans are anti-imperialists, however. It would have taken a far-seeing person to predict, thirty or forty years ago, when it was popular for Central Americans in political life to charge the fruit companies with intervening in their countries's internal affairs, that one day the government of Honduras would approach the government of the United States and plead for financial help to a fruit company to permit it to expand its Honduran operations, but that has occurred; or that Latin American governments long accustomed to denouncing United States oil companies as imperialistic would be asking those same companies for assistance in developing their countries' resources, but that also has occurred.

THE REAL IMPERIALIST

The myth of American imperialism is helpful to Soviet Russia, which has achieved dominion over most of Eastern Europe, and possibly over Cuba. It deflects criticism from Russia and helps to make Russian imperialism more secure. The myth acts as an irritant in relations between the United States and its Latin American neighbors and makes it more difficult for them to engage in the cooperation that is so important to all of them. Those are precisely the effects some anti-imperialists seek.

6
NATIONALISM

NATIONALISM HAS been defined as "a state of mind in which the supreme loyalty of the individual is felt to be to the nation-state."[1] Few phenomena have had the worldwide importance that nationalism has had.

Carlton J. H. Hayes, an early and eminent student of nationalism, did not consider that the imperialism of the late 1800s had principally economic origins as Barraclough later suggested. He maintained that it was sparked by nationalism, by the new national rivalries that had arisen in Europe.

> The economic explanation is not fully convincing. Neither Russia nor Italy had surplus manufactures to dispose of or surplus wealth to invest, though both engaged in the scramble for imperial dominion. Germany acquired an extensive colonial empire before she had much exportable capital, and France obtained an even bigger overseas empire while her industrial development lagged behind Germany's. Great Britain had long had all the supposed economic motives for imperialism—export of manufactured goods, demand for raw materials, supply of surplus capital—though these did not move her in the 1850s and 1860s as they did in the 70s and 80s. On the other hand, Norway, whose ocean-borne commerce was exceeded only by Britain's and Germany's, remained consistently aloof from overseas imperialism.[2]

There is no doubt that nationalism was a powerful force in Europe. Nevertheless it was slow in coming to Latin America. Initially, as we have seen, the colonists had no great urge to set up new nations. The revolt against Napoleon's dominion over Spain was more pro-Spanish than anti-Spanish. There was little talk, and probably little thought, of permanently severing political ties with Spain. At first, that is.

The wars of independence, when they finally came, were bloody. Property losses were severe. The normal life of vast areas was disrupted. Bolívar, among others, tried to insure that the break with Spain would be final. On June 15, 1813, in a Proclamation to the People of Venezuela, he said:

> Moved by your misfortunes, we have been unable to observe with indifference the afflictions you were forced to experience by the barbarous Spaniards, who have ravished you, plundered you, and brought you death and destruction. . . . Let the monsters who infest Colombian soil, who have drenched it in blood, be cast out forever; may their punishment be equal to the enormity of their perfidy, so that we may eradicate the stain of our ignominy and demonstrate to the nations of the world that the sons of America cannot be offended with impunity.[3]

Hatred of Spaniards became real and widespread, but it alone was incapable of holding Latin Americans together.* They formed separate republics following roughly the boundaries of the colonial districts. Paraguay rejected union with Argentina. Mexico dreamed of absorbing Central America but was unable to. As for Central America, it broke up into five tiny states. The task of forming nations in the many new countries was a gigantic one.

The nation-state itself was a relatively new institution. In Europe it had evolved from an intricate set of events and circumstances that had had their effects over a period of centuries. Latin Americans adopted the nation-state as a model but they lacked the experience and the training that had gone into creating the model. Spanish centralism had required that each colony be attached directly to the Crown, and that trade and other communication among the colonies be kept to a minimum. Even within colonies there was little tradition of cooperation. Also, people capable of forming nations were not numerous. The nuclei around which nations could be built were separated not only by distance, and by broad and lofty mountains and vast jungles, but also by inherited characteristics of people. It was no more than natural, then, that Spanish America should split into a number of countries, and that even within countries unity would be difficult and in many cases impossible to achieve.

Typically, most of the population remained outside the nation, politically, culturally, and economically. They were the blacks, most of

---

*Greater Colombia, which Bolívar founded, comprised what are now Venezuela, Colombia, Ecuador, Panama, Peru and Bolivia—hence Bolívar's reference to "Colombian soil" when addressing Venezuelans.

the mixed-bloods, and of course the Indians, who were by far the most numerous group. Nor would the Indians have entered if they had been invited. They wanted to remain separate and apart, and many of them still do. The problem of forming a nation while leaving out many or most of a country's inhabitants has been a perplexing one in Latin America.

Colonial society had been characterized by tensions—between government and people, between *peninsulares* and creoles, whites and colored, rich and poor. The determined centralism of the Spanish Crown, all the more oppressive because it was well intentioned and carried out meticulously by earnest bureaucrats, had sought to direct and control most of the colonists' activities—political, economic, and religious. After independence many of the old tensions remained, while new ones appeared—between competing political and economic groups, between military groups, between the military and civilians, between clericals and anticlericals, between *caudillos,* and between the cities and the countryside.

Antinationalist rather than nationalist sentiments prevailed for decades after independence. The elites of Peru, the only ones who "mattered" in that country, felt much closer to the elites of Ecuador and Bolivia, whom they did not know, than to other Peruvians. Class, not nationality or even religion, was what held people together. Nor was language the bond that it was in Europe and the United States. Indians did not speak Spanish and most of them refused to learn.

There was little incentive for those who were excluded from the nation, or who had excluded themselves, to think in national terms. Governments had meager claim to people's loyalties. They inspired scant respect. Imperial Spain had had little but burdens to offer most people, and it often seemed that this was equally true of the new governments. Chronically short of funds, they were known principally in their roles of tax collector and policeman.

Largely isolated from other centers of population, most communities lived self-sufficient lives, unconcerned with considerations of nationality and even ignorant of them. What loyalties people had were apt to be local—to persons who were close and visible, to the *patrón* who could protect or the *caudillo* who could lead. Moreover loyalty to one community or leader frequently involved hostility to other communities and leaders, whether local or national. In Nicaragua it was hostility between Conservative Granada and Liberal León that led to William Walker's incursions. In Ecuador there still is a rivalry that sometimes approaches hostility between Quito, the capital, where conservative landowners dominate politics, and the port city of Guayaquil, the country's traditional doorway to the outside world and outside ideas. In these and other countries regional animosities have been a cause of civil wars and a barrier to political unity.

ANTI-AMERICANISM

It was not until 1900 that nationalism became a dominant force in most of Latin America, and then it took the form of anti-Americanism. Furthermore it seemed determined to make up for lost time. In that year José Rodó, a Uruguayan, published "Ariel," an essay, that three-quarters of a century later, continues to influence Latin Americans' attitude toward the United States. In it he warned of the materialism of Americans, the little culture they possessed, their "mediocre view of human destiny."

Rodó first extolled Latin Americans. "Perhaps," he began, "there lacks in our South American character the definite contour of a personality. But even so, we Latin-Americans have an inheritance of Race, a great ethnic tradition to maintain, a sacred bond which unites us to immortal pages of history and puts us on our honour to preserve this for the future."[4] He recognized that Americans, too, had qualities that were praiseworthy; that they had made liberty a reality. But his praise of Americans has been little remembered in Latin America. What is remembered, and frequently quoted, is his view that Americans lacked the finer instincts that Latin Americans were blessed with.

> In the ambience of America's democracy there are no heights so lofty as to escape the climbing of the flood of vulgarity, and it spreads and extends itself freely as over a level plain. . . . The ideal of beauty does not appeal to the descendants of the austere Puritan, nor even a passionate worship of the truth; they care little for any thinking that has no immediate practical object—it seems to them idle and fruitless; even to science they bring no selfless interest for discovery, nor do they seem capable of loving its truths only because they are true; investigation is merely the necessary antecedent of practical application.[5]

Rodó set a fashion that many hastened to follow. Rufino Blanco Fombona, a Venezuelan, surpassed Rodó in cutting the American colossus down to size. Gabriela Mistral, a Chilean schoolteacher who was to win a Nobel Prize for her poetry, made certain that Blanco Fombona's message would not be forgotten. Alfredo Palacios, a colorful Argentine Socialist and bon vivant, said that the United States had sold its soul for riches and power. Scores of respected and less-than-respected intellectuals and pseudointellectuals joined the anti-American chorus.

There was plenty about the United States to object to, of course. The war against Mexico was criticized even by Americans. The war with Spain, although it brought freedom to Cuba, reflected little glory on the victors. In spite of Spain's deplorable record in Cuba, its weakness cast the United States in the role of a bully, and the Spaniards' courage would have aroused the sympathy even of a Bolívar. The Panama episode; Theodore Roosevelt's corollary to the Monroe Doctrine, his "big stick" policy; the overconfident, sometimes boastful language of Americans; all awakened legitimate fears in Latin America. President Wilson's meddling in Mexico, and his military interventions in Central America and the Caribbean, irritated even admirers of the United States.

Latin Americans whose views were given prominence took a generally negative attitude toward their northern neighbor. The United States, growing in strength and confidence, was a target for those who felt their own countries diminished. American brashness could not hold a candle to Latin American flamboyance, but still it rankled. Flamboyance could be elegant, as brashness could not be, and the Latin Americans had a feeling for style. The United States, despite its interventions, remained a bastion of freedom in the world, and possibly for that very reason a different and higher standard was applied to it. Its misdemeanors and alleged misdemeanors were examined as under a microscope, catalogued, and broadcast to the four corners of the world.

Latin American nationalism of the early 1900s was largely inspired by intellectuals. But denigrating American culture did nothing to elevate Latin American culture. American culture, whether one liked it or not, was authentic, but Latin America's was largely an imitation of France's culture. Furthermore it was the property of a few of the elite, who were not at all ready to share it with the masses they despised. Nor were the masses receptive to that kind of nationalism. Largely illiterate and too preoccupied with their own troubles to have opinions concerning the United States, they doubtless would have been delighted to share in the material rewards Americans had earned for themselves, and the freedoms they enjoyed. A nationalism that appealed only to those who would isolate themselves from the nation was a contradiction in terms.

By the 1930s, however, a new nationalism was taking root. Industrialization, the growth of cities, and the beginnings of modernization had enlarged and strengthened the middle sectors, the entrepreneurs, managers, professional men, and the bureaucrats. All these had interests of their own, and they needed political power to defend and promote them. They sought it among the workers—the very masses the intellectuals had shunned.[6]

NATIONALISM AND STATISM

The new nationalism took on a populist quality. Its leaders played down the cultural theme, which still had little or no meaning for the masses, and emphasized social and economic themes, which did have meaning for them. They talked of a new, dynamic state that would promote economic development and insure that its rewards were fairly distributed. Among other things the new state would regulate the activities of the large corporations—the "monopolies," as they were called—many of them foreign. Lázaro Cárdenas, in Mexico, and Juan Domingo Perón, in Argentina, were new nationalists.

Some governments expropriated foreign-owned properties and undertook to operate them. The foreign mining and petroleum companies were special targets. The state moved easily from intervention in the economy to participation in it—to entrepreneurship, in other words. In some countries it was to become the principal entrepreneur, the biggest monopolist of them all.

Among the most enthusiastic nationalists were the bureaucrats, and for natural reasons. Wealth and the power that goes with it had long been in the hands of a privileged few, and were closely held. For the many the logical road to advancement and power was government. As populist nationalism added to the economic role of the state it also added to the economic and political role of the bureacracy. The bureaucrats, not surprisingly, reciprocated by promoting populist nationalism. Their power came to rival and at times to surpass that of the oligarchs. Some oligarchs, in fact, entered the bureaucracy in order to protect their own privileges while simultaneously promoting populist nationalism.

Of course it was not only nationalism that influenced the state to enlarge its role. The Great Depression of the 1930s literally forced governments to assume new economic functions not only in Latin America but in most countries of the world. In the United States, for example, President Franklin D. Roosevelt was given near-dictatorial powers over the economy. But rising nationalism increased the pressure on Latin American governments to intervene in the economy.

LA RAZA CÓSMICA

In some countries the new nationalism involved a real effort to create nations out of people who were divided by racial origin, by social stratification, by economic interest, and by excessive regionalism and individualism. Mexico led the way. It developed a cult of the Indian. From a sullen, withdrawn individual of little interest to society the Indian now became a "noble rebel." He was exalted in ways that must have surprised and confused him. His ancestors were hailed as builders of great civilizations, as indeed they were. People began to take pride in their Indian blood. Indian culture became the fashionable thing.

The high place that had been given to the Indian was shared by the mestizo. The old racism gave way to a theory that persons of mixed blood were superior to those of a single race. In 1925 José Vasconcelos, the noted Mexican educator, wrote a book, *La Raza Cósmica,* in which he predicted that the fusion of races in Latin America would lead to a universal race capable of inhabiting the earth in peace. The book had considerable vogue. Mexican nationalism was going to create a new Utopia, and it would be worldwide.

The new nationalism helped to give both the mestizo and Indian (although not the many Indians who refused to be assimilated) a feeling of belonging to the nation. But it also was directed at ends that had little to do with nation building—ends that in fact made nation building more difficult. Marxists used it to advance Marxism, Communists to serve the purposes of Soviet foreign policy. For many of the privileged nationalism was a substitute for action on behalf of the masses, a balm to their consciences.

Chile had long had a healthy sense of nationhood. Crowded into the temperate, fertile center of the country, Chileans, a virile and enterprising people, had little difficulty communicating with one another. They did not need the new nationalism to become a nation. Unfortunately they were not immune to its influence. What it did was steer them in the direction of statism and xenophobia. Instead of attracting new blood, new talent, and new enterprise, they began expelling groups who had been helpful to them and who were prepared to continue to be helpful. When Spain expelled its Arabs and Jews, Spanish aristocrats enriched themselves by taking over their properties. When the colonies became independent the creole aristocracy added to their *latifundia* the lands the Spaniards had abandoned. The expulsion of the foreign copper mining companies, in 1971, did not add to the wealth of Chileans. It did, however, greatly increase the power of the new aristocrats, the politicians and the bureaucrats. The new nationalism, and the new militancy of Chile's socialism, led to the bankruptcy of government and nation and to the near-extinction of Chile's democracy.

Peru, with its large Indian population, has found nationhood particularly elusive. The military government that seized power in 1968 made a banner of nationalism and its accompanying anti-Americanism. They remained a banner until a disastrous economic decline compelled the military leaders to put them aside.

NATIONALISM IN BRAZIL

Brazilians faced many of the obstacles to nationhood that plagued the Spanish Americans. In some ways their problems were more awesome. The immensity of the country—the distances that separated populated areas and the difficulties of communication—the great Amazon Basin, much of it impenetrable and all of it mysterious, and the few people at hand to tie all that vastness together, made nationhood seem remote at times. The racial mixture, the high ratio of slaves and former slaves, and the extreme social inequalities were other impediments to unity. More than one group tried to break away and set up a state of its own, but without success.

Brazil had advantages too. Its size created problems but it also was a source of pride and wonder to its people. Even before independence many were convinced that the far-flung Brazilian kingdom would some day be one of the great countries of the earth. Brazilians sometimes say, cynically, that theirs is a country of the future—and always will be. But the dream persists, and the belief that it will be realized has been strengthened with time.

Brazilians developed a sense of nationhood as early as the seventeenth century when they fought off the French and expelled the Dutch. Since Portugal was too small and too weak to take care of them, Brazilians learned to take care of themselves, to become a nation in other words. For Brazilians the war of independence constituted a minimum rupture with the past. It resulted in little bitterness toward Portugal or Portuguese; after all, the king had lived right there in Rio de Janeiro. The first emperor of Brazil, as we have seen, was the heir to Portugal's throne.

The same absence of bitterness characterized relations among Brazilians. That, too, was helpful to nationhood. There were struggles for power among groups with opposing interests, but they were less divisive than in most Latin American countries. Brazilians had a way of getting along with one another. They were tolerant, with a capacity for compromise. There have been violence and repression in Brazil's history, but conciliation has been the norm. Ideological division has been less sharp than in most of the Spanish American countries. When the powerful state of São Paulo rebelled against dictator-president Getulio Vargas (1930–37 and 1950–54), in 1932, but failed to unseat him, Vargas dealt kindly with the revolutionary leaders, and went so far as to attend the inauguration of the Avenida 9 de Julho, in São Paulo's capital, which was named to commemorate the uprising.

Brazil's excellent diplomacy also helped to build the nation. Its representatives were able to obtain recognition of Brazilian sovereignty over the extensive areas that *bandeirantes* and gold seekers had added to the national territory. Brazil was happily free from small-power complexes. It had little hesitancy in cooperating with the United States, little fear of being labeled a "satellite." It was the only South American country to declare war against Germany during World War I. It participated in the peace negotiations and played an active role in the League of Nations. In World War II it was the only Latin American country to send ground forces to fight against the Axis (Mexico sent air forces to the Far East). They served side by side with the Americans in Italy and the soldiers of the two nations got along with one another. Brazil felt at home with the great powers.

If patriotism is sometimes the last refuge of scoundrels, in Latin America nationalism frequently is a substitute for patriotism. President Vargas did not hesitate to arouse anti-American nationalism when he found the political going rough and his authority weakened. Juscelino Kubitschek (president 1956–64), who was a constant petitioner for United States aid, seemed to be more critical of the United States the more he demanded from it.* And his successor, João Goulart (1961–64), was as anti-American as he was corrupt. But in general Brazilians have gotten along with one another and with outsiders without excessive appeal to demagogic nationalism.

Gilberto Freyre. One of the architects of modern Brazilian nationalism is Gilberto Freyre, author of two tremendously popular studies of Brazil that have been translated into the principal languages of the world. They are *Casa-Grande e Senzala* (The Masters and the Slaves) and *Sobrades e Mucambos* (The Mansions and the Shanties). So important are these books that some Brazilians have suggested that one day their history will be chronicled in two parts: before Freyre and after Freyre.

In *Casa-Grande e Senzala* Freyre described the development of Brazilian civilization from the time of the patriarchal family, the time of negro slavery and the one-crop economy based on sugar. In *Sobrades e Mucambos* he continued the story to the middle of the nineteenth century. Freyre described Brazil exactly as it had been. He painted an infinitely detailed picture of what went into the making of the nation. He wrote of the plantation, of the owner's great house, his wife, his mistress or mistresses, his children, white and mulatto, of the slave, the shanty, the system of justice and injustice, the food, the drink, the city, and the filth. He wrote of the emperor, the church and the priest, of the faithful, of the judge and the judged, of voluptuousness and piety and the arts,

*Our ambassador to Brazil during the Kubitschek administration was Ellis Briggs, a Foreign Service officer whose sense of humor was matched by his vast experience in Latin America. When Kubitschek's spending and his attendant demands for United States aid had risen to unprecedented levels a worried State Department instructed Briggs to suggest to Kubitschek that he do a little belt-tightening. Briggs delivered the message and, predictably, Kubitschek became excited. Jumping up from his chair he threw open his jacket and, fumbling with his trousers top, shouted, "Tighten my belt! I'll show them! I'll show them I can tighten my belt!" Suddenly he ceased to fumble and, looking at Briggs, said apologetically, "I'm sorry. I'm wearing suspenders." Kubitschek continued to wear suspenders, at least in a figurative sense.

and he fitted them all together into something Brazilians could recognize and identify with.

Most of what Freyre wrote reflects the old plantation societies of Bahia and Pernambuco rather than the new vibrant societies of central and southern Brazil. Nevertheless his works continue to have great importance in holding Brazilians together. Despite the centrifugal force of racial differences, geographic dispersion, and widely different economic levels, Brazil has become a nation. Its discovery of the seeds of nationhood in its history and its mixed race is paralleled by Mexico's, but in Mexico nationhood cost years of suffering and a million lives, while in Brazil it was achieved with a measure of joy.

7
MARXISM

KARL MARX had little more than disdain for Latin America and its great men. Of Bolívar, who had worked himself to an early death in an effort to bring freedom to the colonies, he said, "Like most of his countrymen he was averse to any prolonged exertion." He referred to the great liberator as a "most cowardly ordinary wretched rascal." Marx said that "all the vices of the Spaniards—boastfulness, grandiloquence, and quixotism—are found in the Mexicans raised to the third power, but they no longer have the substance that the Spaniards possess." Marx's collaborator, Friedrich Engels, said: "In America we have witnessed the conquest of Mexico [by the United States] and we are happy with it. . . . It is in the interests of its own development that henceforth Mexico should be placed under the tutelage of the United States."[1]

Neither Marx nor Engels knew Latin America, of course, or had much interest in it. Their theories were developed with Europe in mind, and they gave little thought to the less-developed countries. Nevertheless Marxism has had enormous influence in Latin America as well as in other less-developed areas.

Prior to the Russian Revolution and for some time afterward democratic liberalism was the missionary political force in the world. The Declaration of Independence and the Declaration of the Rights of Man were freedom's charter, the American Constitution a model for peoples who aspired to be democratic. Democratic liberalism was a powerful force. It helped to bring empires down, to free nations from tyranny. But once free, nations found democracy difficult to practice. In the 1970s a bare one-fifth of the world's nations were democracies, and many of those were far from being models. Among the newly independent countries democracy was almost unknown. And within the democracies themselves liberalism had lost much of its force. Britain, which had nurtured liberalism and spread it over much of the world, was now a small insular nation beset with economic and social problems. In Latin America the democratic ideal, to the extent that it persisted, was diluted with Marxism. Marxism, which is antidemocratic and antiliberal, had become the revolutionary force.

Marxism was new. It had no record of failure, as democracy had in countries where weak efforts to practice democratic liberalism had produced neither democracy nor liberalism but instability and poverty. In a world in which science had undermined traditional religion Marxism, which claimed to be scientific, became a new religion, one that was attractive to many because it offered not vague spiritual rewards that might be collected in the next world but material rewards that were available here—although not now. Marxism's rewards, like those of other religions, were in the future.

Marxism claimed to have a universal quality that democracy lacked. In contrast to the haphazardness of democratic liberalism which in Latin America often degenerated into near-anarchy, Marxism was systematic and coherent; at least its proponents said that it was. And while many nations were considered, quite correctly, to be not ripe for democracy, Marxism could be imposed. In its complete form it had to be imposed.

INDIVIDUAL AND COLLECTIVE APPROACH TO DEVELOPMENT

Marxism is a collective approach to development while capitalism is an individual approach.[2] Americans, by inheritance, by temperament, and because capitalism has made it possible for them to enjoy one of the highest living standards in the world, have generally favored the individual approach. In contrast Latin Americans, by inheritance, by temperament, and because capitalism, or what passes for capitalism in Latin America, has failed to provide most of them with decent living standards, have frequently favored the collective approach.

Latin Americans, like Americans, are largely products of their histories. Spaniards and Portuguese brought feudalism to America; Englishmen brought the industrial revolution and the joint stock company. They also brought the Magna Carta, which fostered individual initiative in ways that Spaniards and Portuguese had difficulty understanding. Today's Latin American resents government but he also depends on it. He finds ways to influence it. Government corporations, especially when they are labelled "monopolies," are apt to be a source of pride. Large private corporations, on the other hand, often arouse his distrust. If they are not only large but foreign, remote, difficult to influence, with an unnatural and impersonal passion for efficiency, he is particularly distrustful of them.

The Latin American university has had an important role in the spread of Marxism. In many universities Marxism is treated not only as a subject of interest in the history of economic thought but as an important part of contemporary economic theory. As university education has become common, and unemployment, even among university graduates, has risen, many students conclude that the capitalist system as they know it offers them little opportunity, and their interest in Marxism increases correspondingly. More and more Marxist-oriented students graduate directly into politics (others enter politics long before they graduate). Their influence is substantial.

When Latin American Marxists talk to Americans about economic matters each group may find that the other is speaking a different language. The Americans regard private capital as the source of their material progress and well-being. The Latin Americans, in contrast, maintain that private capital is evil in its origins and in its effects. The Americans tend to reject Marxism because it does not accord with their own observations—with what they see and experience in their own country, or with what they may have seen and experienced in other countries. The Latin Americans are more susceptible to Marxism because in their minds it does accord with what they see and experience in their countries. The two groups react differently largely because they have lived in different environments and are the products of different cultures.

ATTITUDE TOWARD CAPITAL

Marxists and non-Marxists differ radically regarding the origin of capital. Marx recognized that capital is required in order to increase the productivity of labor—to make it possible to accumulate labor in one spot where economies of scale can be achieved, and to purchase the machinery that multiplies the output of workers. But he considered too that private capital gave its owners the opportunity to exploit labor, that it was the "surplus value" stolen from labor that permitted capital to earn more capital and enabled the capitalist to concentrate most of the world's wealth in his own hands.

The surplus value that Marxists talk about is made up of profits, interest, and rents, but to the American these are advantages that capitalism offers. They help to make it possible for him to own his own home, to have a car, and perhaps a boat, to fly to Mexico or drive to Canada during his annual vacation, and to do a hundred other things that he considers normal and desirable.

Concerning the United States capital that is invested in Latin America, the Marxists say that it came from two sources. It came, first of all, from England and other European countries and was increased over the years by the reinvestment of surplus value. But much of it, they say, was ground from the backs of slaves, particularly in the American South. In fact much of the capital that came from Europe also was ground from the backs of early workers who were virtually slaves.

Capital ground from the backs of slaves is what the Marxists call "primitive accumulation." All that many Latin Americans have had to do is to look around them to see such examples as large landowners living in apparent luxury while their laborers barely earn subsistence, and factories whose workers are not much better off.

Now the average Latin American is not an economist or a political scientist any more than the average American is. He may have only the faintest idea of what Marxism is. Nevertheless when Marxists, or politicians or intellectuals who are influenced by Marxism, speak of the inequities (and iniquities) of the capitalist system it may occur to the Latin American that those persons have hit the nail on the head so far as his country is concerned. So long as one accepts the premise that capitalism rather than factors such as avarice, history, or politics are responsible for Latin America's economic problems, Marxism as it is presented to the masses can make a certain amount of sense.

MARXISM'S EFFECTS

Since Marxists consider that private wealth has been accumulated through theft and slavery it is not surprising that the Marxist governments of Cuba and Chile moved swiftly to seize foreign-owned as well as other private properties and felt under no obligation to compensate the former owners. Does one compensate robbers when the wealth they have stolen is recovered? And since the capitalist ethic, on the other hand, holds that capital is accumulated through the application of intelligence, courage, ingenuity, and hard work, and serves worthy ends, it was equally predictable that the United States government would be outraged at their actions.

Marx did not agree with everything that was said and done in the name of Marxism. Engels reported that in the 1870s Marx said, with reference to the French Marxists, "All I know is that I am not a Marxist." Nor would he probably agree with most of what the Marxists say and do today. He never visualized the changes that have occurred within the capitalist system: the phenomenal increase in the productivity of machinery, the power of labor unions, the relative affluence of workers, ownership of corporations by millions of large and small shareholders, the frequent distinction between ownership and management. He never foresaw that capitalism would provide much higher living standards than Marxism could or that tyranny, the loss of both political and economic freedom, would mark the final stage of Marxism.

Marxism as a system is now invalid. Much of it has been abandoned in Russia where capitalist devices and cooperation with the capitalist world have been resorted to in an effort to instill a degree of dynamism into the country's economy. More than one foreign Communist has returned from Moscow complaining that few Russians take Marxism seriously. Karel van het Reeve has said, "It is hardly a great exaggeration to say that more university professors in Paris and Tokyo are convinced Marxists than in all Russia."[3]

Nevertheless Marxism's influence on Latin America's politics and economics remains great. It was seen not only in the electoral victory of the Chilean Marxist Socialists and Communists in 1970 but in the ideology of the Christian Democrats who opposed them. Victor Raúl Haya de la Torre, who except for military interference would probably have become president of Peru, was strongly influenced by Marxism; and the military leaders who prevented him from reaching the presidency were equally influenced by it. The United Nations Economic Commission for Latin America (ECLA), which has probably influenced economic thought in Latin America more than any other group, has borrowed liberally from Marxism. In Cuba Marxism was imposed of course. The Cuban masses had nothing to say about it.

Why, in the light of Marxism's failure to prove itself, have so many nations been influenced by it? As early as 1866 Eugen von Böhm-Bawerk said that Marxism had "its most powerful support not in the convinced intellect of its disciples, but in their hearts, their wishes, and their desires."[4] Marxism, in Böhm-Bawerk's view, was less a dogma than a symbol of protest. For today's Marxist leaders it is much more than a symbol of course. For Allende and his followers in Chile it was an avenue to power. For Cuba's Castro, Marxism, with its strict control over people's lives, was a device for retaining power. Under the Marxist system politicians and bureaucrats are supreme. They are the establishment. For many of its leading protagonists that is its principal merit.

Even the Church has been influenced by Marxism.

MARXISM AND THE CHURCH

During the period of colonial rule the Catholic Church occupied a privileged position in Latin America. Its influence in education, in politics, and in economic matters was very great. But independence changed much of that. Many bishops and priests who had continued loyal to the Crown returned to Spain and were not quickly replaced. Relations between those who remained and the new governments were often difficult. Deprived of many of its prerogatives, the Church turned inward. It entered into what some have called its "ghetto" stage, during which it showed little interest in nonreligious matters and had little influence over them.

While I was serving as consul at Puerto Castilla I had as my house guest the Bishop of Honduras. During a long conversation I asked him why the Church seemed always to be on the side of the government although the latter did not always appear to be on the side of virtue. The bishop replied that he tried to avoid antagonizing the government because unless it was friendly to the Church it tended to be an enemy of the Church and its purposes. That attitude was probably characteristic at the time but the Church was already changing.

In 1891 Pope Leo XIII had stirred many churchmen to thought and some to action when he published his encyclical, *Rerum Novarum,* on conditions of labor in the industrialized countries. In 1931 Pope Pius XI endorsed *Rerum Novarum* with his own encyclical, *Quadragesimo Anno,* and gave further impetus to reform. Pope John XXIII's *Mater et Magistra* and *Pacem in Terris,* and the Second Vatican Council, placed the Church among the leaders of those seeking social improvement. Bishops and priests once more concerned themselves publicly with the non-religious issues of the day. A new "jet set" of priests, endowed with ample funds, flew to national and international conferences and made pronouncements on lay matters that concerned them. (The Archbishop of Panama, for example, not only worked earnestly to help the poor; he also lobbied energetically for the return of the Panama Canal to Panama.) The Church had become a destabilizing influence in Latin America, a dynamic force for change.

Among the instruments of change were the Latin American Bishops Conference and a number of priests' organizations whose aim was rapid and radical social improvement. The Bishops' Conference had particular importance. Even the most conservative bishops could not fail to be affected to some degree by the various papal encyclicals and by the demands for social improvement that had come out of the Second Vatican Council. Citing papal authority the bishops, meeting in Medellin, Colombia, in 1968, criticized Marxism and "liberal capitalism" as well. They maintained that "both systems militate against the dignity of the human person."[5]

The bishops had this to say about the conservatives in Latin America's society—those with whom, only a few years earlier, they had been charged, probably with justification, with being too closely identified.

> The Traditionalists or Conservatives show little or no social conscience, have a middle-class orientation and consequently do not question the social structures. In general they are primarily concerned with preserving their privileges, which they identify with the "established order." Their community action takes the character of paternalism and alms-giving, with no concern for changing the status quo.[6]

No one would have been surprised if Marxists had criticized persons who had a "middle-class orientation." Marx himself had only disdain for the middle class and looked forward to its eventual liquidation. But for Catholic bishops to talk in such terms was something new to most people.

The bishops did not spare foreigners. They charged foreign investors in Latin America with such offenses as tax evasion and excessive remission of profits and dividends, matters that were clearly beyond the direct knowledge of most bishops.

Many priests were far to the left of the bishops. Camilo Torres, a Colombian priest, said:

> In order to give [the majorities] food, drink, and clothing, basic decisions are necessary, decisions which can only come from the government. Technical solutions we have or we can obtain. But who decides on their application? The minority, against its own interests? It is a sociological absurdity that a group would act against its own interests. . . . The power must be . . . taken so that structural, economic, social, and political reforms benefiting [the] majorities may be realized. This is called revolution, and if it is necessary in order to fulfill love for one's neighbor, then it is necessary for a Christian to be a revolutionary.[7]

Torres joined a revolutionary band and died in combat against government troops in 1966. He became a martyr of the extreme left. Archbishop Helder Pessoa Camara, a Brazilian, said, "It seems to me that the memory of Camilo Torres or of Che Guevara merits as much respect as that of the Reverend Martin Luther King."[8]

Ivan Illich, a former priest turned reformer, with a considerable following among Catholic clergy and laymen, stressed the need for new and liberal social programs in Latin America, but warned the Church against accepting money from foreign Catholics in order to carry them out. In an article entitled "The Seamy Side of Charity," he said, "The receiver [of money donated by foreign Catholics] inevitably gets the message; the 'padre' stands on the side of W.R. Grace and Co., Esso, the Alliance for Progress, democratic government, the AFL-CIO and whatever is holy in the Western pantheon."[9] For Mr. Illich there were few good things in the Western pantheon.

Following Medellin many bishops and lower clergy embraced the Marxist dogma of class struggle and of the need for "liberation" from "dependence" on the more economically advanced countries. Those persons found themselves in many ways closer to the Marxists than to the non-Marxists. Some clergy frankly preached Marxism.

Referring to contemporary Nicaragua, Father Miguel d'Escoto,* a Maryknoll missioner and publisher of Orbis Books, said in his introduction to Richard Millett's *Guardians of the Dynasty:*[10]

> To . . . actively participate in the construction of a just, noncapitalistic system can only be the result of a moral conversion. If the elite are

*American-born Father d'Escoto became foreign minister of Nicaragua in 1979.

> not up to this kind of patriotic action, then their reluctance will only serve to prove that the *Frente Sandinista de Liberación Nacional* had been right all along in choosing violence and guerrilla warfare as the only viable strategy to bring about change.

By no means all bishops and priests agreed with this identification or near-identification with Marxism. Most of them doubtless disagreed with it. Pope John Paul II himself, inaugurating the Third General Conference of Latin American Bishops at Puebla, Mexico, on January 29, 1979, said that some of the conclusions of the Medellin meeting had been misinterpreted. While he urged the bishops to continue working for social justice he cautioned against political activism and violence. He reminded them that Christ was not a politician, a revolutionary, a warrior against Roman domination, a participant in a class struggle, or a "Nazareth subversive," as some clerics had painted him, and he made clear that it was through evangelization rather than confrontation that the Church could be most helpful. Although he said the Church was concerned with man, not political systems, he defended the right to private property and denounced atheistic humanism. His message was profoundly anti-Marxist.

Despite the Pope's words the prospect was that the Church would remain divided, to some degree at least, on how it should contribute to social improvement in Latin America. Its attitude or attitudes would help to determine which way Latin America would go; whether in the direction of political and economic freedom and social justice or of Marxian socialism and the tyranny that is a part of it.

The future of the Church itself might also be involved. Priests who have the power to forgive sins might be powerless to fulfill the hopes of political and economic improvement that some of them were holding out to the masses. During the colonial period, and for some time after independence, many of the Church's successes in the temporal field were at the cost of its authority and influence in the spiritual field. In today's infinitely more complex world failure in the temporal field might have similar consequences, while success might alter the nature of the Church with even graver consequences for the Church and for society.

III

DEVELOPMENT: PROMISE AND PROBLEMS

8
POVERTY AMID PLENTY

IN 1945, when I was serving in Paraguay, an American writer visited Asunción, the capital. He noticed that most people were modestly and even poorly dressed, that dwellings were far below United States standards, that only the principal streets were paved, and that there were few automobiles. The city's best hotel had very simple accommodations, and the writer was unable to find a really good restaurant. He was appalled at what he considered Paraguay's poverty.

About the same time another American visited Paraguay. He was a businessman and banker, one of the first presidents of the US government's Export-Import Bank. He walked up and down Asunción's streets and drove out through the countryside. And he looked into the eyes of Paraguayans. Later he said to me, "I hope nothing we may do will change these people." The banker remarked that Paraguayans seemed to be well-fed. They were a sturdy, vigorous people. Their clothing was usually very clean. While he noticed the scarcity of automobiles he saw, too, that nearly everyone who came in from the country had an animal to ride. He said he would not soon forget the sight of a country woman trotting into market on her burro, her baskets of vegetables slung behind her, a black cigar in her mouth. To him she was a free woman, one of nature's capitalists, self-confident and independent. The banker saw in Paraguayans not poverty but pride, an inner tranquility that he had missed in many countries, possibly including his own.

The writer thought the Paraguayan government, and the government of the United States, should do more to help Paraguay's masses who were living in conditions that he considered intolerable. The banker, who had come to Paraguay to see what he might do to help, was expressing a wish that his efforts, wise or unwise, successful or unsuccessful, would not unwittingly offend the dignity of Paraguayans or lessen their pride; that he would not needlessly and thoughtlessly disrupt a way of life that, simple as it was, and doubtless in part because it was simple, brought rewards that were real and lasting and that might not survive mere material improvement, or the wrong kind of material improvement.

Until comparatively recently the few persons who managed to visit Latin America regarded most of the countries as quaint, and it was generally agreed that the world was better off for the quaintness Latin America contributed. Quaintness sold stereopticon slides and Chautauqua lectures. Quaint countries were more interesting than our own, and even though few of us might have chosen to live in one of them it seldom occurred to us to feel sorry for those who did. But attitudes have changed. Much of what we used to consider quaintness in Latin America, and in the less-developed countries generally, is now regarded as poverty, and most of us have come to feel, and indeed correctly, that poverty in another country concerns not only the people of that country; that it concerns us as well. But how it concerns us, and what if anything we can or should do about it, even how we should define it, is not nearly as clear as some of us have been led to believe.

Of course not only attitudes have changed. Conditions also have changed—many of them radically. Today's Latin America is quite a different place from yesterday's. It is better in many ways. Health conditions in general have improved, as has education. Most countries are becoming industrialized, some of them rapidly. But problems have not lessened. Rather they have increased and some old problems are more serious than they used to be.

One new problem is an explosive increase in population, a result of improved health and a continued high birthrate. Latin America has the highest population growth of any area in the world. Increased production is eaten up by increased population, so that per capita income remains low. Millions whom the land no longer supports have fled to the cities, where many of them are added to the already growing numbers of unemployed. Living closely together in cities has made Latin Americans more politically conscious, more aware of problems they face, more exposed to the influence of demagogic leaders, and more susceptible to that influence. Better communications, the radio, the television, and the daily press have revealed to the underprivileged that the masses in many countries live much better than they do.

The Church, concerned traditionally with things of the spirit, is taking an increased interest in people's material welfare. In some countries the military have taken the lead in bringing about economic and social change after taking over the government by force. In Cuba a gifted demagogue, after capturing a democratic revolution against the country's dictator, betrayed it to the Communists. In Chile a Marxist coalition, running against a divided opposition, was voted into power in free elections. It socialized most of the country's economy and added to the poverty that afflicted Chileans before it was overthrown.

People frequently see in Latin America what they want to see or have been led to think they should see. Americans may see one thing; Latin Americans may see something quite different. And among Americans, as among Latin Americans, there are apt to be varying views of the same thing. Are the poor in Latin America victims of foreign imperialists? Of domestic oligarchs? Of both? Are they victims of their own ignorance and of demagogues who exploit ignorance in order to advance their political careers? Are they victims of all those things? Is affluence in the more-developed countries a cause of poverty in the less-developed countries? Or would less affluence in the more-developed countries result in more poverty in the less-developed countries? If those questions are difficult to answer, they are no more so than many other questions that relate to Latin America's economic and social problems and to what other countries can and should do to help solve them.

LAND AND CLIMATE

As we have already noted, there are two kinds of resources required for development: human resources and material resources. Human resources—the kind of people who inhabit a country, their work habits, their ability to cooperate in the common interest—are very important. The development that has taken place in Japan, which is overpopulated and depends heavily on imports of food and raw materials, is startling evidence of that. But material resources also are important. Economic progress in the United States was greatly facilitated by the wealth of the land and other physical features that favored growth. How can we characterize Latin America's material resources? How do land and climate affect development?

Latin America is a land of extremes. It extends from the Rio

Grande, on Mexico's northern border, to Cape Horn, some 7,000 miles to the south. It has an area twice that of Europe and two-and-a-half times that of continental United States. It occupies nearly one-sixth of the land surface of the earth.

The Andes, which stretch from Venezuela and Colombia to the Straits of Magellan, are the world's longest mountain range and contain some of its highest peaks. The Amazon is the mightiest river in the world. It drains 40 percent of all South America. More than 100 miles wide at its mouth, its annual discharge is at the rate of 3.4 billion gallons a minute, 11 percent of the water drained from all the continents of the world.

Despite its large and beautiful cities, its rich farms, and the impressive economic growth that characterizes some sections, Latin America as a whole is still a less-developed area, and geography furnishes some of the reasons. Mountains and desert make much of the land useless for agriculture or living. Three-fourths of the area lies in the tropics. Much of it is lowland, where heat is continuous and rainfall excessive.

There can be little development without communication, and nature has created formidable obstacles to communication in Latin America. The jungles and rain forests are among them, of course, and so are the mountains. England, some six thousand miles away, was for many years more accessible to most Argentines than was Chile, their neighbor across the Andes. Mountains have divided many countries into separate cultural and economic regions. They have hindered political as well as physical communication. On much of South America's west coast they descend to the very edge of the sea, leaving no room for natural harbors. Even on the east coast mountains have hindered communication. Rio de Janeiro has one of Latin America's few natural harbors, but Brazil's Great Escarpment reaches almost to the port and has to be crossed before people and goods can reach the interior.

Nor have rivers been as helpful as one might expect. In all Mexico and Central America there are no navigable rivers. On the Pacific coast of South America only the Guayas, in Ecuador, is navigable for light vessels. At the same time the Amazon, which empties into the Atlantic, is navigable for ocean vessels as far as Manaus, Brazil, 900 miles from its mouth, and for smaller vessels as far as Iquitos, Peru, some 1,400 miles farther west. There is little of immediate value along that enormous stretch of river, however, and once one leaves the river communication tends to be extremely difficult.

Besides the Amazon there are three other large river systems, all in South America. One is Colombia's Magdalena-Cauca System, which empties into the Caribbean. It is navigable for 900 miles but is shallow. Another is the Orinoco in Venezuela, which is navigable for large vessels for some 700 to 1,000 miles. The third is the Paraná-Paraguay System, which empties into the 170-mile estuary of the Rio de la Plata. The system drains 1.5 million square miles of Argentina, Uruguay, Paraguay, Bolivia, and Brazil. Oceangoing steamers ascend it to Rosario, Paraná and Santa Fe, in Argentina, while smaller vessels can reach Asunción, in Paraguay, and Corumbá, in Brazil, which is some 1,800 miles north of the Rio de la Plata. The Paraná-Paraguay is not as satisfactory a river system as it might be. It meanders, snakelike, past the Argentine *pampa,* frequently doubling back upon itself as though it had more than enough time to get anywhere. It shifts its channel from time to time and sandbars sometimes interfere with navigation. But it is the most important river system in all Latin America. Until early in the twentieth century it was Paraguay's only outlet to the sea. Buenos Aires, on the Rio de la Plata, is not a natural port but at great expense to Argentina it has been made a very useful one.

While Latin America is far from being an El Dorado it nevertheless contains areas of great natural wealth, as well as areas whose wealth has not yet been explored. The extensive humid *pampa* of Argentina is the finest area in the world for growing grains and raising cattle. Coffee is one of the most important commodities in world trade. Latin America produces most of it. Sugar, cotton, soybeans, and other valuable products of the tropics and the temperate zone are grown, many of them under especially favorable conditions. Latin America can be made to yield any animal or vegetable product that is found anywhere.

The area is rich in the precious metals that beckoned *conquistadores* to its farthest reaches. It is also rich in minerals that have brought it incomparably more wealth than gold and silver have. Venezuela is the world's third largest exporter of petroleum. Together with Brazil it has some of the world's largest and richest iron ore deposits. Chile and Peru are rich in copper, and Chile is a monopoly producer of natural nitrates. Mexico is a major exporter of many metals and has a newly discovered capability of becoming one of the world's leading exporters of petroleum. Bolivia is the world's second largest tin exporter.

If water is a valuable resource, and if pure water is a particularly valuable resource, then the Amazon basin is immensely rich. Water in the Rio Negro, the Amazon's chief tributary, is as pure as distilled water. Thousands of factories could take water from the lower Amazon without diminishing the supply noticeably. Because the Amazon overflows its banks there is a common impression that the basin is a huge swamp. As a matter of fact most of it is above the flood plain. It was once the world's principal source of natural rubber but lost its near-monopoly, and most of its rubber trade, when the British grew trees from Brazilian seed and planted them in Malaya and Sumatra. In the 1920s the Ford Motor Company tried to introduce scientific rubber production in the Amazon. It invested large sums in plantations. There were problems but they were being overcome. The plantations were productive, health conditions were good, and workers were efficient. The trouble was that there were not enough of them; too few Brazilians were willing to live in the Amazon Basin.[1] On the basis of per capita exports, however, the basin has been one of the world's most productive regions.*

Japanese immigrants have shown what can be done when the basin's manpower problem is solved. Due to their efforts pepper, which they introduced, has become the most valuable product of the state of Pará. Thanks to their efforts, also, jute, which formerly was imported, is now produced in the basin, and Brazil, which grows more coffee than any other country, ships the beans in bags produced at home. Preston James has said that "the subsistence farmer [in the Amazon Basin] is condemned to poverty. But he is not condemned to poverty because of the land on which he works or because of the climate, or any other elements of the habitat. He is condemned to poverty because of his own attitudes, objectives, and [inadequate] knowledge of technology."[2]

For years American fruit companies have been opening large jungle areas throughout Latin America to profitable banana growing. Keeping the jungle from encroaching on the plantations and protecting the health of workers have not been great problems. Yellow fever, which at one time was a serious impediment to development, has been largely eliminated, and the incidence of malaria has been greatly reduced.

Temperate Tropics. Surprisingly, perhaps, heat is less extreme in tropical America than it is in the United States, although it is more continuous and humidity is higher. Air-conditioning has made many

---

*Nevertheless in 1979 there appeared to be reason to fear that the military government's extensive program to develop the Amazon Basin would not only fail but would also cause serious harm to the basin's ecology.

tropical cities quite as comfortable for living and working as cities in the United States. Of course Latin America also has is own natural system of air-conditioning. The conditioner is altitude. Following the Indians' example, the Spaniards built cities in cool places. Many of the most important cities of tropical America are at an altitude of several thousand feet. Mexico City is 7,500 feet above sea level; San José, Costa Rica, 3,725; Bogotá, Colombia, 8,750; and Quito, Ecuador, 9,350 feet. Except for the few people who are bothered by altitude those cities have delightful, healthful climates, often likened to perpetual spring.

Nearly one-half of Mexico lies within the tropics but a majority of its people live on the cool Central Plateau at altitudes varying from 3,600 to 8,600 feet. And although the widest part of Brazil is just south of the equator most of it has a healthful, temperate climate. A great plateau, covering almost 1 million square miles and ranging in altitude from 2,000 to 3,000 feet, extends from northeast Brazil far to the south and southwest.

And not only altitude tempers the heat. On the Atlantic coast of tropical America cooling trade winds create an agreeable climate and a booming tourist industry, while along the Pacific coast of South America a cold antarctic current produces pleasing temperatures well into tropical Peru. It also has made much of the area a desert, little suited to habitation but a source of great mineral wealth to the nations that have been its owners.

Clearly there are two frontiers in Latin America. One is the geographical frontier, which still is extensive. The other is the scientific-technological frontier, which has scarcely been breached. It may never be possible to exploit the first frontier successfully without also exploiting the second, but both are accessible.

No nation and no area has the resources that, ideally, it should possess, but nations with resources that are greatly inferior to those of Latin America have long enjoyed prosperity. Since the Latin Americans have not been equally successful, reasons must be sought in other circumstances. We have already considered history and politics. Let us address ourselves directly to Latin America's efforts to achieve satisfactory economic development.

9

THE ECONOMIC COMMISSION FOR LATIN AMERICA

DEVELOPMENT—The improvement of countries' economies, the raising of living standards of their people—is the most important subject in Latin America, economic or political, domestic or international. Development is an economic objective that has to be achieved through economic means. But it will not be achieved except in the presence of political conditions that favor it. Elections, when they are held, usually revolve around which man or group offers greatest promise of achieving rapid development. Even when governments are changed arbitrarily, the new regime almost invariably justifies its extralegal seizure of power by promising economic improvement that the ousted regime has not been able to bring about. Development is a domestic phenomenon. It affects the people of a country and it must be achieved principally by them. But it is not attainable in the absence of reasonably satisfactory relations with other countries.

Since development is given such importance it is natural that a great deal should have been said and written about it, not only in Latin America but also in the more-developed countries, particularly the United States. Political leaders, political scientists, economists, editorialists, and columnists have produced a formidable literature on it. Because the discussion, in its present proportions, is new, and since it is largely theoretical, in the sense that the impressive literature devoted to it has not been matched by equally impressive results, there have been many approaches to development and to the related subject of economic aid.

In Latin America, groups styling themselves "liberal" and "progressive," and some other groups as well, have tended to follow the doctrines enunciated by the Economic Commission for Latin America (ECLA), a United Nations body on which all Latin American governments are represented and which, for all practical purposes, represents Latin America's views. ECLA has made the following points, among others.[1]

THE CENTER AND THE PERIPHERY

According to ECLA, the world economic system is divided into two parts: "the center," that is to say the developed countries; and "the periphery," which is made up of the less-developed countries, including the countries of Latin America. Under the "outdated" pattern of international division of labor, in which each country produced and traded what it could best produce, the task that fell to Latin America, as part of the periphery, was that of producing food and raw materials (primary products) for the great industrial countries of the center. The pattern, if it was to work fairly, involved two assumptions. The first was that the cost to Latin America of goods manufactured in the center would be lessened as technology improved. The second was that the center's demand for Latin America's primary products would grow as fast as its income grew. In practice, however, neither of those things has occurred. In the first place, technical progress in the center has brought not lower prices for the products Latin America imports from the center but higher wages and profits in the center. At the same time, prices of the primary products Latin America ships to the center have not improved, or have improved less than prices of manufactured goods, because, contrary to the second assumption, demand for those products has not increased in proportion to increased income in the center.

For example, while people in the center (and in the periphery too) have an almost limitless desire to acquire the cars and the many other products that the center manufactures, the amount of coffee a person can drink is limited, and the center's demand for coffee therefore does not increase in proportion to its income. As a result of the limited demand for primary products, ECLA points out, income from exports to the center has been kept unfairly low. One effect of this is that the Latin American countries have been unable to accumulate the capital they require in order to truly progress.

The measure of these inequalities is the "terms of trade," which have swung against primary products. To illustrate: if country X has to ship twice the amount of coffee, sugar, and iron ore that it used to ship in order to pay for the same quantity of imports from the center, then the terms of trade, from country X's viewpoint, have deteriorated. This, ECLA reminds us, is the kind of thing that has taken place. Not only have the Latin American countries been denied their proportionate share of the gains brought about by technological improvement in the center, but a part of the gains from their own increases in productivity has been transferred to the center in the form of continued low prices for their products. It follows that the center should take steps to insure that prices for imports from Latin America bear a closer relationship to prices Latin America must pay for products imported from the center.

But, ECLA maintains, the center has not been content with profiting from structural defects in the world economic system that work in its favor. While preaching the virtues of the international division of labor it violates the principle by erecting tariff and other barriers against commodities that Latin American countries can produce more economically than the center can. Sugar is an example of this. Production of sugar, which the Latin American countries grow more cheaply than the center, has been subsidized in center countries to the detriment of trade with Latin America. The center countries should practice what they preach by eliminating such unfair and uneconomic practices.

Trade and Industrialization. Even when such barriers to trade are removed, however, Latin American countries still will be unable to provide employment for the natural increase in their populations, and they still will have to face the economic, social, and political problems that this gives rise to. The solution lies in industrialization on a much broader scale and at a more rapid rate than in the past. And that, too, ECLA claims, requires the understanding and the active cooperation of the center.

If industry in the Latin American countries is to prosper it will require protection against competition from the center, from the more efficient producers that is, and the center should understand and accept that. Furthermore, protection must be continued so long as productivity in the Latin American countries is lower than in the center. And productivity will continue low until such time as the Latin American countries have been able to accumulate capital in amounts comparable to those in the center countries, plus of course the technical skills they require. In short, protection may continue for a very long time.

In contrast center countries, ECLA indicates, should move in the opposite direction. They should eliminate tariff and other barriers to imports of Latin American manufactures; that is to say they should give them more favorable treatment than they give to imports from other center countries. Such treatment, ECLA says, will not only assist industrialization in Latin America; it also will benefit the center countries themselves, and the reasons are clear. Latin America has an almost limitless need for products from the center, but it can acquire only as much as it can pay for with its exports. It follows, then, that the more Latin America exports to the center the more it buys from it. The level of trade is raised and both parties benefit. But the opposite is not true. Latin American countries are not in a position to bring about an increase in exports to the center by increasing their imports from the center. The center's imports from Latin America reflect other circumstances than Latin America's purchases. All Latin America is apt to get when it increases its purchases from the center is a headache—a balance-of-payments problem, to be exact. The center is in a position to obtain spontaneous reciprocity for its tariff concessions and for other facilities it extends, but Latin America is not. The key to improved trade with Latin America therefore is in the hands of the center, especially the United States.

The Role of Government. But ECLA goes still further. It maintains that industrialization in Latin America requires not only special facilities from the governments of the center countries and protection from the center by the Latin governments; it requires also that the Latin American governments should have a direct role in development. They naturally should invest public funds in needed economic and social overhead, such as highways, port works, power plants, schools, and hospitals, but if circumstances require (and ECLA believes they will) they should also invest directly in industry and agriculture. The objective of that kind of investment would not be socialization. ECLA suggests that socialization, if it should come about, would be the result rather than the objective of government action (although to countries that might be socialized that would appear to make little difference).

That, then, is ECLA's principal thesis regarding trade and development. It has been widely adopted by less-developed countries, not only in Latin America but throughout the world. Dr. Raúl Prebisch, an Argentine, who is the principal author of ECLA's doctrine and who was the organization's executive secretary for many years, became secretary general of the United Nations Conference on Trade and Development (UNCTAD), which first met in Geneva in 1964. Thanks to the affirmative votes of seventy-seven less-developed countries UNCTAD adopted the ECLA thesis as its own. In addition UNCTAD was given permanent status, with the result that there is continual pressure from that source to alter the world trading pattern to the advantage of the less-developed countries.

Many of ECLA's and UNCTAD's proposals have been resisted by the more-developed countries, but the UNCTAD proposal that manufactures from the less-developed countries should be given preferential tariff treatment has prospered. In this case the United States, after having first resisted the proposal, later assumed leadership in obtaining approval of it by the more-developed countries, with the result that Japan, members of the European Economic Community, and, eventually, the United States itself agreed to adopt it.

EVALUATION

John Pincus has said that Prebisch's views (which are embodied in ECLA and UNCTAD doctrine) "are, in some aspects, modern translations of Marxist writing on imperialism."[2] At the same time Americans will find some of ECLA's proposals quite familiar. Its demand for better prices for Latin America's primary products will remind many of their government's agricultural price support program, which provides that kind of help to American farmers. The protection ECLA asks for Latin America's industries corresponds to the protection the United States has given to its own "infant industries." And the preferential treatment ECLA asks for Latin America's exports of manufactured products may be compared to the preference the United States government, in awarding certain kinds of contracts, has given to depressed areas of the country. ECLA's thesis that the Latin American countries have been on the periphery of the world economic community does not differ greatly from the claim long made by southerners in the United States that discriminatory freight rates and other devices made their area an economic colony of the north, or from the claim of some minorities in the United States that they have been victims of the "system" rather than participants in it.

ECLA's program, it will be seen, is aimed at inducing the more-developed countries to extend to Latin America benefits similar to some of the benefits those countries already extend to their own nationals. ECLA argues that the benefit to the world community, including the more-developed countries themselves, will more than justify the cost of the program. But not everyone in the more-developed countries finds the problem as simple as ECLA defines it or the remedies as easy to apply, and some believe that experience supports their skepticism. In the United States, for example, despite a widespread opinion that the farmer, without government assistance, is unable to share in the general prosperity, it has been difficult to discover the precise formula for helping him. Programs have been costly and difficult to administer. They have involved strict governmental controls. An inordinate portion of their benefits has gone to those least in need of them—to many whom Latin Americans would call "oligarchs." The problem of helping the poor also has been a difficult one. Billions of dollars have been spent in efforts to relieve poverty; all kinds of benefits for the needy have been voted and many persons have been helped. But the needy we still have with us. Many Americans suspect that the needy countries, or a large number of them at least, we shall also continue to have with us.

Persons in the more-developed countries not only foresee practical problems in trying to carry out ECLA's program; many of them are also doubtful about some of the principles involved. By seeking preferential treatment for some of Latin America's exports ECLA is asking the more-developed countries to abandon a principle that has served them and, they believe, the international community well: the principle of equality of treatment, of nondiscrimination among nations. ECLA is saying that where Latin America is concerned nondiscrimination should sometimes give way to discrimination—in its favor. The more-developed countries foresee a continuing and growing demand for new discriminations and new exceptions that might be difficult to grant, and that might lessen pressure on the Latin Americans to solve their problems by their own efforts.

Furthermore, since ECLA emphasizes the state's role as entrepreneur, and since some Latin American governments have responded with enthusiasm, ECLA seems to be asking the more-developed countries to discriminate in favor not only of Latin American products but, in some cases, of products of statist economies. Agreeing to that, some persons fear, would limit rather than encourage development since it would weaken support for private enterprise, which has been chiefly responsible for development in the past.

Not only persons in the developed countries question ECLA's thesis; many Latin Americans also do. The masses, of course, are little familiar with it, and are influenced chiefly by the antiforeign interpretation given to it by politicians. Industrialists tend to welcome ECLA's demand for protection against foreign competition and tariff preferences for their exports; producers of primary products agree that they are entitled to higher prices for those products. But many entrepreneurs have little confidence in government's ability to carry out the dominant economic role that ECLA seeks for it.* They are too familiar with the weaknesses of government—the frustrating delays in making even minor decisions, the interminable paper shuffling, the partisanship of politicians and the quibbling of bureaucrats. The Brazilian saying, "Our country grows at night while the politicians sleep," may reflect the attitude of Latin Americans more accurately than ECLA does. Nevertheless ECLA's has been the most powerful single voice in the economic field and its influence among those who wield political power has been great.

Pincus has suggested that ECLA's analysis of Latin America's trade problem may be correct but that the solution it proposes may not be the most adequate. Nevertheless, he indicates, the facts around which the controversy revolves are clear. He reminds us, among other things, that:

1) The per capita income of the less-developed countries is growing very slowly, and among the reasons is scarcity of foreign exchange.
2) The present structure of international trade is in some respects a serious barrier to rapid economic growth in many less-developed countries.
3) Promotion of exports of both primary products and manufac-

*ECLA's headquarters are in Santiago, Chile. Former Chilean president Jorge Alessandri, in conversation with me in April 1975, placed much of the blame for the economic excesses of the Socialist-Communist regime of Salvador Allende, in the early 1970s, on ECLA's influence over the years. Pedro Vuskovic, a Marxist who had worked with ECLA for twenty years, became Allende's first minister of economy. The program he carried out nearly destroyed Chile's economy before he was replaced by Carlos Matus, another Marxist who had also served with ECLA.

tures is among the possible remedies open to the less-developed countries.

4) Trade growth of many less-developed countries is being held back by inelastic demand for primary products and by agricultural protectionism in the more-developed countries.

5) World demand for manufactures, on the other hand, is buoyant. But tariffs and other governmental restrictions in the more-developed countries have made it difficult and sometimes impossible for the less-developed countries to share in meeting that demand.[3]

Pincus thinks "it is important for the rich countries to be aware that they are, in effect, choosing to help keep [the less-developed countries] poor."[4]

There is no room for doubt that the less-developed countries, including the countries of Latin America, have trade problems that are real and urgent. There is no room for doubt either that the more-developed countries have an indispensable role in helping them to meet those problems.

10
PLANNING AND INTEGRATION

TROTSKY ONCE said that capitalism was a system in which "each man thinks for himself and no one thinks for all." Today's Marxist theorists, like Trotsky, believe that government planning is more rational than the market; indeed, they insist it is planning that chiefly distinguishes socialism from capitalism. In Communist countries planning is a substitute for freedom. To paraphrase Trotsky, if citizens are not permitted to plan for themselves then the government must plan for them—adequately or inadequately.

Government planning is an imprecise operation, especially in free societies where plans, if they are to succeed, must to a great extent be carried out by private persons and groups that may not believe in government planning or may disagree with the plans government has drawn up. Even persons in government who are outside the planning process, and whose cooperation is essential if plans are to be carried out, may be hostile to the planning process or may disapprove of plans that have been officially approved. For these and other reasons planning has prospered (not necessarily succeeded) most in countries where economic freedom does not exist or is severely limited. By the same token the mere act of planning, of persistence in the planning process, tends to lessen freedom.

The issue is to some degree a matter of semantics, of course. All governments must plan in the sense that they must look ahead, foresee problems to the extent they can, and prepare to meet them. The alteration of a tax rate, the elimination of exchange controls, the offering of incentives to private investment—all may be considered a part of planning, and all governments engage in planning of that kind. But the preparation of a detailed plan to which an economy and a society is expected to adhere is quite a different thing.

The Latin American country that has experienced most rapid growth in recent years is Brazil. Brazil also has one of Latin America's freest economies. On the other hand in Velasco's Peru, while the economy deteriorated rapidly, planners sat around a table and drew up plans in virtual isolation from the rest of the government and from the community, and the more grandiose the plans the more satisfied the planners often were with their work.* In Allende's Chile Marxist planners destroyed the country's free economy and brought about economic prostration in three years.

ECLA is a staunch proponent of planning, which it prefers to call "programming." But it is quick to deny any tendency toward statism, although it recognizes that in a country where planning flourishes the state may to a great extent supplant private enterprise. Not surprisingly ECLA's most enthusiastic followers have been those who seek to greatly expand the state's economic role.

Although the United States itself had little or no experience in national planning the United States thinkers who conceived the Alliance for Progress, the program of inter-American aid and cooperation undertaken in the 1960s, insisted that Latin Americans should engage in it. "Such targets as land and tax reform, broader educational opportunities and additional mobilization of domestic capital will become reflected in national programs," they predicted. Following their counsel President Kennedy, talking to the Latin American ambassadors whom he had called to the White House, said, on March 31, 1961:

> If our alliance is to succeed, each Latin nation must formulate long-range plans for its own development—plans which establish targets and priorities, insure monetary stability, establish the machinery for vital social change, stimulate private activity and initiative, and provide for a maximum national effort. These plans will be the foundation of our development effort and the basis for the allocation of outside resources.

Early plans of the Latin American governments were drawn up for the principal purpose of attracting United States aid under the Alliance

*General Juan Velasco Alvarado led the military revolt that overthrew the freely elected government of Fernando Belaunde Terry on October 3, 1968, and served as Peru's president until he in turn was overthrown by the military on August 25, 1975.

for Progress. They succeeded in doing that, but otherwise they were little more than expressions of aspirations. Nevertheless planning fitted in with the increasing importance Latin Americans in government were giving to their own role in the development process. As time went on it seemed to many observers that the planners were taking their mission much too seriously. In a warning clearly intended for the Latin American governments one of the American authors of the Alliance wrote, in some dismay:

> Planning for development does not mean centralized control of the whole economic structure on totalitarian lines. It means planning that is concentrated on two essential elements: (1) an integrated program of public investment in economic and social infrastructure for which government has direct responsibility . . . and (2) provision of a framework of institutions and incentives within which private enterprise can function efficiently. The government development plans, in a sense, may be likened to the arteries of a healthy human being, with private enterprise providing the blood cells which flow through those arteries.[1]

The warning was clearly called for, but many persons intimately familiar with Latin America feared that if the blood cells of private enterprise were expected to flow through the arteries of government planning many Latin American economies would continue in a state of anemia unless new and more successful efforts were made to insure that the blood cells were richer and more plentiful, and the hardening process that tends to attack government arteries in Latin America were reversed.

In the 1960s ECLA was frank to recognize planning's weakness. It said that planning had been far from effective and listed a number of reasons why. One was an acute shortage of competent planners. Also, it noted, there had been little support for planning either within government or within the private sector; both groups had either ignored plans or opposed them. By the 1970s, however, planning had taken firmer hold, and not only ECLA but also officials of the important Inter-American Development Bank were extolling the merits of Latin America's planners.

All Latin America's planners are committed to integration of the area's economies. Integration accords with ECLA's thesis that development must include industrialization, that industrialization requires larger markets, and that creating larger markets requires positive action by the Latin American governments.

One result of the world depression of the 1930s was that Latin Americans received sharply lowered income from their exports, so that many manufactures they had previously imported were now beyond their power to acquire. In order to free themselves from this precarious dependence on foreign sources of supply, as well as to improve their foreign exchange positions and provide jobs for workers, the larger countries initiated, or in some cases intensified, programs to manufacture such items at home—programs of "import-substitution" as they were called. With import-substitution the process of industrialization had begun in earnest, and soon all the countries were engaged in it. Results were on the whole impressive. In the larger countries domestic production rapidly outstripped exports and imports in growth. And imports, which had consisted largely of consumer items, now comprised primarily semiprocessed goods, fuels, and machinery and other capital goods, typical imports of a developing economy.

By the early 1950s, however, import-substitution had nearly reached its limit. Industrialization beyond that point was going to be difficult. It was evident that something new had to be added if the area was to avoid stagnation. As we have seen, one proposal sponsored by ECLA was that the more-developed countries should give improved treatment to Latin America's exports, thus expanding the market for them. Another was that, following the strikingly successful examples of the European Economic Community and the European Free Trade Association, the Latin American countries should integrate their economies; that they should join together in a common market which promised a number of advantages. It would replace the small national markets of the separate countries with a regional market of some 230 to 250 million persons. It would make possible economies of scale—larger, more modern, more efficient plants that could produce goods more cheaply. It would permit the establishment of capital-goods industries without which full industrialization could not be achieved. It would convert Latin America from a loose geographical and cultural grouping into a responsible economic unit and perhaps open the way to converting it into a responsible political unit.

CACM AND LAFTA

In 1960 two integration agreements were signed: an agreement for a Central American Common Market (CACM), and an agreement among

Mexico and several countries of South America to establish a Latin American Free Trade Area (LAFTA). LAFTA finally came to include all the South American countries. It fell short of being a common market in that it had no common external tariff.

CACM had spectacular success until war broke out, in 1969, between two of its members, Honduras and El Salvador, and Honduras withdrew from the market.* Despite that development, intrazonal exports of CACM countries increased from 8.5 percent to 26 percent of total exports in six years.[2] But the civil war in Nicaragua and the resulting overthrow of Nicaragua's president Anastasio Somoza Debayle, in July 1979, created new obstacles to successful Central American integration.

LAFTA had little success. Although the member countries had agreed that tariffs and other restrictions on substantially all trade among them would be removed by 1975 nothing like that occurred. Members took full advantage of the large number of escape clauses in the vaguely worded agreement. Vested interests succeeded in blocking concessions they opposed. Sometimes it seemed as though every member country wanted its own steel mill, its own automobile manufacturing plant, and its own petrochemical plant together with protection from competition by similar plants in other member countries. Nevertheless intrazonal exports of LAFTA countries increased from 7.6 percent to 12.3 percent of total exports in six years.[3]

ANCOM

By the early 1970s LAFTA was moribund. A disproportionate amount of the increase in intrazonal trade had gone to the "Big Three", Argentina, Brazil, and Mexico. In order to improve their competitive position six South American countries agreed, in 1969, to form an Andean Common Market (ANCOM) within LAFTA. By 1978 Bolivia, Colombia, Ecuador, Peru, and Venezuela were members. Chile, an original member, had withdrawn following the overthrow of the Allende regime in that country. The new government considered that the aims and rules of the Andean group, especially the strict limitations and

*In June 1971 Honduras signed bilateral integration agreements with Costa Rica, Nicaragua, and Guatemala, but El Salvador's trade with Nicaragua and Costa Rica had to be routed in a way to avoid Honduran territory.

controls over foreign investment and the high external tariffs that were envisaged, were incompatible with its purpose of restoring economic freedom in Chile.

ANCOM members were enthusiastic planners. A favorite device of theirs was the "sectoral program for industrial development" under which production of key products would be allotted to member countries. But agreeing to programs proved to be difficult indeed. After seven years of effort only three programs had been approved. Furthermore, the economies of scale that the programs were going to make possible were being sacrificed to nationalism and to politics. Many persons doubted that the extremely detailed and complex agreements, which had to be implemented by legislation in the member countries before they could go into effect, would ever have the results desired.

Meanwhile not only the government of Chile had changed; changes, some peaceful and others violent, had also taken place in the other Andean countries. And the economic picture had changed as well. Rising oil prices had created grave problems for importing countries. From a position of discouraging new foreign investment most countries began to court it. Achieving a common market was still a distant objective. The value of trade among member countries increased by some 500 percent in six years.[4] But a large part of the increase was due to higher prices of Venezuelan and Ecuadoran oil.

Despite government plans and programs, resistance to integration remained formidable. The smaller and poorer countries feared that the benefits of integration would continue to go principally to the larger countries of the region, and that existing inequalities would thus be continued and even increased. Industrialists who had long enjoyed monopolies in protected national markets were seldom pleased with the prospect of having to face competition from other Latin American countries. Some persons feared that the principal gainers from integration would be the large, non–Latin American companies. Societies most of which had been unable to achieve reasonably satisfactory cooperation within themselves were finding it difficult to achieve cooperation with one another. The prospect of a fully integrated Latin American economy was remote. Nevertheless efforts in that direction were expected to continue.

11
AGRARIAN REFORM

AS WE HAVE seen, Latin America's failure to achieve satisfactory development has been explained in many ways. Among the reasons cited are geography, climate, race, the "economic imperialism" of the more developed countries, and also the area's colonial heritage. Many persons believe that the land tenure system, an important part of that heritage, is a principal source of the area's problems, and that permanent progress will not be achieved until the system is changed.[1] Agrarian reform is an important feature of ECLA's program for Latin America.

Agrarian reform in Latin America is not new; in some countries it is nearly as old as independence. During a period in Mexico's history known as *La Reforma* (1855–76), and dominated by Benito Juarez, one of Mexico's most revered patriots, a Liberal government enacted and carried out a law designed to modernize the country's landholding system. The Liberals had read the right books and were sure they had the right ideas. They wanted Mexico to become a country of independent landowners living and working in a free society, as in the United States for example. There were two obstacles to realizing such a dream. One was the extensive church lands on which Indians lived under the generally benign protection of priests; the other was the centuries-old system of Indian *ejidos,* or communal villages. In a doctrinaire effort to carry out their ideas the reformers broke up both the church lands and the *ejidos,* with the result that the rich and the unscrupulous moved in and built up vast new estates, or added to existing estates, while millions of Indians were left landless, and many of them homeless. It was not the first example of doctrinaire agrarian reform in Latin America nor would it be the last.

LATIFUNDIA, MINIFUNDIA, AND COMUNIDADES

Pre-Columbian Indians allotted land according to family and community needs. Europeans rejected that and proceeded to distribute it (and frequently its Indian occupants) among favored persons. They brought the *latifundio* to America. Avarice rather than need became the criterion for land distribution and land use.

The typical *latifundio* covered an enormous area and was largely self-sufficient. It produced foodstuffs, fuel, building materials, skins, and fibers. These met the meager needs of the workers and most of the owner's needs as well. The owner also enjoyed many luxuries—a spacious home, for example, and abundant personal service. Luxuries that the *latifundio* could not furnish directly the owner could obtain by exchanging surplus produce in the nearest town or city, or by exporting it. Many owners had homes in the city and spent most of their time there, while the *latifundia* were left to the impersonal care of managers. A *latifundio* did not have to produce much to maintain a single owner and his family in luxury. As a result many, perhaps most, *latifundia* were not very productive. They contributed relatively little to the general economy.

It was not until the twentieth century that the colonial system began to crack, and even then change came slowly. In Mexico the 1911 revolution brought about drastic change. In the 1950s redistribution of land was carried out in Guatemala and, on a larger scale, in Bolivia. Venezuela expropriated a large acreage and distributed it to peasants. In Chile a Christian Democratic government and, later, a Socialist-Communist government and a military government, redistributed large areas of land. In Peru a military regime broke up *latifundia* and restored land to the Indians. Castro's agrarian reform placed Cuba far to the left of such communist countries as Poland, Yugoslavia, Bulgaria, and Hungary. All political groups in Latin America have given thought to agrarian reform, and all governments have enacted some kind of reform.

Today's *latifundia*, more than yesterday's, are market-oriented, but in many countries the colonial heritage weighs heavily upon them. Owners can still live well even when *latifundia* are operated inefficiently, and many continue to be operated inefficiently.* The typical *latifundio,* today as yesterday, requires the services of low-paid workers who are tied to the land. Practices do not differ greatly from those followed in colonial times. Commonly a worker is ceded a small plot of land where he can plant a garden and perhaps keep a few animals. He then has to labor part-time for the owner, or sell the owner a part of his produce at prices fixed by the owner, or both. Whatever course he follows his income is no more than he and his family require for subsistence.

In the early days of independence the *latifundista* dominated his peasants politically no less than economically. He no longer has the political power he once had, but frequently he can still "deliver" not only his own vote but also the votes of peasants who live on his land. Many proponents of agrarian reform believe that neither development, nor social justice, nor democracy will be achieved until peasants are freed from the political control of the large landowner—until the *latifundio* is broken up, that is.[2]

Not all peasants live on *latifundia*; many live as owners, tenants, or squatters on tiny plots of land, *minifundia* as they are called. But a large number of these *minifundistas* are forced to supplement their inadequate incomes by laboring on nearby estates. The effect of some agrarian reform programs has been to take workers off the large estates and place them on their own *minifundia* where their situation is little improved. Not only may the *minifundista* still be compelled to work part-time on an estate; the estate may be the only market for his crops and his only source of credit. He may be as dependent on the estate as when he lived on it.

There is a third major type of landholding, the Indian *comunidad*, a survival of the pre-Columbian system of community ownership. It is found mostly in the Andean region of South America. Over the years *comunidades* have eroded in area and most of them are too small to meet the needs of a rapidly growing population. It was the violent occupation of private estates by land-hungry Indians that helped to bring on the

*In contrast, plantations, many of them very large and some foreign-owned, which produce bananas, coffee, cotton, sugar, and some other crops for export, tend to be operated very efficiently. The military government which assumed power in Peru in 1968 was criticized for expropriating sugar plantations owned by W. R. Grace and Company which were among the country's leading foreign exchange earners.

1968 revolution in Peru and a radical program of agrarian reform. The *comunidad* permits its occupants to live as Indians in practical isolation from the rest of the nation, as doubtless is the wish of most of them, but it has few other merits. Agricultural methods are primitive, individual initiative is stifled, and there is little contribution to the national economy.

Still another form of landholding, reminiscent of the *comunidad*, is Mexico's *ejido*, made up of land expropriated from large owners and distributed to landless villages at the height of the revolution. *Ejidos* were formed out of some of the best lands in Mexico and some of the worst. They could be cultivated individually or collectively, as the *ejidatarios* determined. Once regarded as the solution of Mexico's agrarian problem, the *ejidos* have been a great disappointment. Poorly conceived, poorly organized, poorly supported by the government, and victims of partisan and corrupt politics, a few have managed to have some success, but more have been failures. Some have simply disintegrated. They are not an attractive model for today's agrarian reformers.

Agrarian reform, then, has three principal objectives. The first is to improve the condition of peasants who for centuries have lived a serflike existence. The second is to increase production of the agricultural products a growing population urgently requires. The third is to improve opportunities for the practice of democracy. And it is often stressed that agrarian reform also is needed in order to make possible the industrialization that Latin Americans regard as essential to economic and social improvement.

In the more-developed countries the farm population and the rural population generally are an important market for industrial products. But that is not true of Latin America. The rural population is poor; its purchasing power is insignificant. Clearly if rural workers could earn enough to acquire the city's products, and if they could produce enough, and cheaply enough, to supply the city's agricultural needs adequately, both rural and city workers would enjoy greatly improved living standards. The rural and urban sectors of the economy would reinforce each other.

Agrarian reform will also contribute to industrialization in another way, its proponents say, namely, by helping to finance it. In its early stages industrialization is costly; mills and factories have to be installed and a vast infrastructure built. Those things must be paid for. Eventually most of them have to be paid for out of a nation's earnings, particularly its foreign exchange earnings, and in all Latin American countries agricultural exports are an important source of foreign exchange.

The agrarian structure is not static of course. Subdivision of privately owned properties through sale and inheritance has been going on for centuries. The pace is excruciatingly slow however. More significant is the spontaneous migration every year of thousands of rural families to the cities and to the virgin jungle and highland. Such migration does not reduce the size of *latifundia* or the power of the *latifundista* but it provides some escape for the growing number of persons whom the *latifundia* can no longer support. At the same time migration to the cities usually has the effect of adding to unemployment there; the migrant may find himself no better off than he was before. And migration to virgin lands also can bring its own disappointments, such as poor soil, poor health conditions, and distance from markets.

Some large owners have acted independently to make land available to the landless or indeed to anyone who might work it. For many years American fruit companies have encouraged local farmers to grow bananas and have offered their own lands for the purpose.[3] The Catholic Church has transferred properties to families that have been working them. Some owners have subdivided their properties in anticipation of expropriation. Such measures have been helpful but they have not greatly reduced the problem.

The Alliance for Progress called for "programs of comprehensive reform" to insure that the land would become, for the man who worked it, "the basis of his economic stability, the foundation of his increasing welfare, and the guarantee of his freedom and dignity." The republics seemed to be clear about where they wanted to go but they were less than clear about how to get there. Most have kept to the indirect and relatively tranquil road of evolution. A few have chosen the direct and rougher road of revolution. Neither group has come close to reaching the goal outlined in the Alliance for Progress.

INDIRECT REFORM

Indirect reform is designed to accomplish its objectives without radically altering the social system or the existing power structure. For example many countries have enacted laws designed to bring about a balance in the bargaining power of landlords and peasants. Among the most common are laws regulating work and tenancy contracts. Proponents of direct reform say, however, that such laws do not help much—that like countless other laws in Latin America they are seldom observed. They point to cases where landlords have actually evicted tenants in order not to have to comply with the laws, leaving the tenants worse off than they were before. They suggest that laws of that kind are more useful to governments and landlords than they are to peasants because they give the impression that there is preoccupation with agrarian reform when the real objective is to maintain the status quo.

Another common instrument for increasing the productivity of land and improving the lot of the landless is tax reform. Since productive farmers tend to be taxed at higher rates than those who leave their land idle, the latter are encouraged to hold on to properties, taking advantage of the historic tendency of land to increase in value, and using the land as protection against inflation. Higher taxes on unused (or underused) land, it is urged, would encourage owners to make the land more productive and therefore more useful to the economy, or to sell it to others who will. Laws providing for such taxes have been enacted in many countries. Here again, however, it is claimed that frequently they are not enforced. High inheritance taxes aimed at forcing the subdivision of estates also have been enacted in some countries. But many landowners have found ways to make them ineffective. A favorite device is to incorporate family holdings so that when a member dies no inheritance tax is paid and no subdivision takes place.

Still another example of indirect reform is colonization. It naturally occurs to some persons that instead of expropriating or confiscating lands that are already under at least partial cultivation, the state should add to those lands by opening up jungle and mountain areas that have never been exploited. Successive governments in Peru have tried to lure colonists to the eastern slope of the Andes, while Brazil has tried to attract them to the Amazon valley. Neither has had much success. Proponents of direct reform tend to belittle such efforts. They point out that colonization programs are costly; that if they are to have a chance of succeeding they involve not only transporting families and giving them land but also helping them to clear the land, furnishing them homes, tools, seeds and technical assistance, building roads, bridges and drainage systems, and taking steps to maintain or improve public health. Argentina has spent as much as $17,000 a family in land settlement projects, and even Guatemala and Ecuador have spent $3,000 a family.[4]

At the very best pitifully few families could be resettled with the funds available to the average Latin American government. Proponents of direct reform point out, further, that jungle and mountain land is usually poor land; that there is very little good new land to offer Latin America's rapidly growing rural population; and that the only lands that have immediate potential are the underdeveloped *latifundia* in the more-or-less settled areas. Breaking up and parceling out the *latifundia* is the answer, they say.

DIRECT REFORM

In contrast to indirect reform, which is carried out within the existing rural power structure, direct reform is aimed at radically changing that structure. Advocates of direct reform recall that it was the French Revolution that brought agrarian reform to France, and that it also took a revolution to bring it to Mexico. Since effective reform transfers not only property but power from one group to another it is by its very nature revolutionary, they say.

Proponents of direct reform point out that large landowners do not voluntarily relinquish power. They do not willingly give up their lands, or any large part of them. Their lands have brought them wealth, security, status, a privileged social and political position that they have come to take for granted as a kind of natural right. At the same time, if they are to be compelled to give up lands they expect to be paid for them. That, unfortunately, is beyond the means of most Latin American governments. As we have seen, land values often have little relationship to productivity. Little-used farm land on the savannah of Bogotá may sell at a higher price than farm land in France's Normandy, one of the most productive areas in Europe. No government could afford to pay commercial prices for such land. Nor is land the only cost of reform. The new landowner requires assistance from government, as in the case of colonization projects. Without such aid, land redistribution might represent a loss to the peasant as well as to the community.

Many Latin Americans do not agree that direct reform is needed. They include most of the landowners of course, and many persons in political life. Such persons tend to think that the Latin American tendency to seek solutions by revolution is a fatal weakness that hinders rather than advances true reform, and they base their attitude on their own observation.

Although one of the announced objectives of agrarian reform is to increase food supplies, the result of revolutionary reform, initially at least, is often to reduce them. Many new landowners are not skilled enough, or lack the equipment, to produce efficiently. Others lack incentive; they are content to engage in subsistence farming. Even though new landowners, over a period of time, should become efficient producers, as some clearly are capable of doing, revolutionary reform still may lead to long periods of food shortages. Only timely United States aid prevented widespread starvation in Bolivia following the 1952 revolution, with its agrarian reform, in that country.

Opponents of direct reform allege that what would help to increase agricultural production and promote the welfare of agricultural workers is less rather than more government intervention. Instead of working to keep agricultural prices remunerative, as the United States government frequently does, Latin American governments more often impose controls in order to keep prices down. But, critics point out, not even the best-inclined farm owners can reward workers adequately or continue to produce in quantities that are needed, if prices are kept lower than production costs. Critics remind us also that government efforts to force agriculture to pay the costs of industrialization have often had the effect of weakening agriculture while saddling countries with inefficient industries. Argentina's Juan Domingo Perón, an early proponent of industrialization, went so far as to make agricultural exports a government monopoly. He bought products at low prices, which the government itself fixed, and sold them abroad at the highest prices the market would bring (he and his close followers pocketed a share of the profits). Quite naturally, farmers and ranchers, who objected to operating at a loss, planted less and allowed herds to become depleted. The total economy deteriorated.

The fact that direct reform often involves confiscation or virtual confiscation of properties is deeply disturbing to many investors and potential investors, who tend to regard it as an attack on all property—an effort to undermine the free enterprise system. Communists are the most ardent proponents of direct reform, and they of course want to free the peasant from subjection to the landowner in order to impose their own kind of subjection upon him, and upon the country. That is what took place in Castro's Cuba, and what was taking place in Allende's Chile.

In most Latin American countries the Church has espoused agrarian reform. In some countries, notably Mexico, Boliva, and Peru, militant peasants have forced governments to enact reform. But reform is carried out by politicians or by the military acting as politicians. The politician claims to speak for the peasant, but he may know very few peasants. Most peasants are inarticulate of course. Many have more confidence in the *latifundio* owner, the *patrón* whom they know, than they have in the politician whom they do not know. The *patrón* is godfather to their children. He is someone to go to in sorrow or trouble. On the *latifundio* they are assured of a place to live, however modest, enough to eat and, one day, a decent burial. In the outside world they may not be confident of having any of those things. Even if peasants should consider that direct or revolutionary reform is what they most need many still would approach it with doubt and fear.

THE FAMILY FARM

Most Latin American governments are committed, on paper at least, to the ideal of the family farm. Americans, of course, are also enthusiastic supporters of the family farm, and in their aid programs, as well as in their oratory, they have pressed the family farm concept. But many Latin American supporters of agrarian reform have little enthusiasm for the family farm. They base their position in part on history. While the family farm is common in some parts of Latin America, in Costa Rica and in parts of Colombia for example (it also was common in parts of pre-Castro Cuba), and while many *minifundia* might be classified as family farms, although woefully inadequate ones, there is no family farm tradition in Latin America comparable to that in the United States or Western Europe. In its place is the tradition of landlordism. In Latin America many families who are on the edge of poverty employ servants who are even poorer than they are. Similarly the owner of a tiny farm may hire some landless person to work it for him while he enjoys his ease. Customs of centuries are not quickly overcome by legislation. Furthermore in many countries there is not enough good land to place peasants on family-size farms; in the best conditions they would be settled on what could only be called *minifundia*. Given that circumstance reformers tend to think in terms of cooperatives and collective farms. The risk is that these will become state farms on the communist model; that the private *latifundista* will be replaced by the state as *latifundista*.

As against the collectivist urge there is great pressure to preserve the large private farms such as one finds in Argentina, for example, farms that have furnished Europe with much of its meat, Europe and other parts of the world with much of their grain, and Argentina with most of its foreign exchange. Owners of those well-run farms, and economists and persons in political life as well, point out that in the United States itself the family farm may be becoming an anachronism; that it would be uneconomical and pointless to break up large, productive entities in Latin America out of devotion to the "quixotic" ideal of the family farm.

THE U.S. ROLE

The United States has had a difficult and controversial role in connection with agrarian reform. Increasingly concerned that the economic aid it was extending would not have the desired results until the system of land tenure and land use was changed, it began, as early as the Eisenhower administration, to prod the Latin Americans into enacting reform. Political leaders of both parties eloquently supported reform and roundly denounced the Latin American "oligarchs" who they considered had frustrated it in the past.

Following the establishment of the Alliance for Progress, during the Kennedy administration, a report by members of the Senate's Foreign Relations Committee said:

> One of the reasons US prestige has increased in Latin America in the last 18 months is that . . . the United States has moved to dissociate itself from the extreme conservatives at the top of the Latin American oligarchies. This element is out of sympathy with every current US policy except anti-Castroism. Its days as a political influence in Latin America are numbered. It will either be overthrown by a Castro-type revolution, or it will be pushed aside by the kind of peaceful revolution envisaged by the *Alianza para el Progreso*. Although the members of this element proclaim themselves the real friends of the United States, they are not in fact. If the United States once again identifies itself with

> those elements, it will lose the good chance it now has to win the friendship of the rising liberal forces who are going to determine the future of Latin America, either through the democratic processes or through a Castroist perversion.

The signers of the report were Senator Wayne Morse, a Democrat who frequently backed liberal causes, and Senator Bourke D. Hickenlooper, a Republican who, despite the harsh words he had for the "extreme conservatives" in Latin America, was a supporter, in the United States, of the presidential candidacy of Barry Goldwater.

AID representatives in Latin America were encouraged to press for reform, and some did so with enthusiasm. In one South American capital that I visited in 1963 I talked to the AID director about the changes I had noted since an earlier visit. "There have been changes," he admitted grudgingly, "but not enough. You see, this country hasn't had its revolution yet." It was clear from his attitude that he thought the country should have its revolution soon and that he wanted to take part in it.

Some Latin American governments pledged support of reform in part because they estimated that in the absence of such a pledge United States aid would not be available to them.

But Americans soon learned that agrarian reform is a political as well as an economic and social phenomenon and that in espousing it they had entered a thicket in which it was easy to lose their way. Property owners, and many persons in political life, accused them of intervening in Latin America's politics. Meanwhile governments proceeded to expropriate US-owned properties that had nothing to do with agrarian reform. In Bolivia, where the United States had supported revolutionary agrarian reform with large-scale aid, a new regime responded by seizing the properties of the Gulf Oil Company. Peru not only expropriated large US-owned sugar plantations; it also expropriated US-owned mining properties and seized a US-owned petroleum company. Chilean *latifundistas,* vexed at United States support of agrarian reform, urged their government to take over the large US-owned copper mining companies, and the government did. Many Americans, including some who had advocated agrarian reform, resented such measures and their resentment lessened their enthusiasm for reform, and also for aid. A disillusioned Senator Hickenlooper introduced an amendment to the Foreign Assistance Act which prohibits American aid to governments that have expropriated American property without arranging for prompt and effective compensation to its owners.

But in Latin America agrarian reform remained very much on the agenda. Most governments hoped that indirect reform would do the job, but the possibility that additional countries would take the direct road, the revolutionary road that is, was by no means remote.

12
COMMODITIES

ECLA WAS NOT the first official body to protest the inequities that resulted from Latin America's role as supplier of primary products to the industrialized countries. The Latin American countries and other less-developed countries had long sought ways to obtain higher and more stable prices for their exports.

COMMODITY AGREEMENTS

One device the countries had urged was the "commodity agreement," which required the cooperation not only of the principal exporting countries but also of the principal importing countries. The idea behind the commodity agreement was that prices would be improved and stabilized by regulating supplies. The exporting countries would reduce or at least limit exports while the importing countries would limit imports. The international coffee agreement of 1962 was an example of such an agreement. Agreements covering sugar and wheat had been in effect, off and on, for many years.

Coffee has been Latin America's second most important export and its principal agricultural export. It has represented as much as one-third of Latin America's exports to the United States. In 1977 coffee represented 66.8 percent of all export proceeds for Colombia, 62.2 percent for El Salvador, 44.3 percent for Costa Rica, 21.1 percent for Brazil and a high percentage for seven other Latin American countries. The unsettling effects, political as well as economic, for those countries of excessive fluctuations in coffee prices are difficult to exaggerate.

An inter-American coffee agreement was signed by the United States and fourteen Latin American countries during World War II, but it was allowed to lapse in 1948. The United States had little faith that commodity agreements, which involved complex controls by the governments of both exporting and importing countries, were the best solution to the problem of unsatisfactory prices. It did not relish the role of international policeman, the tedious job of keeping track of imports and of trying to detect the inevitable efforts to evade restrictions. Its attitude changed in the 1950s, but more for political than economic reasons. The cold war was threatening to heat up. Castro had taken over in Cuba. The United States wanted the free world's good opinion and its cooperation. It joined a study group and a coffee agreement was reached in 1962. Sixty-seven producing and consuming countries became members.

Results for producing countries were generally good, and there was naturally talk of agreements covering other commodities, but the possibilities were meager. Of the products Latin America produced in quantity very few had no clear substitutes; reducing trade in most products would bring lower rather than higher income to producers. Nor were all economists convinced that commodity agreements were desirable. They tended to limit exportation of a commodity to the countries that were already exporting it, to create a kind of monopoly that stifled initiative. By raising prices they discouraged efforts to reduce costs. They lessened pressure on countries to diversify their economies and reduce dependence upon a single product or a very few products. They placed floors under prices but they did not place ceilings over them. Between 1965 and 1978 the average price of green coffee varied from $0.3633 a pound to $3.3347 a pound, a price that provoked consumer boycotts in many parts of the world.

In mid-1979, the United States was a participant in international agreements covering coffee, wheat, and tin, and had signed a sugar agreement that the Congress had not yet approved. The prospect for additional agreements was not favorable.

PETROLEUM

Latin Americans tend to believe that subsoil rights, the right to ownership of mineral resources that lie below the surface of the land,

and the right to exploit those resources, belong not to owners of the land but to the state, and their constitutions and laws reflect that belief. There is a strong feeling, too, that foreigners should be enjoined from exploiting Latin America's mineral wealth.

Brazilians are by no means the most nationalistic Latin Americans. Nevertheless they say, *O petroleo e nosso* ("The petroleum is ours"). Brazil has a state petroleum monopoly; so have Mexico, Peru, Chile, Argentina, and a number of other Latin American countries. While it might be difficult to demonstrate that any of them except Mexico's has been truly successful, their position (political, not economic) has been virtually unassailable. Juan Domingo Perón was the most nationalistic of modern Argentina's presidents. So great was Argentina's need for petroleum, however, that he flew in the face of his and Argentina's ideology when he negotiated a contract with a large American company to come in and help the state monopoly to increase production. The contract was one of the causes of Perón's downfall.

Ousting Perón did nothing to lessen Argentina's burden of paying for imported petroleum when it could—with outside help—have been producing its own. When Arturo Frondizi became president, in 1958, those imports were costing $300 million a year, which was roughly equal to the deficit in the country's international balance of payments. Frondizi had been a leader in the movement to keep the foreign oil companies out of Argentina. Nevertheless one of the early acts of his government was to enter into drilling contracts with foreign companies for the purpose of making Argentina self-sufficient in petroleum. That purpose was substantially accomplished.

The contracts were simple service contracts. The companies had no concessions. They owned no land. They never at any point had ownership of the petroleum they produced. They worked for the state monopoly and were paid a percentage of the value they added to the monopoly's production. Nevertheless President Frondizi, like President Perón, was forced out of office, and the elected government that followed proceeded to annul the contracts as "unconstitutional" and contrary to Argentina's interest.* When petroleum production again declined a later government renegotiated the contracts, but there was still political opposition to them.

*The contracts with the companies were not the principal reasons for the ousters of Perón and Frondizi but they helped to make the ousters popular.

Argentina's actions in the petroleum field did not involve the government of the United States, but the seizure of US-owned properties by a number of other governments created serious difficulties in relations with those governments.

Bolivia. On March 13, 1937, the Bolivian government, without warning, confiscated the properties of the Standard Oil Company of Bolivia. The company had invested some $17 million in the country but had lost interest in further drilling and had offered to sell its assets to the government. Unfortunately the company also had become a pawn in Bolivia's Chaco War against Paraguay. The decree ordering confiscation charged it with evading taxes and also with shipping oil illegally to Argentina, which the Bolivians believed had favored Paraguay in the war. But the charges seemed to be pretexts rather than reasons for the confiscation.

Early in the war the company had declined the government's request for a loan of several million dollars. In the government's view it had also refused to cooperate in other ways in the war effort. Ironically the Paraguayans, at the same time, were charging the company with having incited Bolivia to enter the war, and with having financed the purchase of military equipment by the Bolivian government. Paraguay was convinced—mistakenly, it would appear—that the disputed Chaco territory was oil-rich, and it had no difficulty convincing itself further that the Standard Oil Company of Bolivia coveted the oil and believed it could gain access to it more readily if the oil lands were Bolivian rather than Paraguayan.

In explaining the confiscation of the company's properties the Bolivian minister of foreign affairs told the United States minister in La Paz that the Bolivian government "had to dispel the impression current throughout the world that the weak and impoverished Bolivia had been merely an instrument of the all-powerful, imperialistic world monster, the Standard Oil Company—that the Chaco War had been fought merely to protect the Standard Oil properties."[1] A few days later the minister said: "We had to drive the Standard Oil Company out of Bolivia for political reasons. It will never be allowed to return." He said, further, that "it was a natural aspiration of a country to control its petroleum resources." There was an implication in what he said that when a foreign company operates in Bolivia under a concession granted in accordance with Bolivian law, abides by Bolivian law in its operations, and pays taxes under provisions of Bolivian law, the Bolivian government has lost control of its petroleum resources.

Despite the minister's statement that Bolivia wanted to control its own resources his government, shortly afterward, signed an agreement with Argentina for joint exploitation by the two governments of Bolivian-owned oil lands. At the time Bolivia possessed no proven oil resources except those it had confiscated from the Standard Oil Company, and the company still was contesting the confiscation. To make the matter still more complex, the agreement with Argentina responded to Bolivia's hope that Argentina would prevent Paraguay from gaining control of the oil fields, which Paraguayan troops could see from the cease-fire lines.[2]

For the United States, Bolivia's seizure of the Standard Oil properties was a disappointing response to President Franklin D. Roosevelt's "Good Neighbor Policy," which it had hoped would usher in a new and better era in US–Latin American relations. The US minister in La Paz considered it "perfectly clear that the Bolivian government would never have dreamed of applying a similar policy of confiscation to the property of any one of its neighbors, as, for example, Chile, which has a large amount of capital invested in Bolivia."[3] There was little dissent from that in Washington. The State Department reminded Bolivia that the Good Neighbor Policy could not be one-sided; that "it must in its very essence have a reciprocal character"; but the Bolivian government was little impressed. Meanwhile the United States was denying Export-Import Bank loans and technical assistance to Bolivia, and relations between the two countries could have been described as poor. War in Europe was probably most responsible for bringing the two governments together. On December 17, 1941, an American economic mission headed by Merwin L. Bohan, a Foreign Service officer, arrived in La Paz to discuss aid to Bolivia. On January 27, 1942, the Bolivian government agreed to pay the Standard Oil Company $1.5 million plus 3 percent interest, and the United States considered the case closed.

When the Bolivian minister of foreign affairs told the United States representative that the Standard Oil Company would never be allowed to return to the country he may have been right. But some years later the Gulf Oil Corporation, another American company, began operations there, and after it had invested some $100 million and greatly improved Bolivia's oil production, its properties, in turn, were seized by a revolutionary government. A later government reached a settlement with the company. The Gulf Oil Corporation was happy to be out of Bolivia but results for Bolivia were not happy. When world oil prices quadrupled overnight in the mid-1970s, it looked as though the increased production the foreign companies had brought about might spark the development Bolivians had long hoped for. But it did not work out that way. By 1979 producing fields were being exhausted, no new fields were being developed, and a costly refinery that was still unpaid for was processing crude oil imported by the government-owned company at prices Bolivia could ill afford. Bolivia, which had been a net exporter of oil for twenty-five years, was running out of the product when it was most needed.

The Bolivian case illustrates a feature that is common to all such cases: they do not occur in a vacuum. Seizing a foreign company may be a means to a totally different end, such as gaining support for a war, or for a political party or a political candidate, or achieving some other political purpose. But the circumstance that it is "a natural aspiration of a country to control its resources" provides a special temptation for governments to seize petroleum and mining properties even when results are apt to be harmful rather than helpful to the country in question.

Mexico. On March 18, 1939, Mexico's president, Lazaro Cárdenas, expropriated the properties of the British, Dutch, and United States oil companies that were operating in the country. The companies valued the lands they owned at $200 million and the lands they held under concession at $500 million. They claimed that their investment in drilling and other equipment amounted to an additional $60 million.[4] In comparison, the confiscation of the Standard Oil Company of Bolivia was a minor incident except to the degree that it might have encouraged events in Mexico.

The Mexican government, it should be emphasized, did not confiscate the oil companies' properties, as Bolivia had done; it expropriated them. And although the companies rejected the legality of the expropriation the US government did not. Mexican willingness to compensate the companies was always present, although at no time did the government contemplate paying anything like the value the companies placed on their properties.

Furthermore President Cárdenas maintained that expropriation never would have been resorted to if the companies had been willing to accept in full a decision by the Mexican Labor Board in a two-year-old labor dispute. The companies did in fact refuse to accept the decision. They were uncompromising in their attitudes, evidently confident that their governments would successfully support their position.

The companies took the view that the labor dispute was merely a pretext for expropriation; that President Cárdenas had planned to expropriate the companies just as he had planned to expropriate (and in fact had expropriated) many of the large *haciendas* in Mexico. Whether he had planned it or not, the oil companies provided him with excellent legal and political grounds for his action. Expropriation of the oil companies quickly became an integral part of the Mexican Revolution and of President Cárdenas' program for implementing it more vigorously than earlier presidents had been able to or had chosen to.

The expropriations led to a dispute between the United States (and the British and Dutch) and Mexican governments that lasted four years. It was characterized by firmness on the part of the Mexicans, intransigence on the part of the companies, dissension within the US government, and some remarkable diplomacy by the US ambassador to Mexico, Mr. Josephus Daniels.* As in the Bolivian case the war-time interests and needs of the United States finally prevailed. After having unsuccessfully urged the Mexicans to accept international arbitration the United States accepted Mexico's proposal that a commission of two experts, one to be named by each government, should appraise the companies' properties. The United States agreed even though the companies withheld their consent.

Meanwhile the Sinclair Oil Company had reached its own direct settlement with the Mexican government. Finally the remaining American companies were awarded $29,137,700.84 and the Mexican case, also, was closed.

Peru. The Standard Oil Company lost its Bolivian properties in 1937 and its Mexican properties in 1938. Thirty years later it was in trouble in still another Latin American country. On October 3, 1968, Peru's armed forces overthrew the elected government of President Fernando Belaúnde Terry. Within a week troops had occupied the

*As secretary of the navy in 1914, when American warships seized Veracruz, Daniels might have been persona non grata to the Mexicans. But he sympathized with their cause, applauded their speeches, including the anti-American ones (he understood no Spanish), and earned their approval and affection.

installations of Standard Oil's subsidiary, the International Petroleum Company (IPC) at Talara, in Peru's northern desert.

Why the military government chose to seize the IPC properties will doubtless be debated for years. The company had a long history of litigation and negotiation with the Peruvian government. Many, although by no means all, of the facts are clear but the conclusions to be derived from them are far from clear. As in the case of other Latin American countries Peru's law provides that ownership of subsoil rights is vested in the state. There was one exception to that rule, however: the La Brea y Pariñas oil field belonging to IPC. The exception had not been sought by IPC or granted to it; in fact it had become an embarrassment to the company, which for some years had been trying to reach a new agreement with the Peruvian government consonant with the general law.

IPC was the latest of many owners of La Brea y Pariñas. The first owner was a Spanish aristocrat, Don José de Quintana, who had aided Simón Bolívar in his struggle to liberate Peru, and in return had been deeded a pitch (*brea*) mine at Amotape. Under the deed to Quintana Bolívar's government renounced all its rights to the mine. The deed was the basis of the later claim by La Brea's owners to possession of subsoil rights, a claim that the Peruvian government rejected. In 1868 oil was discovered on the property and the Peruvian government took a new interest in it. In 1888 the property was sold to two British citizens who leased it to the London and Pacific Petroleum Company.[5] The company worked it unprofitably for some twenty years.[6]

The Standard Oil Company acquired the property in 1913, and in 1914 the government began to press for tax payments in accordance with the general law. During the following eight years IPC used every available expedient to protect its special privileges. Finally Peru's president, Augusto B. Leguia, agreed to submit the case to the International Court of Justice. In March 1922, however, before the court could consider it, the Peruvian minister of foreign affairs and the British minister in Lima (IPC was incorporated in Canada) signed an agreement to end the dispute. The terms of the agreement, which were considered favorable to IPC, were later incorporated by the court in its arbitral award.[7]

Far from settling the issue the award pushed it into the realm of politics. Feeling against IPC mounted. In August 1957 the company offered to accept regular concession status under Peru's petroleum law, but the government by that time was unwilling to go along. Meanwhile it had kept petroleum prices in the country so low that the company, which sold most of its product locally, was losing money.[8]

In 1959 Pedro Beltrán, a conservative political leader and businessman who owned *La Prensa,* one of Peru's leading newspapers, became premier. Shortly thereafter the government decreed a substantial increase in the price of gasoline. Charles T. Goodsell has described the reaction to the measure:

> This brought a storm of protest in Congress and in *El Comercio, La Prensa's* rival daily. . . . The company was charged with all manner of crimes, including treason in Peru's recent border conflicts and complicity in two murders. Huge sums of money were declared as owed to Peru by IPC because of alleged illicit profits or unpaid taxes. All charges, no matter how wild, were given instant publicity in *El Comercio.* An almost incessant drumbeat of attack continued for some two years, making life not only uncomfortable but dangerous for IPC officials resident in Lima.[9]

Despite the political furor the company reached an agreement with the Belaúnde government in 1968. But the armed forces quickly took over the government, cancelled the agreement, and seized IPC's properties. Far from recognizing that the company was entitled to compensation, the new military regime took the view that it owed the government much more than the value of the assets that had been seized.

The IPC was definitely not the sole reason, and probably not the principal reason for the 1968 military coup. It was, however, a welcome pretext; the seizure of IPC's properties was politically popular in Peru. Not surprisingly, it produced a crisis in United States–Peruvian relations. Following the seizure the government proceeded to expropriate a number of other large United States investments, including the seventy-year-old Cerro de Pasco Mining Company, some fish-meal properties, and some industrialized sugar plantations owned by W.R. Grace and Company. While it recognized an obligation to indemnify the owners of such properties it persisted in the view that it owed nothing to IPC.

The United States reduced bilateral aid to Peru and opposed loans by international agencies. Peru accused it repeatedly of exerting economic pressure, of intervention in Peru's internal affairs, of imperialism, and of other offenses against international comity. The United States, on its part, sent a special emissary to Lima who conducted quiet negotiations with the Peruvian government. On February 19, 1974, the two governments signed an agreement providing that Peru would pay the United States $150 million in settlement of the claims of US citizens and that the US government would determine how it would distribute that sum among the claimants. One of the claimants compensated for its losses was IPC.

Venezuela. In 1934, when President Juan Vicente Gómez died, Venezuela was the largest exporter of petroleum in the world. Gómez, a dictator, had ruled his country with firmness and cruelty. Cooperation between him and the foreign oil companies had been excellent. He had even gone so far as to permit the companies to draft the country's petroleum laws.[10] Following Gómez's death the companies shared some of the odium that attached to his name. Nevertheless successive Venezuelan governments chose the path of collaboration rather than expropriation or confiscation.

Marxists in Venezuela not unexpectedly urged strong government action against the companies, and expressed confidence that President Roosevelt, under his own Good Neighbor Policy, would take no steps to retaliate. The non-Marxist view, in contrast, was aptly expressed by *El Heraldo* of Caracas which asserted that "Marxist dogmatism" would ruin Venezuela; that Venezuela, while recognizing the evils attending foreign economic influence, should try to gain the greatest advantage from it for the people of Venezuela. That is a fair description of the attitude the Venezuelan government took. The first post-Gómez regime defined its policy as "one of partnership in a common enterprise in which the companies have a legitimate interest by virtue of their very large contributions in capital, organization, and technique."[11] The companies themselves could not have suggested a better policy.

With the Bolivian and Mexican examples before them the State Department and the companies adjusted their attitudes toward the problem in Venezuela. The State Department gave high priority to the free world's need for Venezuela's petroleum, especially after war had broken out in Europe. But it also took the view that the government and people of Venezuela should "receive a more equitable share of the proceeds of the [petroleum] business," and initiated steps to discourage conflicts.[12] Venezuela did likewise. It engaged Herbert Hoover, Jr., a petroleum engineer and son of a former president of the United States, as a consultant, and even sought and obtained the advice of Secretary of State Cordell Hull's petroleum adviser. On their part the companies, after some prodding by the State Department, decided that it was in their interest, as well as in the general interest, to cooperate more broadly with the Venezuelan government, and they began to assist the government in such fields as agriculture.

On March 13, 1943, a new petroleum law, agreed to by the companies after prolonged negotiations, was approved by the Venezuelan congress. The companies' concessions were confirmed but the government obtained important new benefits for the nation. It continued to exact higher and higher returns from the companies; by 1960 it was by far the greatest beneficiary of the companies' operations.

On January 1, 1976, Venezuela nationalized its oil industry. The companies were paid the book value of their properties. They had already agreed to short-term contracts under which they would continue to market Venezuelan oil and would extend technological assistance to the new government-owned companies. Many of the five hundred or so foreigners among the twenty-three thousand oil industry employees were expected to remain as employees of the Venezuelan companies, at least for a time.

The Venezuelan government had won a great political victory by nationalizing the petroleum industry. At the same time, recognizing that it was not yet able to operate the industry, it had arranged for the companies to continue operating it during the crucial early period. There were problems in carrying out the agreement, as was probably inevitable. Nevertheless the largest expropriation in Latin America's history was being carried out with a minimum of acrimony.

OPEC. Venezuela's latest gains vis-à-vis both the private companies and foreign consumers were made possible principally by its membership in OPEC, which it had a leading role in creating.[13] OPEC stands for Organization of Petroleum Exporting Countries. By 1978 it had brought about profound changes in world patterns of trading and consumption. It may also have inaugurated a new era in international relations.

It had long been suggested that commodity agreements such as the one on coffee, which had to be approved by importing countries and policed by them, were really not needed—that in the case of certain commodities at least, producing countries, by forming cartels, could themselves control exports and insure more satisfactory prices. OPEC succeeded in doing just that, and importing countries were greatly concerned over the results.

The Persian Gulf, North Africa, and Venezuela have long been the primary oil-exporting areas of the world. (Nigeria also has become a leading exporter in recent years.) The Persian Gulf countries have by far the largest oil reserves. Furthermore their competitive position and the competitive position of the North African countries are much better than Venezuela's. Flat desert terrain makes exploration costs much lower. Wells have a much greater flow. And wages have been lower. The countries could easily undersell Venezuela. But increasingly, and under the urgings of Venezuela, they have chosen the way of cooperation (some would say collusion).

OPEC was created in 1960. In 1978 its members were the Persian Gulf states of Abu Dhabi, Iran, Iraq, Kuwait, Qater, and Saudi Arabia; the North African states of Algeria and Libya; plus Indonesia, Nigeria and, in Latin America, Ecuador and Venezuela. Their oil exports represented 90 percent of the free world's trade in oil. OPEC's aim was not only to increase its members' share of the "take" from petroleum production but also to gain control of the instruments of production. In a series of negotiations, or confrontations, beginning in the early 1970s, most of the OPEC governments proceeded to take over the oil companies' properties in whole or in part, and all of them raised the prices of oil to consuming countries by some 700 percent. The Arab countries, taking further advantage of their newly acquired power, went so far as to institute an oil embargo against the United States in an effort to force it to modify its attitude toward the Arab-Israeli conflict.

The sellers' market in petroleum was brought about by a dramatic increase in world consumption, from 10 million barrels daily in 1950 to 30 million in 1970. Projected consumption for 1980 was much higher. OPEC reminded the rest of the world that oil was an exhaustible resource. It took the view that it was not only in OPEC's interest but in the interest of importing countries that oil consumption should be reduced so that future generations would not be deprived of that source of energy. The Shah of Iran referred to petroleum as a "noble" commodity out of which hundreds of useful products, including fertilizer without which millions might be doomed to starvation, were made.

It was a pity, the Shah considered, to burn such a commodity unnecessarily. The Shah demonstrated that he practiced what he preached by undertaking to develop nuclear power in Iran.

The OPEC countries explained, too, that since oil was exhaustible it was their duty to use it, while it lasted, to build up economies that would make it possible for their people to maintain decent living standards after the countries' oil wealth had been exhausted. And OPEC's idea of what was required, in income, to accomplish that was, in simple terms, all the traffic would bear. Since the consuming countries were desperately in need of oil to keep their own economies operating, and since only OPEC could supply it in sufficient quantities, it was evident, too, that for a time, at least, the traffic would bear a great deal.

The OPEC countries had a good case. It was too much to expect that they would continue, indefinitely, to let other countries burn their oil without limit in order to maintain life styles that were tragically wasteful. Architects and builders, industrialists, governments, and private citizens in the affluent countries, and in many that were not particularly affluent, had acted as though the world's natural resources, no matter how finite, were theirs almost for the asking. In New York City a single skyscraper was consuming enough energy to supply a medium-sized city—more energy perhaps than some of the exporting countries had been consuming only a few years earlier. It was time that recourse was had to other sources of energy: nuclear sources, coal (which had been downgraded in favor of petroleum), the sun, the wind, and the tides, and the heat in the depths of the earth.

One problem, of course, was that the oil-importing countries had not foreseen the crisis that confronted them; OPEC had given them no time to adjust to the new circumstances. Overnight, almost, oil had gone up from less than $3 a barrel to as much as $17. Some of it had cost less than thirty cents to produce. Nor were OPEC countries themselves without problems. Higher oil prices soon boomeranged. Newly rich Iran, which had embarked on ambitious programs of industrial and military development, found itself short of funds. Forgetting for a time that oil was too precious a commodity to burn needlessly it urged the industrialized countries to buy more. Consuming countries, on their part, intensified their own search for oil and began to seek alternative sources of energy. But change came about very slowly. Consumers remained heavily dependent on oil imports from the OPEC countries.

COPPER

As in the case of petroleum most countries of the free world are heavily dependent on a few Third World countries for their supplies of copper. The United States is the world's number one producer of copper but it is also the number one consumer. Chile is the free world's second largest producer and its number one exporter. Other producers in Latin America are Peru, Mexico, and Cuba. But there are differences among the countries that production figures do not reveal. In the United States reserves of copper ore are being rapidly depleted, and exploitation of lower-grade ores makes the metal increasingly costly to produce. Chile, on the other hand, has enormous reserves, and Peru's deposits are believed to rival Chile's.

Until the late 1960s United States companies were the principal copper producers in both Chile and Peru, but circumstances resulted in quite different policies toward them in the two countries. Peru's copper resources were largely unexploited. Since Peru itself could not exploit them, the military government that seized power in 1968 exerted pressure on the Americans to increase their investments. The alternative was to lose their concessions. The pressure succeeded; the companies made large new investments.

In contrast to the situation in Peru, Chile's copper mining industry was already highly developed. Many persons in political life charged that the companies were giving too little attention to the interest of Chile, and that this would continue so long as the mines remained in foreign hands. Pressure on the government to take over the companies mounted.

Under President Eduardo Frei Montalva, a Christian Democrat who was elected in 1964, progress toward the "Chileanization" of copper was dramatic. The companies agreed (reluctantly it is true) to admit the government as majority partner in their enterprises. Payments by the government for the shares it acquired would be invested in expanded operations, and taxes on the companies' earnings would be frozen for a period of years. The companies invested an additional $55 million of their own funds in mines and plant. The Export-Import Bank, as well as international financial agencies, joined in supporting this cooperative effort to give Chile greater participation in the copper mining industry. The government was now receiving more than 80 percent of the companies' gross profits.

With Socialist-Communist support (in Chile, it will be recalled, the Socialists were to the left of the Communists) Salvador Allende, a Socialist, was elected president in 1970 with 35.8 percent of the popular vote. Expropriation of the foreign copper mining companies had been one of Allende's principal campaign pledges, but he needed new legislation to carry it out the way he wished to. He had no trouble getting it. Chilean politicians had been saying for so many years that the foreign copper companies were "exploiting" Chile that the congress was quite ready to give him the powers he asked for. Some might not agree with the economies of expropriation but most were convinced that politics required it.

Allende had no intention of paying for the expropriated companies, and he knew that the question of compensation could bring him into conflict with Chile's courts. In order to avoid that he asked the congress to approve an amendment to the Constitution that would provide for expropriation and set up rules for compensation. Again the congress went along. The amendment it approved provided that any compensation due the companies should be reduced by the amount of "excess profits" they had earned since 1935, and that the president himself must determine what those excess profits had amounted to (what constituted "excess profits" was never defined). The amendment provided further that the companies could appeal the president's decision only to a Special Copper Tribunal, to be established, thus making any appeal to the Supreme Court impossible. To the surprise and shock of many Chileans, Allende determined that the companies had earned $744 million in excess profits; that instead of receiving compensation for the properties that had been taken from them, they now were in the position of owing money to the government (Allende had taken a leaf out of the Peruvian book). When the Allende-appointed Special Copper Tribunal declined to hear an appeal the companies found themselves without legal recourse.

The military regime that took power on September 11, 1973, proceeded to reverse nearly everything Allende had done in the economic field. It restored the banks, the coal mines, the five hundred or so factories, and many of the other properties Allende had seized, to their rightful owners. And although hard pressed for funds it compensated the copper companies for the loss of their properties. The Chilean government, whether it wished it or not, was now the undisputed owner of one of the world's greatest copper mining industries.

CIPEC. In 1967 the leading copper exporting countries joined in an effort to gain greater control over production and distribution of the product. As in the case of OPEC it was a Latin American country that took the lead. Largely under the leadership of Chile the Intergovernmental Council of Copper Exporting Countries (CIPEC) was formed by Chile, Peru, Zaire, and Zambia. They were joined later by Australia and Papua New Guinea as associate members. The CIPEC countries were as interested in stabilizing prices as they were in increasing them. A variation of one cent per pound meant $22 million to Chile's revenues, and fluctuations of 30 cents and more were not unusual.

Cooperation among CIPEC countries was not easy. As in the case of OPEC, production costs varied greatly among the members, so that what might be a losing price for one could be quite remunerative for another. And of course the degree of dependence on copper varied greatly among them.

CIPEC's efforts to increase and stabilize prices had little effect. Petroleum can be stored in the ground and released with the turn of a valve. But copper production cannot be controlled so easily. Prices of the metal continued to fluctuate widely. Between 1960 and 1976 Chile's yearly income from copper exports varied from $800 million to $2 billion 1976 dollars.

Third World countries did not limit their price-raising efforts to petroleum and copper; they sought higher prices for other exports too. An Association of Iron Ore Producing and Exporting Countries (AIOPEC) was formed. Governments of bauxite-producing countries increased their "take" from the trade. Meanwhile free-market prices of many agricultural products had risen. The United States, the greatest industrial nation in the world, was hoping to improve its balance of international payments through larger exports of grains and other foodstuffs and fibers. Increases in world population and improved living standards in many countries were causing demand for food to increase more rapidly than supply. The great value of all primary products had become evident, and countries rich in such products, as many Latin American countries are, were being recognized for what they had become or could become—wealthy countries.

13
PRIVATE ENTERPRISE AND THE STATE

PRIOR TO World War II most Latin American governments depended on private persons and groups to bring about development, and all except Cuba continue to depend on them in varying degrees. But government, itself, has more and more assumed the role of entrepreneur. In countries such as Argentina, Mexico, and Peru it has become the principal entrepreneur. Whether government entrepreneurship has contributed to development, however, is questionable.

Latin American governments fill the role of entrepreneur naturally, and even gladly, but they rarely fill it efficiently. They seldom perform efficiently even their primary role—to do those things that only the state can do and that are themselves essential to development—to maintain order, to provide mass education, to protect the public health, and to build and maintain highways, bridges, port works, and other infrastructure.

The weaknesses of government entrepreneurship are well-known and are particularly acute in the less-developed countries which, by definition, are capital-poor and lack experience in the complex task of development. It frequently occurs that the capital that a government has invested in building a factory might more usefully have been spent in meeting a need that only the government can meet. If private investors had been permitted, or persuaded, to build and operate the factory, the need could have been met and the economy would also have its factory. Of course much state entrepreneurship in Latin America has resulted not from building factories or opening mines, but from taking over factories and mines that private investors, usually foreigners, have built or developed. In those cases the state either pays for the property or takes it without payment. In either event the economy may be damaged. If the state pays, the amount usually is less than the property is worth, and the state's credit is affected. If it does not pay, the damage to its credit is even greater. In neither case is new wealth created, and the possibility that foreigners or even citizens will invest funds that will create new wealth is lessened.

Also, experience suggests that a privately owned factory or mine would make a greater contribution to the economy than one owned by the state because it would be better run. There are, of course, some well-run state enterprises, and some poorly run private firms but, in general, the private firm is more efficiently conducted because it has to be. Unless the private firm enjoys a monopoly it must meet competition. It must operate with some efficiency, and it has a corresponding need to employ persons who will contribute to efficiency. A government-owned enterprise, in contrast, seldom is under such compulsions. It has little fear of competition because its losses are absorbed by the state. Its manager may be less interested in making a profit than in pleasing his political superiors, in giving jobs to their relatives and friends (as well as to his own relatives and friends). The more jobs he finds for deserving politicians and their friends the higher he may be regarded in government. Overstaffing is a chronic defect of state enterprises as it is of government itself.

SOCIALIZATION'S FAILURES

The Chilean government's Development Corporation has said, starkly: "The deficit of state entities is part of Chile's economic history. . . . These entities, sometimes described as pillars of development, have in fact contributed notably to the impoverishment of our country."[1] The Latin American countries have moved steadily in the direction of socialism but at different rates and along different roads. In some countries government has assumed the role of entrepreneur because there is scant private interest in investing. In others it has assumed the role after its own acts and attitudes have discouraged investment that might otherwise have taken place. That is to say, socialization has been surreptitious. And of course some countries have moved openly and deliberately to socialization.

Argentina has alternated between open and surreptitious socialization. The Argentine government owns and operates not only telephone companies, power companies, steel mills, rail, air, and steamship lines, and a petroleum monopoly (such enterprises are commonly state-owned in Latin America) but also a very large number of industrial plants. So far government entrepreneurship has produced unsatisfactory results, and the military government that assumed power in 1976 adopted a program to reduce it. For many years democratic Uruguay engaged in both surreptitious and open socialization. As economic distress grew so did protest. The Tupamaros, a secret terrorist group, kept the country in a state of near-anarchy until the military, in 1973, forced the congress to close and converted the elected president into a military-supported dictator.

Socialization in Brazil also had been both surreptitious and open until the military government that took control in 1964 moved away from socialism. It quickly achieved one of the highest economic growth rates in the world. In Chile the Allende regime drastically accelerated the rate of socialization, but results were disastrous, as we have seen, and the military government that replaced it in 1973 moved sharply to the right. Peru, in contrast, turned leftward. The military government that seized power in 1968 expropriated plantations, oil properties, mining companies and other industries developed by private interests, both domestic and foreign. Economic results were very harmful. A bloodless coup in August 1975 brought a more moderate military group into power, and elections for a constituent assembly were held in June 1978. But Peru's economy remained in a state of acute crisis.

Mexico has taken the open road with least disruption: large areas of the Mexican economy have been socialized. At the same time other large areas have remained open to private investment. Furthermore the government has been careful not to change investment rules in the middle of the game. Mexico's economy has great difficulty supporting the country's rapidly growing population, and millions of Mexicans have crossed into the United States, legally and illegally, in an effort to improve their lot. But the economy would be still weaker (and the country's political stability would be seriously threatened) if it were not for the flourishing private sector.

Of course the country that most emphasizes the economic role of the state is Cuba, where the role has become nearly total. Results have not been impressive. In 1977 it was estimated that Cuba's economy was being subsidized by the Soviet Union at a rate of some $2 to $3 million a day. Cubans appeared to have enough food to maintain health, and for some that was probably an advance over pre-Castro days. But few had much more than that. And tyranny had been institutionalized.

FOREIGN INVESTMENT: A FORCE FOR GROWTH

If you were a poor farmer in a depressed area of the United States and an oil company asked permission to drill on your land, and you gave permission, and the company struck oil, and you received 60 to 70 percent of the profits from the operation, without having had to invest a penny yourself, you would probably think you had done handsomely. And if the oil company hired many of your relatives and friends to work for it, paid them more than the prevailing wages in the area, built homes for them, and provided them with medical attention and schools, your relatives and friends would probably think they were doing handsomely too. Also if the company bought materials from local firms and engaged local contractors to help it in its work, the community in general would feel that it was doing well. This is the picture the foreign oil and mining companies that operate in Latin American have of themselves, and it is not far from being accurate.

But there is also another side to the picture. In Chile the copper mining industry, when it was predominantly American-owned, supplied one-fourth of all the government's revenue and 60 percent of the country's foreign exchange. Chile had once been in the position of the poor farmer in the United States, and the American companies had come down and transformed the country. Did the Chileans think they had done handsomely? Not all of them did.

In November 1971 Chile's Socialist president, Salvador Allende, appeared on national television in the United States. One of the panel members questioned him concerning his government's seizure of the American copper companies. The president replied with a question of his own. "How would Americans feel if the automobile industry in the United States were owned by foreigners?" he asked. Many Americans could see the point.

Pincus has said:

> If coincidence of material interest were the only criterion for capital flows, then private investment in underdeveloped countries would be the primary technique for transferring capital from rich to poor

> countries. The foreign investor seeking profit, and the host seeking more rapid growth of income and opportunities would bask in the warmth of their mutual gain.[2]

As a matter of fact prior to large-scale foreign aid the relationship was the one Pincus described. Private investment was the medium through which foreign nations extended economic cooperation to Latin America and to other areas. The English were the first large-scale investors; later Americans became predominant. The cooperation that private investors extended to Latin America was welcomed in the area. What Latin America needed and wanted from abroad were resources it lacked: funds, equipment, materials, and techniques. All these were available from private sources and were supplied by them.

Foreign investment continues to be a dynamic force for growth in Latin America, but it is not always welcomed in the manner Pincus described. In some countries it has been increasingly resented and its properties have been increasingly coveted. To revert to the once-poor farmer in the United States: it might occur to him that, once the oil company had made its investment and the oil was flowing in quantity, he could seize the company's installations and get not 60 or 70 percent of the profits but all of them for himself. In that case, if we assume he could run the business properly, he would be even better off than when the company was running it. And if the courts supported the farmer the company could do little about it. That is what happened to the copper companies under Chile's Socialist-Communist government.

Many Latin Americans would say that the poor farmer is not a good analogy, that there are many educated, enterprising men in Latin America who require only capital and technology to do anything that people do in the more-developed countries. That of course is true to some degree, and the United States, in its aid programs, has tried to insure that resources, to the extent possible, are channeled to private users. But governments frequently want more than that. As entrepreneurs they want to receive the same kind of aid that private entrepreneurs expect to receive. While the United States has been quite ready to help finance typically governmental activities such as building roads, dams, and portworks, and even power plants and steel mills, it has been less ready to advance funds for activities ordinarily undertaken by private groups. It has taken the view that the purpose of aid is not to displace private capital but to add to what private capital is doing and is willing to do. For example it has been unwilling to finance exploration activities of the numerous state-owned oil companies because there are many privately owned companies that are quite ready to search for oil in any part of the world where there is a likelihood of finding it, and to agree that most of any profits they may earn will go directly to the state.

The United States has also been unwilling to lend money for exploration activities by governments for another reason—because they are so costly and so risky. A private oil company that operates in many parts of the world can lose $100 million or $200 million in one country and make it up in another. For a Latin American government to lose $100 million looking for oil might mean that the government would be overthrown. It clearly would mean that citizens of the country, poor already, would be saddled with an additional and needless economic burden. It would doubtless mean, too, that the US government, if it had financed the effort, would be blamed for helping to bring that disaster upon the country.*

A common criticism of foreign investment is that through profit remittances, payment of salaries to foreigners, and other practices, it drains Latin America of resources as the Spaniards did in colonial times. But Stacy May, an American economist, and Galo Plaza, a former president of Ecuador and former secretary general of the Organization of American States, in a study of the much-criticized United Fruit Company, revealed that the company had left in the countries in which it operated seven dollars for every dollar it remitted abroad; and that it had also pioneered in health measures, in scientific research, and in the planting of new crops that were of much greater value to the countries' economies than to itself.[3] Instead of draining the countries of wealth the company created enormous wealth and left most of it in Latin America.

Sears, Roebuck and Company, which conducts an entirely different kind of operation, aims at acquiring all its merchandise in the countries in which it operates. In order to do this it has carried out a true technical assistance program, without cost to Latin American governments or to

---

*When I was ambassador to Argentina, President-elect Arturo Frondizi informed me that unless the United States helped to finance the operations of the country's state-owned oil company he would be forced, as president, to accept aid from Soviet Russia. I told him that United States aid would not be available for that purpose. He did not appeal for Russian aid nor did Russia offer its aid. Furthermore, as already noted, his government signed service contracts with a number of foreign companies with the result that Argentina quickly became self-sufficient in petroleum.

any foreign government. It has been so successful in encouraging and teaching Latin Americans to produce needed goods, and in helping to finance their efforts, that in some countries it purchases almost nothing abroad (in Colombia, as early as 1971, it was actually purchasing nothing abroad; in Brazil 99.41 percent of its purchases were made in the country; in all Latin America it purchased from 14,000 domestic suppliers, a majority of them small). In addition nearly all its officials and employees are Latin Americans (that is true of all large American companies in Latin America), and employee participation in ownership of its stores is very high.[4]

Of course through the tax mechanism a major part of the earnings of all, or nearly all, the large foreign companies goes directly to the Latin American governments.

Dignity or Progress? Some Latin Americans (and some Americans too) say that what is involved in developing natural resources is not dollars and cents, or even social justice, but human dignity. President Allende implied that dignity was an important factor in his government's decision to seize the copper companies. It seems clear that each country has to strike a balance—to make up its mind where its best interests lie. No country, even the most powerful, can have all its desires satisfied. Which is more important: dignity or progress? And how does one define those terms? If the properties of a foreign company, "in justice," should be in the hands of people of the country, does that mean that the government should seize them without compensating their owner? Is there no justice on the owner's side? Is a country's good name, its moral and commercial credit, worth nothing? Were Chile's economy and its democracy less secure when the copper mines were in the hands of foreign companies, with the government free to tax them heavily and regulate them strictly, than they were later when they were in the hands of a government that was seeking to grasp total political and economic power?

Is it necessarily true that help received from foreign private capital is offensive to the dignity of those who are helped, while help received from foreign governments is not? The United States was developed with the help of foreign private capital. Was that offensive to its dignity? Few Americans thought it was. How high a price should a government pay to defend what it considers to be its citizens' dignity? Do political leaders sometimes confuse their own dignity (or pride, or vanity, or personal interest) with the dignity of citizens? Is human dignity enhanced by inhuman poverty? Do Latin Americans lose dignity working for foreign companies that pay them higher wages than they can earn elsewhere, and that treat them as human beings rather than as serfs, which may have been their previous condition? And does confiscation of foreign properties enhance a nation's dignity, or the dignity of citizens? Some evidently believe it does. Others have doubts.

Granted that state enterprise is rarely efficient, some observers remind us that it is at least indigenous. The real conflict in Latin America, they maintain, is not between state and private enterprise but between indigenous and foreign enterprise. But that has not been true in the past, and there is little reason to believe that it will be true in the future. Mexico's early history is an example.

Mexico's revolt against Spain brought it independence, but early effects on the nation's economy were disastrous. *Peninsulares* who returned to Spain took their liquid capital with them. In any case fiscal irresponsibility and political instability that often approached anarchy discouraged new investment. By 1867 Mexico had pledged 95 percent of its customs revenues to the service of debts. That same year there were 15 miles of usable railroad in the country. The United States, at the time, could boast of 30,000 miles of track.

The meager economic growth that took place was largely the work of foreigners. The mining industry was a case in point. Until 1864 there was not a single private bank in all Mexico that miners could go to for credit, and those merchants who acted also as money lenders charged such fantastically high rates of interest that it was not practicable to borrow from them. In an effort to lure foreign money into mining the government modified the old Spanish code so as to grant foreigners not merely concessions to exploit mines but virtual ownership of the mines. The result was a new gold rush. The British invested some 25 million pesos in old and new mines. They were followed closely by the French and the Germans. Americans, too, tried their luck but their role was less important. In the two generations following independence foreigners invested a possible $100 million in mining ventures. Results for Mexico were good. By 1868 gold and silver production was only a trifle less than in 1818, just before independence. Results for the foreign investors were less happy. It is doubtful that they were able to extract from the mines as much as they had put into them.[5]

A century later Latin America's need for foreign investment was still great. Goodsell has given us a vivid example of what foreign investment has meant to one country, Peru.

> The SPCC [Southern Peru Copper Corporation] joint venture was put together for the purpose of developing an open-pit copper mine in southern Peru called Toquepala. Although the presence of copper ore bodies had been known at Toquepala for decades, they had not been exploited because of the enormous cost involved in extracting and refining 1 percent ore located 8,500 feet up in the Andes and transporting it some 50 air miles to the sea. The job eventually cost over $240 million, the largest single private investment in the history of Peru. Involved was not only the removal of vast quantities of overburden, but the construction of a town and mill near the pit, a port and smelter near the fishing town of Ilo (plus additional housing), and a 114 mile railroad connecting the two. The project was in part financed by a $100 million loan from the US Export-Import Bank and went into production in 1959.[6]

Peru's choice in the 1950s was not between an indigenous Toquepala and a foreign Toquepala; it was between a foreign Toquepala and no Toquepala at all. Toquepala was far beyond the capacity of either Peruvian private interests or the Peruvian government to develop, and probably beyond the capacity of either to operate. There are many Toquepalas throughout Latin America. Some are the mainstays of the economies they contribute to. And there are many more enterprises that are smaller than Toquepala but still very important to Latin America's economies, which would not exist if foreign investors had not been able and willing to build them.

Without foreign investment Toquepala would not have been developed nor would Chile's great copper mines. Without it neither Argentina's nor Mexico's railroads would have been built nor would Venezuela, today, have the flourishing petroleum industry that makes it one of the rich countries of the world. And without foreign investment tomorrow's Latin America will be condemned to very slow growth or no growth at all. Its needs and its desires are beyond its ability to meet alone, or with the help of foreign governments. It is not only a question of private or public investment, or of foreign or indigenous investment. What is also involved is employment or unemployment, growth or stagnation, and perhaps growth or retrogression.

Not all Latin Americans will agree with that. Some believe that the development "package," which consists of capital, technology, management, and marketing, can be split up; that the capital can be borrowed, the technology hired, the management learned, the market developed, and the need of new foreign investment thus eliminated. Some countries might accomplish that over a long period of time, and with great difficulty, but such a sophisticated approach to development is far beyond Latin America's present capability. Foreign private investment continues to be a vital ingredient of development.

Are Joint Ventures the Answer? Many devices for making foreign investment palatable have been tried. Oil companies are no longer granted concessions; rather they operate under contracts, which may provide that their properties will revert to the state after a fixed number of years. Another device is the joint venture in which the foreign investor enters into partnership with a local investor. Some countries require this in certain circumstances. The device has worked well in many cases. But like other devices it is not a panacea, and insisting on it may retard development for reasons that are evident.

Latin American investors are not nearly as anxious to go into partnership with foreigners as some may imagine. In the first place they tend to insist on higher dividends than foreigners are accustomed to. In many countries local investors can earn 25 percent (and frequently much more) merely by lending their money. Moderate earnings do not interest such persons. In addition, foreign investors usually want to reinvest a large share of their earnings, which means foregoing dividends, but the Latin American tends to be more interested in quick profits. Frequently it turns out that the only available local partner is the government, which makes for an uneasy partnership, and even governments are often short of capital—except perhaps in inflation-ridden countries that offer little attraction to foreign investors.

The Multinational Corporation. While the joint venture, to a small degree at least, has attenuated antagonism to foreign investment, the multilateral corporation may have increased antagonism and the fear that inspires it. The expression, "multinational corporation," is new, and the phenomenon is new in its present dimensions. We have long had experience with the large oil companies that operate in many countries although they are incorporated and principally owned in the United States and Europe. But the number and size of companies with investments and operations in many countries have grown so rapidly that many governments fear that the sprawling giants will create difficult problems for them. What criteria should governments follow in taxing them, for example? Can they know, in detail, how an enterprise allocates profits among many jurisdictions, or what countries its policies favor? Won't governments have to devise new kinds of cooperation among themselves in order to effectively regulate the enterprise? Many of the problems are not new, but there are more of them today, and they are more complex.

Some governments have welcomed the multinational corporations with wariness. Others go out of their way to invite them in. In Europe the Common Market presented special opportunities to them. They responded by making a notable contribution to the market's growth, as they did later to the growth of the Central American Common Market. Brazil also welcomed them and they contributed to that country's rapid growth. The Andean Common Market on the other hand enacted an elaborate investment code aimed largely at regulating the operations of multinational corporations. The code went so far as to require that foreign corporations wishing to take advantage of common-market preferences should lower their investment in local firms to not more than 49 percent (the common market later modified the code, and member countries even ignored it, so that its effects were not nearly as great as was planned).

At the same time that foreign countries seek to restrict the activities of the multinational enterprises, organized labor in the United States charges the US-owned enterprises with exporting jobs and technology to the benefit of foreign countries and to the detriment of United States workers. Early in 1978 the world's two largest tire companies, Goodyear and Firestone, announced that they were closing down their passenger-tire plants in Akron, Ohio. One month later, Goodyear had another announcement to make: according to the *Washington Post,* the company was planning to invest $30 million and employ 2,000 workers in a new tire plant—in Chile. The role of the multinational corporation clearly is important. Equally clearly, it is difficult and controversial.

UNEMPLOYMENT

A major tragedy in Latin America is the steady emigration abroad, especially to the United States, of persons with education and skills that the countries require if they are to progress. This "brain drain" parallels a similar drain of dollars that Latin Americans send abroad for investment and safekeeping. Together they serve to negate much of the effort foreign governments and the international agencies are making to support development in Latin America. In theory the educated and skilled persons who emigrate to other countries, if they remained in Latin America, would help to insure the progress to which the area aspires. But while skills promote progress they also require a degree of progress, a certain momentum in the development process, in order to be used effectively. An industrial manager needs a plant to manage. A scientist needs a laboratory and a project that is adequately financed. Foreign private capital can add to the momentum of development, but its cooperation is frequently spurned by governments for political or ideological reasons.

It is not only the educated and the skilled who have trouble finding employment. The unskilled, who make up the mass of workers, have even greater difficulty finding jobs. Latin America leads the world in population growth, but employment has not grown correspondingly. It was estimated in the early 1970s that 140 million new jobs would have to be created during the remainder of the century merely to absorb the increases in population. The prospect of creating them was not good.

In the United States unemployment on the scale we find in Latin America has been a result of severe economic depression, but in Latin America it exists and even worsens in the presence of economic growth that, of itself, is excellent. Many measures that have brought about substantial growth have had little effect in lessening joblessness. When the more highly developed countries had their industrial revolution there were not enough men and women (and children) to satisfy the need for workers. In contrast, today's highly mechanized and (often) automated plants require only a few skilled operators. They have little to offer the growing millions of unskilled who are looking for jobs.

Agricultural mechanization, growth of the rural population, and the lure of urban life have resulted in a continuing exodus to the cities. One result has been the immense shantytowns that ring the great cities—the *callampas* of Chile, the *villas miserias* of Argentina, and the *favelas* of Brazil—many of whose inhabitants are unemployed. It is obvious that while capitalists, landowners, business and professional men, and many workers are enjoying the benefits of economic growth, an increasing number are denied its benefits.

Not only does Latin America have a high unemployment rate, and one that is growing in many countries; it also has a high rate of underemployment, of persons who would not remain in their occupations if they could find jobs that were more suitable and more remunerative. Household servants are in that category; if they could find jobs that paid them better and offered them better working hours, most would take them. This has occurred in cities such as Medellín, Colombia, where a prosperous textile industry created new job opportunities, especially for women. But such examples still are not common, and many Latin Americans who are not affluent still have servants in their households while even wealthy persons in the more-developed countries have some difficulty managing that. Gracious living, that is to say living attended by personal service, is increasingly rare outside the less-developed countries, where it makes underdevelopment not only tolerable but very pleasant for privileged persons.

Many persons consider that Latin American governments have had the United States and Europe too much in mind as models of development. In Latin America, as we have seen, development has been equated with industrialization. Although Latin America has an excess of labor and a shortage of capital it has given priority to building mills and factories that are capital-intensive and employ little labor. Some believe that this is the wrong road to follow; that providing jobs should be not merely a by-product of development but its main purpose; that men and women can and should be the principal beneficiaries of development no less than its principal instruments.

United States industries have contributed in special ways to alleviating the problem of joblessness in Latin America. Some automobile manufacturers have been producing components in Brazil and importing them into the United States. The electronics industry has moved most of its labor-intensive production to Mexico and to such places as Taiwan, Hong Kong, and South Korea, where components are assembled and returned to the United States. Hundreds of small US-owned industries serving the United States market have sprung up in Mexico close to the border. Other industries, on the United States side of the border, employ workers who live in Mexico and commute daily. But that kind of "private aid" rests on a precarious basis since organized labor in the United States charges, as in the case of the multinational corporations, that it results in "exporting American jobs." Ironically, other critics charge that it "exploits" low-wage foreign workers.

There will be no easy solution to the dilemma of economic growth that is accompanied by growth in unemployment. Barend A. de Vries, a senior economist in the World Bank, has given a great deal of thought and study to the dilemma. He urges greater attention to labor-intensive agriculture and manufacturing in the less-developed countries. At the same time he also maintains that "it is extremely difficult to conceive a lasting solution to the employment problem without a rapid growth in . . . foreign exchange earnings and the availability of mass-produced consumer goods," and that "both of these may—for many products and in many countries—be achieved most rapidly by capital-intensive technology."[7] What is needed, we are left to conclude, is more attention to labor-intensive technology and opportunities and also more attention to capital-intensive technology and opportunities—better managed economies in other words. That is easier to prescribe than it is to achieve, as Mr. de Vries well knows. Many persons feel that it will not be achieved in most countries in the absence of continuing foreign aid.

14
UNITED STATES AID

I WAS AMBASSADOR to Colombia when the Ninth International Conference of American States met in Bogotá on March 30, 1948. The US delegation was headed by General George C. Marshall, secretary of state and author of the Marshall Plan which was bringing about dramatic economic recovery in war-ravaged Europe. Nearly every Latin American country was represented by its foreign minister, and nearly every foreign minister had come to Bogotá prepared to request a Marshall Plan for Latin America.

The evening before the secretary was to address the conference he assembled his principal advisers to go over the speech that technicians had prepared for him. The main topic, of course, was how he would confront the inevitable demand for a new Marshall Plan. Averill Harriman, who had headed Marshall Plan activities in Europe, appeared to be leaning toward a similar plan for Latin America. I demurred. I said that Latin Americans were not Europeans, nor were Europe's problems theirs; that they would not respond to Marshall Plan treatment as Europeans had responded.

During the discussion I referred to recent acts of Latin American governments in expropriating US-owned properties without compensating their owners. At that point Harriman turned to me and said, "Do you know how we got our railroads in the United States?" I acknowledged that I did not know. "We stole them," he said tartly. He indicated that our entrepreneurs had engaged in some very sharp and very dubious practices at the expense of European investors. Since Mr. Harriman had inherited one of the largest railroad fortunes in America his statement was impressive. I maintained, nevertheless, that what he had said was not relevant to Latin America. I said that confiscation of foreign-owned properties discouraged what Latin Americans sorely needed, namely, additional domestic and foreign private investment; that in the absence of such investment there was no possibility that, with or without foreign aid, they would achieve the economic and social gains they rightly aspired to.

I told Secretary Marshall that I believed in foreign aid. I reminded him that as ambassador to Paraguay, before the Marshall Plan had proved itself in Europe, I had appeared before a skeptical committee of Congress and pleaded for a continuation of the wartime aid we had been extending to Latin America. But I also suggested that because it affected the lives of foreign peoples it should be extended cautiously; that we should build upon success. Thirty years later Theodore H. White, after a lifetime of experience in the international world, expressed more clearly and eloquently what I was trying to convey when he wrote that "competence must play bodyguard to good will, for without competence American good will can become political plague." American aid, he continued, was becoming "an addictive political drug, as dangerous to its recipients as would be our outright political hostility."[1] If some countries on which we have showered aid have repaid us with a measure of hostility, the fault may be more ours than theirs.

The following day the secretary told the assembled delegates that there would be no Marshall Plan for Latin America. The Colombian people, as well as the delegates, heard his words but they showed no resentment. A few days later Jorge Eliecer Gaitan, a Liberal party leader who had promised to free the masses from the poverty and distress in which they lived, was assassinated in downtown Bogotá, close to where the conference was meeting. The city erupted. Much of it was destroyed. Some 1,500 persons lost their lives on Bogotá's streets in three days. Minutes after Gaitan's assassination I found myself in the middle of a frenzied mob. But no one threatened me. No American lost his life or was injured in the *Bogotazo,* even though Communists, screaming over the radio, tried to turn the mob against the United States. Latin Americans had not learned to blame the United States for their economic and social woes. That would come with large-scale aid, after American political leaders had voluntarily assumed a major share of the blame for those woes, and Latin American leaders had enthusiastically agreed with them.

As late as the 1920s the private enterprise system seemed to be meeting the needs of the international community. But the early 1930s brought tremendous changes. Economic depression spread over the earth. Hundreds of banks closed their doors. Latin America's exports, and the prices they brought, dropped sharply. Governments found themselves unable to service the loans that foreign bankers had made available to them so freely, and the loans went into default. Latin America's needs were greater than ever but its credit with private banks had dried up. The US government went into the lending business in order to help fill a vacuum created by the collapse of the private lending system and the near-collapse of the private enterprise system itself.

The Export-Import Bank of Washington was established in 1934 to promote United States trade with other countries. Although in practice the bank has concentrated on financing exports, the fact that its charter stresses that it "should supplement and encourage and not compete with private capital" means that its projects have been, in varying degrees, additional to what would have been carried out without its help. In that sense they have constituted true aid. Latin America is dotted with power plants, steel mills, and factories that the Export-Import Bank has helped to finance.

Organized technical cooperation was undertaken in Latin America during World War II by a newly organized Institute of Inter-American Affairs. The program had various objectives. One of course was to maintain the best possible relations with the Latin American countries. Another was to help the Latin Americans provide strategic materials the United States needed for its war effort. Still another was to help them produce things that they normally imported from the United States or Western Europe but that were now in short supply or difficult to ship because of shortage of transport. After the war had ended the United States decided to continue the program until it could be evaluated under conditions of peace.

At the same time the United States undertook to extend relief and aid on a global scale. It contributed more than half the cost of the United Nations Relief and Rehabilitation Administration (UNRRA), which helped to meet the emergency needs of the devastated and occupied nations. The next effort, carried out by the United States alone, was the program of economic and military aid to Greece and Turkey, countries that found themselves under powerful Communist pressure. That program, initiated in 1947, was followed shortly by the Marshall Plan. The United States expended nearly $15 billion on Marshall Plan aid. It clearly was money well spent. Aid was hailed everywhere as an effective economic and diplomatic instrument.

POINT FOUR

In his January 1949 inaugural address, President Harry S. Truman recommended four courses of action in the international field. His fourth recommendation was that "a bold new program" be instituted "for making the benefits of [United States] scientific advances and industrial progress available for the improvement and growth of underdeveloped areas." From this recommendation came the so-called Point Four program of technical cooperation, which reached most of the less-developed countries of the free world. It was an enlarged version of the technical cooperation program that was being carried out by the Institute of Inter-American Affairs in Latin America. The Congress had only limited enthusiasm for Point Four. It was conscious of the tendency of programs to expand. It wanted assurance that Point Four would not become a giveaway program; that it would not be the beginning of an effort to place on the shoulders of the American taxpayer a large share of the burden of financing development throughout the world.

The Congress's fears were not entirely unjustified. Programs grew steadily larger and more numerous as one aid agency succeeded another or was added to the others. Besides the Economic Cooperation Administration (ECA), which administered Marshall Plan aid, and the Institute of Inter-American Affairs (IIAA), there were the Technical Cooperation Administration (TCA), the Mutual Security Agency (MSA), the Foreign Operations Administration (FOA), the International Cooperation Administration (ICA), the Development Loan Fund (DLF), and the Agency for International Development (AID), which was created in 1961 and, in the 1970s, was still administering aid.

We are frequently told that massive United States aid to Latin America resulted from studies and resolutions of the Organization of American States and from such proposals as Operation Panamerica, a "plan" of Brazil's president, Juscelino Kubitschek, under which the United States would help to finance development in Latin America; and all those things, plus studies conducted within the US government itself, did indeed play a role in bringing it about. But the presidents who committed the United States to extend massive aid were impelled less by such developments than by circumstances they were more directly familiar with—circumstances that caused them great concern.

It was in 1958 that the then vice-president, Richard M. Nixon, tried to debate with university students during a visit he made to South America and was stoned and spat upon by students and alleged students in Lima, Peru, and attacked in Caracas, Venezuela. The Nixon incidents created headlines all over the world. Reporters, columnists, commentators, editorialists, many of whom had never even visited Latin America, discussed them and tried to assign reasons for them. Political leaders in Washington engaged in prolonged soul-searching. The assumption most of them started from was that the United States must be doing something wrong in Latin America, or failing to do something right. The assumption was almost bound to be correct, but few persons experienced in Latin American affairs believed that it was an adequate explanation of the Nixon incidents. Some US diplomats had warned the vice-president against debating with students, and when he insisted on doing it they had predicted accurately what would happen to him.* The opportunity to demonstrate against the United States and to embarrass the United States by attacking its vice-president was simply too tempting for extremists to resist. The Nixon incidents had little meaning other than that. But after the press had published millions of words about them, after commercial television had squeezed every ounce of salable sensation from them, and after the administration and the political parties in Washington had made appropriate statements concerning them with one eye fixed on the 1960 elections, Americans were left with the impression that a continent was hostile to them. Seldom had so much been made of so little.[2]

It became axiomatic that it was not extremists and political punks who had demonstrated against Mr. Nixon; it was Latin America that was demonstrating against the United States. The Lima and Caracas mobs were no longer seen as mobs. They had become soldiers in the revolution of rising expectations. The Voice of America stepped up its propaganda to Latin America, which overnight had become a prestige

*Mr. Nixon had not been invited to address the students. The idea was his. As ambassador to Argentina I myself flew from Buenos Aires to Washington in an effort to dissuade him from carrying out the idea, but without results. An American professor who had lectured to Latin American students over a period of years without incident happened to be in my office when news of the attack on the vice-president in Lima reached me. When I read him the message he said, "The vice-president made a political approach to the students and he got a political response." In my view the professor accurately described what had taken place.

area for American diplomacy; an area, that is, in which the United States was in trouble.

If the Nixon incidents aroused concern over the attitude of Latin Americans toward the United States, the Cuban Revolution greatly increased that concern. In January 1959 Fidel Castro took over the government of Cuba. The revolution he led had helped to topple President Batista, a corrupt tyrant whom thinking Cubans had long since repudiated. Castro, a charismatic leader, was acclaimed in the United States, where he had become a hero to many newspapers and their readers. But the honeymoon was short-lived. Castro quickly assumed an attitude of systematic hostility to the United States. He seized American and other foreign properties (and Cuban properties too) without thought of compensation, and gradually but purposefully delivered Cuba over to communism. At the same time he tried to carry his antidemocratic, anti-American revolution to other Latin American countries.

THE ACT OF BOGOTÁ

The United States government was dismayed and alarmed at what was going on in Cuba and at the danger that Castroism would spread to the rest of Latin America. President Eisenhower visited a number of the larger South American countries and talked to their presidents. Other Latin American leaders came to Washington and talked to President Eisenhower.* On July 11, 1960, the president held a news conference at the summer White House in Newport, Rhode Island. He said:

> During my trip to South America in February and in numerous talks in Washington, I have obtained the views of leading Latin Ameri-

---

*Although Secretary of State Christian A. Herter and numerous political and economic advisers accompanied President Eisenhower in Latin America, neither any of those persons nor the resident American ambassador attended the summit meetings the president had with the chiefs of state of the countries he visited. President Eisenhower himself knew little of Latin America, of course, and he had little time and perhaps no inclination to read the voluminous briefs that had been prepared in Washington. From later conversations I had with Argentina's President Frondizi it was evident that each of the presidents had misunderstood much of what the other said to him. It took me several weeks to disabuse President Frondizi of the overoptimistic impression he had obtained at the meeting—a melancholy commentary on the utility of some summit meetings.

> can statesmen on the problems which their countries and the area in general now face. They have told me of the aspirations and needs of their peoples for homes and land and a better life, and of their efforts to meet those needs.

The president went on to list the needs he thought the United States should help the Latin Americans to meet, particularly the needs of the masses for land, homes, education, and decent living in general.

United States representatives took President Eisenhower's program to an inter-American economic meeting that was held in Bogotá two months later. A few days before the meeting began the Congress, at the president's request, had authorized the appropriation of $500 million to establish a social development fund to be administered by the Inter-American Development Bank (IDB), which had just been set up. The fund was to provide "soft" loans (long-term loans at low rates of interest, some repayable in local currencies) to promote social improvement in Latin America. The president's program was substantially approved in the Act of Bogotá.*

THE ALLIANCE FOR PROGRESS

The Act of Bogotá was basically a list of intentions. Those intentions were reiterated and broadened in the Alliance for Progress, which President John F. Kennedy launched a few months later. President Kennedy, in his inaugural address, said:

> To those people in the tents and villages of half the globe struggling to break the bonds of mass misery, we pledge our best efforts to

*In June 1960, a month before President Eisenhower made his dramatic announcement at Newport, Pedro Beltrán, a dynamic Peruvian newspaper publisher and political leader, and at the time his country's prime minister, visited him in Washington. In reply to the president's question as to what could be done about Fidel Castro's spreading influence in Latin America, Beltrán suggested that the United States announce that it was prepared to work with Latin America in a program that would offer hope that its people could achieve what they most wanted—land and homes. The president was impressed with Beltrán's suggestion. I dined with Beltrán in Lima in September 1963. He confirmed the report of his conversation with President Eisenhower, which he believed had helped to bring about the Act of Bogotá. He said, however, that if he had had any idea that the conversation would eventually lead to the Alliance for Progress, with its oversimplifications of Latin America's problems and the direct involvement of the United States in Latin America's affairs, he would never have spoken in the terms he used.

> help them to help themselves, for whatever period is required—not because the Communists may be doing it, not because we seek their votes, but because it is right. . . . To our sister republics south of our border, we offer a special pledge—to convert our good words into good deeds—in a new alliance for progress—to assist free men and free governments in casting off the chains of poverty.

As a candidate Mr. Kennedy was familiar with the Eisenhower administration's economic program for Latin America before it was presented at Bogotá, and he planned, if elected, to carry it out, but with more verve and flair. A group of Kennedy advisers drawn from political, university, and business life met at the Faculty Club of Harvard University and on December 19, 1960, subscribed to a document entitled "Alliance for Progress, a Program of Inter-American Partnership." It set forth most of the principles and aims that later were embodied in President Kennedy's own Alliance for Progress.

The document reflected the mixture of idealism, fear, and faith in government that was to characterize the Kennedy administration's attitude toward Latin America. "Programs and planning must be an adventure in partnership," it proclaimed. And despite what the president was to say later, the proposed Alliance was to be directed at communism and Castroism in Latin America. "The Sino-Soviet alliance," the document noted, "is actively working to topple . . . democratic leaders in the conviction that many nations of Latin America are ripe for a takeover." It added: "We believe that unless the United States adopts new postures, this Sino-Soviet goal is attainable."

"Development of self-sustaining economies is the target," the document declared, and it continued: "In many Latin American countries this is feasible within a decade." While the document recognized the importance of private investment it placed its hope for improvement principally on a larger economic role for government. "Public investment supported by loans from the US Government and international agencies, such as the IDB and the IBRD must play a major role—perhaps the predominant role in the immediate future," it said. And it went on to suggest that "there is need also for substantial capital on a soft-loan basis . . . and for grant funds."

The document maintained that the United States itself should launch the Alliance. "The initiative should be undertaken in a manner that will produce an impact comparable to General Marshall's historic offer [to Europe]," it insisted.

As president Mr. Kennedy did his best to carry out that advice. Addressing the assembled Latin American ambassadors he said, on March 13, 1961:

> I have called on all the people of the hemisphere to join in a new Alliance for Progress—*Alianza para el Progreso*—a vast cooperative effort, unparalleled in magnitude and nobility of purpose, to satisfy the basic needs of the American people for homes, work and land, health and schools—*techo trabajo y tierra, salud y escuela.*

The Alliance for Progress became a program of all the American republics, except Cuba, when its charter was signed on August 17, 1961, at Punta del Este, Uruguay. Its objectives were these:

1) To insure an economic growth rate of at least 2.5 percent for every country
2) To increase income and living standards of the needy while at the same time a higher proportion of the national product was devoted to investment
3) To achieve economic diversification
4) To accelerate industrialization
5) To raise greatly the level of agricultural productivity, reform tax laws, and redistribute the national income
6) To encourage agrarian reform
7) To eliminate adult illiteracy and assure that by 1970 every child in Latin America would have access to six years of primary education
8) To increase life expectancy at birth by a minimum of five years
9) To increase the construction of low-cost houses for low-income families and provide necessary public services to both urban and rural centers of population
10) To maintain stable price levels, avoiding inflation or deflation
11) To prevent the harmful effects of excessive fluctuations in the foreign exchange earnings derived from the export of primary products.

In short, the Alliance was aimed at accomplishing the basic economic and social objectives that the framers considered desirable and that the Latin American countries, by themselves, had been unable to accomplish during their long histories. And, reflecting the view of the planners at the Harvard Faculty Club, the signatories expected that those objectives would be substantially accomplished within ten years.

What was striking about the Alliance for Progress, of course, was the role that the US government was willing to assume. "To supplement the domestic efforts of [the Latin American] countries," the Charter of Punta del Este said, "the United States is prepared to allocate resources which, along with those anticipated from other external sources, will be of a scope and magnitude adequate to realize the goals envisaged in this Charter." Douglass Cater referred to this as a "monumental commitment which for size and complexity makes the Marshall Plan look puny by comparison."[3] He did not exaggerate.

If one were asked how much the Alliance for Progress cost the United States he could not respond. All kinds of cooperation were extended. Technical assistance was greatly expanded. Loans were increased. Some were made at near-conventional rates, others at very low rates. Some loans were repayable in the borrower's currency, which meant, in practice, that they were hardly distinguishable from gifts. And some aid was in the form of gifts—"grants," in aid parlance. Large amounts of foodstuffs were donated under the Food for Peace program, but one purpose of that program was to rid the United States of food surpluses that tended to depress prices. Another difficulty in assessing the cost of the Alliance for Progress is that no one can say when the Alliance died. It was as much a phrase as a cooperative program, and the phrase did not survive the Johnson administration. Nor can we calculate what the Alliance cost the Latin Americans. Their expenditures for economic and social improvement increased, too, but how much they would have expended in the absence of the Alliance we cannot know.

What we do know is that by the mid-1970s cooperation of all kinds extended to Latin America under the various programs amounted to several times the aid extended to Europe under the Marshall Plan. Had it measured up to the high expectations it aroused in Latin America? It had not. There was a tendency on the part of the Alliance's detractors to conclude that because some of the wildly optimistic predictions of progress the Alliance would bring had not been met, it had brought no progress to Latin America. There was an equal tendency on the part of its supporters to give credit to the Alliance for all the gains the Latin American countries had made, including improved weather on the Argentine *pampa*. Some gains had been offset by losses. Improved health had brought about unmanageable population increases. Some improvements in agriculture had siphoned rural people into city slums where their condition might be worse. Latin America's economic and social problems had probably increased rather than diminished.

In all Latin America Brazil was making the most dramatic progress. While Brazil had been a favored aid recipient, its progress was due principally to the government's vigorous support of private enterprise, domestic and foreign. The Central American countries, which had received moderate aid, also had experienced impressive growth after joining together in a common market, but again, new private investment had been a dynamic ingredient. Mexico had shown substantial improvement, but it had received almost no direct aid from the United States or other countries. Its most notable progress had been related to stable government, support of private investment, aid from the privately supported Rockefeller Foundation, and the discovery, with extensive assistance from foreign private firms, of vast new petroleum reserves that promised to make it once more a leading petroleum exporter. Panama, which continued to receive generous aid, was moving ahead rapidly; it had become a center for international banking. Colombia, which also had received generous aid, was making rapid progress and had announced that it would no longer apply for direct aid; high coffee prices and a dynamic private sector had helped to spur growth. Venezuela, which had received very little aid, had benefited greatly from the higher prices of petroleum. It had nationalized not only its petroleum industry but also its rich iron mines, both of which had been developed by foreign private interests. Argentina, in the presence of moderate aid, had made little progress; the deterrent, in its case, was the state of its politics, which only Argentines could improve. With improved politics Argentina would progress rapidly with or without aid.

Over-socialized Uruguay, which had received moderate aid, was trying, with little success, to restore its once-flourishing economy. Paraguay, which also had received moderate aid, has burst into the modern world as a result of economic cooperation with its larger neighbors, Brazil and Argentina. Bolivia, whose social revolution had been supported by massive United States aid, was still a very poor country. Peru had become one of the world's leading fishing countries, but its success was short-lived. The military group that seized power in 1968 had nationalized the fish meal industry, which accounted for most of the production, and subsequent overfishing had drastically reduced the catch. The government was trying to restore the industry to private hands, but the foreign investors who had made the greatest contribution to success were reluctant to return. Political difficulties with the United States had had the effect of limiting aid; Peruvian peasants had been given land, but the economy was in dire straits. Ecuador, which had received moderate aid, was progressing, chiefly as a result of increased petroleum production and higher prices. Again, foreign companies had discovered and developed the deposits.

The Dominican Republic, a favored recipient of aid, was progressing rapidly under improved government. Haiti, next door, had received only intermittent aid. Political problems, which it had experienced since the early days of independence, continued to hinder development. In Chile, another favored recipient of aid, an elected Socialist-Communist government had seized US-owned copper mining properties and laid the country economically and politically prostrate before the armed forces overthrew it and reversed the country's direction. Cuba, which had become an economic dependency of Soviet Russia, was confirmed in its communism. In all the countries growing needs had cancelled out much of the improvement that had taken place. Another factor that had cancelled out improvement was inflation in the United States and the accompanying drop in the international value of the dollar: the United States, donor of aid, had become a source of concern to the Latin American countries because of the difficulty it was having in managing its own economy.

THE AID DILEMMA

Aid's failure to meet the high expectations that were held out for it caused disillusionment among many Latin Americans. And since it had been largely United States optimism and United States promises that had aroused those expectations there was a certain amount of resentment against the United States. Why had aid failed to fulfiill the high hopes its proponents had for it? A brief story may offer a clue.

Quite a few years ago an American company obtained a concession to exploit a large area of tropical pine in a Central American country where I was serving. Since ships could not dock in the open roadstead that was to serve as harbor, the project involved devising a system for placing the timber aboard vessels for export. After careful consideration the company decided that the logs should be dumped into the sea and floated out to the vessels. Equipment to carry out the operation was brought down from the United States. Appropriate ceremonies were arranged to inaugurate the new venture. The president of the company arrived from New Orleans aboard the ship that was to carry back the first cargo of logs. A representative of the president of the republic made the arduous journey from the capital to give testimony to the government's enthusiasm for the project. Officials and citizens were present in great numbers. Speeches were made. A military band, resplendent in new uniforms, was there to give added drama to the occasion.

At a given signal a tiny locomotive gingerly pushed a flatcar loaded with logs on to the pier that had been constructed for the purpose. The band struck up a martial tune, the car was tilted, and the logs rolled off into the sea. They promptly sank. The company's plan to float the logs out to vessels was based on the assumption that Central American pine behaves as American pine behaves. But the Central American pine insisted perversely on behaving as Central American pine behaves.

To many persons in the United States the Latin American problem was disarmingly simple—as simple as floating logs out to sea. Latin America had low living standards. Its people wanted those standards raised. They wanted to eat better, dress better, live better. They wanted improved education for their children. They were embarked on what had become known as a "revolution of rising expectations." In order to carry out that revolution they wanted United States cooperation. The United States was in a position to extend cooperation and it was in fact already extending a great deal, although not enough apparently. Clearly then, if it would only cooperate more, presumably by having bigger programs, better coordinated programs, or programs that permitted long-term planning, Latin America's problems would be solved.

All that was equivalent to saying that if Americans did all they are capable of doing to help the Latin American countries, and if Latin Americans did all they should do to help themselves, the problem of development would be solved. But nearly all human problems would be solved if human beings did all they should do to solve them. Why, then, do so many problems go unsolved? Why have some of Latin America's problems worsened despite earnest efforts on the part of the US government to help solve them?

The Marshall Plan was the first and by far the most successful large-scale aid program. Its success is not apt to be duplicated in circumstances that we can envisage. Whereas the problem of European recovery and reconstruction was urgent and of vast dimensions, its solution, in retrospect, was comparatively simple. Large areas of Western Europe had been devastated by war, but most of the physical plant remained intact. More important still, Europe possessed a reservoir of experience, traditions, and skills that were the accumulation of centuries. When the United States was able to add a small percentage of aid, over and above what Europe itself was able to provide, its contribution acted as a catalytic agent, and the European countries, helped by a newly found ability to cooperate with one another as well as with the United States, restored their economies rapidly.

But the task of cooperating with the less-developed countries is infinitely more complex. Indeed it is only beginning to be understood. Basically, the problem in Europe was one of reconstruction, of restoring modern, sophisticated economies that had been long developing. What the United States has been trying to do in many of the Latin American countries is to help them reach a point that Europe reached a century or more ago, after earlier centuries of effort and training. Europe has been the home and the fountain of material progress. The miracle of Europe was Europe's miracle. Most areas, however, are not yet in a position to perform miracles.

Responsibility for aid's failure to accomplish as much as it was expected to must be borne by both Americans and Latin Americans. Proponents in the United States had many jobs for aid to do. Some wanted to defeat communism, or they wanted to promote democracy. Others saw aid as a device for influencing policies of governments. Some believed that countries had to be either for the United States or against it, and they wanted to reward those they considered friends. Some were looking for gratitude—love, even. When they failed to get either they were disappointed and showed it. Some were for aid because it was the "new thing." Others were for it as they were for motherhood. Such diverse purposes and attitudes were bound to produce a great deal of pulling and hauling—and confusion in the aid program.

Latin Americans also were confused concerning United States purposes, in part because Americans themselves were confused about them. Many Latin Americans suspected United States motives. Early in the program some said, frankly, "We wouldn't do this for you, so why are you doing it for us?" As late as 1956 persons in the Argentine government maintained that Argentina would never permit itself to accept aid from the United States. Not only did Argentina accept aid but within a few years some Argentine officials were recommending threats against the United States as a device to force increases in aid. Many countries cultivated relations with Soviet Russia as a means of exerting pressure on the United States to increase aid. In more than one country where an aid program evoked little gratitude and was quickly taken for granted, reductions that were later made in the program were promptly labelled "economic aggression." Some Latin Americans regarded the program as little more than a subsidy to American farmers and manufacturers whose exports were being financed by AID. Some regarded aid as a form of conscience money: they took the view that the problems of the Latin American countries had to do more with trade than aid; that aid merely replaced in part what the United States was taking away from Latin America through its trade practices. That view tended to grow as ECLA's influence grew. Others regarded aid as a new form of intervention.

The charge that aid is a form of intervention is made freely, often with considerable sincerity. The truth is that the line that separates cooperation from intervention can be very thin. When a government offers aid—help, that is—it assumes that foreigners want help. Now in principle they doubtless do, but in practice they may not all want it. The political opposition may not want it if it is going to strengthen the party in power. The foreign government, for its part, may not want to be helped if a concomitant to help is doing things that are politically unpopular. Latin Americans differ among themselves as to how their countries can best progress. When the United States preached the merits of free enterprise, persons who favored a predominant role for the state attacked it. When it made a loan to a state enterprise, those who favored a strong private sector criticized it. When it sponsored tax reform and land reform persons whose taxes were apt to be raised or whose lands might be taken from them protested. Without wishing to, the United States, as aid donor and development counselor, became a factor and, in the view of some Latin Americans, a participant in the internal politics of the countries it was trying to help.

The long-term plans that the Alliance for Progress sponsored depended for their success on a degree of continuity in the development process. But continuity has not been easy to achieve. It is difficult to exaggerate the disrupting effects of the arbitrary changes in government that have been so common in Latin America. Some such changes have brought improvement, as in Brazil in 1964 and in Chile in 1973, but in each of those cases improvement was measured against a disastrous economic decline under an elected government. Other arbitrary changes have been less helpful. Even orderly change frequently cancels out progress already made. A new administration may not like its predecessor's priorities. It may have its own set of priorities. This makes orderly and confident private planning difficult. And, of course, it makes meaningful government planning difficult too.

New administrations in Latin America are not alone in wanting to act differently from the ways their predecessors have acted. The same tendency exists in the United States. A new administration wants to make a record for itself. This, it usually feels, means doing things differently from the way its predecessors did them, or at least giving the impression it is doing them differently. It wants new programs that will impress people with its dynamism, or if that is not possible, then new names and new images for old programs. Seldom have two simple words had so much meaning for so many people as "Point Four." The expression had no planned appeal to people's emotions. It had nothing to do with Madison Avenue. It was not intended to inspire enthusiasm or gratitude. And yet it did both. It conveyed to hundreds of millions of people throughout the world whom the United States was trying to reach, and whom it needed to reach, the fact of America's wanting to help. When a new administration took over in Washington, however, it stopped using the expression, and its representatives abroad were discouraged from using it. The United States threw an inestimable amount of goodwill and potential for helping people out the window because its government had no enthusiasm for an expression that was associated with an earlier administration.

Of course a new administration feels it needs new men, too. The administrator of the Agency for International Development, or whatever its current name may be, must be changed. He must be a man who is politically acceptable if not necessarily technically qualified.

When the United States launched the Alliance for Progress it was suffering from an illusion of omnipotence. It had emerged from World War II as the mightiest nation in the world, militarily and economically. It was the undisputed leader of the free nations. Through the Marshall

Plan and NATO it had become Europe's savior, and probably freedom's savior. Nothing seemed to be beyond its power. Under the Alliance for Progress United States aid personnel multiplied many times. A Latin American might have been pardoned for thinking that for every problem his country had the United States had sent down one of its citizens to solve it. Many AID officials were strangers to the countries where they had to work, to the problems they had to address themselves to, and to the cultures to which they had to adjust if they were to succeed, indeed if they were not to do harm.

An AID director in Paraguay once told me that it had taken him five years to learn what Paraguay's problems really were. He was a highly intelligent, splendidly educated man. He spoke the two languages that Paraguayans speak. He was there on the spot. And yet it had taken him five years to learn what Paraguay's problems were—the problems, not the answers. In contrast, during the early years of the Alliance for Progress more than one White House staff assistant prescribed remedies for Latin America's problems without ever having visited the area and without knowing the people who must carry out the prescriptions.

The Alliance for Progress was a frontal attack against ignorance, disease, and poverty in Latin America, and the United States was its author and principal sponsor. But it is doubtful that a government should engage in a frontal attack in someone else's country, whatever it may feel needs correcting. It is not an appropriate tactic for a foreign government, particularly one as powerful as the United States, with a historical penchant for intervention. Some persons abroad may applaud it. But others will object, and they are apt to include many who are important to the United States and to the purposes it has in common with Latin America.

Frontal attacks smack of the colonialism that Americans deny they practice, and that they abhor when they think they see it in others. Frontal attacks may be useful in war, but diplomacy, including aid diplomacy, is more in the nature of a guerrilla operation where frontal attacks are eschewed. I suggest that the frontal attack be left to the people whose burden we are trying to lighten. It is theirs to carry, and foreigners should be careful not to give them the impression that others can lift it from their shoulders. If they get that impression then development will be retarded rather than advanced.

By the mid-1970s the feeling of omnipotence Americans had when they launched the Alliance for Progress had vanished. Aid missions had been cut down. Domestic problems, to which many Americans had long been strangely insensitive, and failure in Viet Nam, had caught up with them. The bloom was off the aid rose.

MULTILATERAL AID

In the 1970s the United States was directing more and more of its aid through multilateral channels; principally, in the case of Latin America, through the Inter-American Development Bank. A number of reasons for that were adduced: for example, that multilateral aid aroused less resentment on the part of recipients (an allegation that must have appeared ironic to those who expected that aid would earn gratitude); and that recipients were less likely to charge that aid was being used for "political" purposes, for acts of intervention.

Persons with experience in the aid field recognize that multilateral aid does indeed have advantages, as its proponents point out. But they consider that it has disadvantages as well. For example, if bureaucracy can be a problem in US aid institutions, the problem is multiplied in multinational institutions, where patronage has to be divided among a large number of member nations. Nor are most multilateral institutions as ready as the United States government is to insist that countries receiving aid engage in the kind of self-help measures that, in American eyes, are needed to insure that aid will have helpful effects.

Even under the Alliance for Progress, which was basically a bilateral aid program, it was difficult to insure that aid receivers would take needed self-help measures. The Charter of Punta del Este provided for a panel of experts who would monitor the performance of aid recipients, but it soon became evident that the "experts" lacked either the knowledge or the courage to become a useful mechanism. They were replaced by the Inter-American Committee on the Alliance for Progress (CIAP), which had little more success. Neither was the Inter-American Development Bank, to which the United States is by far the largest contributor and which has only the Latin American and Caribbean countries as borrowers, willing to impose upon borrowing countries (the same countries who largely run the bank) the kind of self-help measures that a purely American bank might have considered wise. The agency that most insisted on self-help was the International Monetary Fund (IMF), which became as unpopular among Latin American borrowers as the United States was.

It appeared that the trend toward multilateral aid reflected not so much confidence in that form of aid as disillusionment with bilateral aid and skepticism in the United States toward aid in general.

A TWO-WAY STREET

The seizure of oil company properties in Peru and Bolivia, and of copper company properties in Chile, contributed to disillusionment with foreign aid in the United States. Whether justified or not by unilaterally determined "moral law" or by "elementary justice," these actions were in clear violation of the norms that have governed cooperative relations among states during many centuries. In an effort to discourage new seizures and improve the basis for future aid, President Nixon, on January 19, 1972, issued a policy statement in which he noted that private investment, as a carrier of technology, trade opportunities, and capital itself, was a major factor in promoting industrial and agricultural development. "A kind of symbiosis exists," he said, "with government aid efforts not only speeding the flow of, but actually depending for their success upon, private capital, both domestic and foreign. And of course, from the investor's point of view, foreign private investment must either yield financial benefits or cease to be available." The president left little doubt that in the future one of the criteria for aid would be the degree to which it helped to encourage private investment.

Mr. Nixon maintained that the United States had a right to expect that in the future: (a) any expropriation of US private property would be nondiscriminatory (that is, properties would not be singled out for expropriation because they were American); (b) expropriation should be for a public purpose (presumably a government's coveting a property would not, of itself, constitute a public purpose); and (c) US citizens would receive prompt, adequate, and effective compensation (for example, compensation would not be reduced or eliminated by the application of ex post facto rules, as in the case of Allende's Chile, nor would payment be made in worthless bonds or inconvertible currencies). In the absence of those conditions, the president indicated, there would be a presumption that the United States would not extend new bilateral assistance, and that it would withhold support from loans under consideration in multilateral development banks.

Secretary of the Treasury George P. Shultz described the United States attitude succinctly during the 1973 meeting of the Board of Governors of the Inter-American Development Bank.

> We do not see how the funds from the United States can be expected to flow to a country where United States property has been taken without prompt, effective, and adequate compensation. This is not an infringement on anybody's national sovereignty; it is . . . not simply a question of our law or your law or international law, or whatever; it is a matter of common sense.[4]

President Nixon's policy toward the treatment of United States private capital invested abroad, and its relationship to aid, differed little, if at all, from the policy that existed when aid was first undertaken. It restored private investment to the high place it had occupied as an instrument of development. It recognized, once more, that there is not enough public capital to bring about satisfactory development in the world, and that countries that reject the cooperation of private capital can not be considered as serious bidders for US government aid.

Despite disappointment and disillusionment foreign aid had become institutionalized, not only in the United States but throughout the world. In fact some countries of Western Europe were investing a higher percentage of their gross national product in aid than the United States was. Aid is a form of cooperation. Indeed "cooperation" is a better name for it than "aid." "Cooperation" connotes a two-way street. It suggests that what we do to help others also helps us, that the act of accepting aid, and using it wisely, is itself an act of cooperation. It suggests, too, that what we can do to promote development in another country depends on what the people of the country are prepared to do for themselves; that what we can do is to add something, usually a very little, to what they do. Neither Americans nor Latin Americans understood that sufficiently when the Alliance for Progress was launched. But experience had taught them a great deal. There was some reason to hope that future aid would be on a sounder basis and that it would therefore be more effective.

15
THE FUTURE OF DEVELOPMENT

DR. ANTONIO ORTIZ MENA, President of the Inter-American Development Bank, said, at a meeting of the Council on Foreign Relations on November 17, 1971:

> In the course of the past decade development as a conscious policy of government has become so common that we now take it for granted. Left and right as designations of government are virtually obsolete. The uniform standard of measurement is that of a government's commitment to economic and social development and how effective it is in carrying out this objective. No government, regardless of how it comes to power, whether it is civilian or military, democratically elected or a result of insurrection, can ignore this basic fact. . . .
>
> This development consciousness is no longer an elitist concept confined to a select, highly educated segment of the population, arguing esoteric points among themselves in a closed world comfortably isolated from the masses. Modern communications—the transistor radio, the written word, satellites, television, the movies—have transformed development consciousness into a mass phenomenon. Expectations have been awakened; the genie of awareness cannot be put back in the bottle.

Dr. Ortiz Mena is a former minister of finance of Mexico and an experienced practitioner of development. His background and his accomplishments require us to take his remarks seriously. But there is also another viewpoint, one that does not necessarily conflict with what Dr. Ortiz Mena has said but that casts doubt on the viability of the development process, not only as it is being carried out in the less-developed countries but also as it has been carried out and continues to be carried out in the more highly developed countries. In this view the gap between the richer and the poorer nations, if it is to be narrowed at all, may be narrowed as much by lowered consumption in the rich countries as by higher consumption in the poor countries.

Economists, political scientists, developers, politicians, and writers for the magazine sections of the Sunday papers have long equated production gains with human improvement. President Nixon hailed the trillion-dollar gross national product in the United States as a milestone of progress with which he was happy to identify his administration. Even the poorest nation, as Dr. Ortiz Mena suggests, now is development-conscious. Development, in the minds of many, has replaced freedom as the primary human objective after survival. Some view it as a requisite for survival. Development is a new and effective instrument of demagogy and a pretext for revolution and for tyranny. And some think it threatens our survival.

Nations produce in order to consume. Production is a good word and so, still, is consumption. But consumption is losing much of its luster, and promises to lose more. Conservation, which may demand less rather than more consumption, is beginning to precede it in the list of human priorities. Many observers are pointing with alarm at increased consumption, especially of raw materials that may be irreplaceable. It is becoming clear that resources that are not depleted through consumption may be lost through pollution, another by-product of development. Ecology has become a subject of urgent concern in the industrialized countries and is being talked about also in the less-developed countries.

In the extreme view, the crisis in development is reached when population growth is excessive, when people occupy too much land that should be used to produce food, when they demand too many manufactures that use up too many raw materials, and in the process pollute the land, the air, and the water. When those things happen growth stops. People starve, or raw materials give out, or pollution takes over, or the strains of overcrowding provoke war. A sinister feature of population growth is that it is exponential. It will have taken centuries to travel half the distance to crisis. But then, through the exponential doubling process, the crisis may be upon us almost overnight.[1]

Many observers believe that this view is too pessimistic. They say that it underestimates technology's ability to meet new needs. They suggest that raw materials are not nearly as scarce as they may appear to be; that lower-grade ores of many metals are almost inexhaustible and will be exploited when they are needed. Nevertheless few deny that overpopulation in some areas is already a fact and that no solution is in sight, or that pollution, alone, is a threat even in the absence of further large-scale development.

The less-developed countries occupy most of the planet. Their populations vastly outnumber those of the industrialized countries. If the problems we face are grave today, think of what they will be when the whole world achieves industrialization—if that should ever occur! At its present rate of growth China will soon have a billion inhabitants. In the early 1970s its income per capita was perhaps $100 a year. Suppose it should become industrialized, a nation of belching smokestacks and two-car families. Where would the raw materials come from? Think of the pollution the winds would bring us! And if a billion industrialized Chinese would not bring about those results would adding India, with another billion inhabitants, do it? Not to mention Latin America, with the fastest-growing population in the world. Meanwhile, of course, the United States and Western Europe, Russia and its satellites, and Japan will continue to be engaged in the process that even today threatens our environment.

Latin America is already experiencing some of the unsought by-products of development. I have on my desk a copy of Preston E. James's *Latin America,* an extraordinarily useful book that my son used in one of his university classes. On page 544 there is a beautiful photograph of Santiago, Chile, with the snow-covered Andes in the background. My son has lived in Santiago. Under the photograph he had written, for his own eyes of course, "It will be a cold day in hell when you have that good a view." The expression is inelegant but it is apt. Santiago has achieved the blessings of industrialization, and one of them is a smog so thick that at times it is difficult to see more than a few city blocks. In the United States, Pittsburgh, the erstwhile "smoky city," has been more or less cleaned up. But in Latin America the process of pollution is just beginning, and neither the resources nor the will to contain it may exist.

Some observers suggest that before the less-developed countries become fully committed to the kind of uncontrolled growth that the industrialized countries have experienced they may wish to explore possible alternatives. Fifty years ago industrialization in Chile had barely begun. Population was less than half of what it is now. Food was almost taken for granted; like air and water it was part of the natural condition.

Santiago's air was pure and clear. Most people lived on the land, and no one lived far from the land. Today Chile's industrialized cities are ringed with shantytowns. Food prices are cruelly high, and malnutrition is common. Outside the large cities Chile still has clean air, clean water, and clean land. If it can preserve these it may be a triumph greater than an industrialization that helps to reduce the quality of life upon the earth.

But will Chileans, and others in their position, agree with that? Will governments and candidates for government office, absorbed in the effort to meet today's needs and today's desires, agree with it? Can population growth, which is reducing some "sovereign" nations to the status of international beggars, be stopped or even slowed down materially? Do free people have the discipline to plan a livable world? Is tyranny essential to survival? Can even a tyrant force a nation to turn round and retreat from development? And even though the less-developed countries should be willing and able to revert to a simpler way of living, would the industrialized countries slow down or reverse their "progress"? Can the economists tell them how to do it without acute economic depression and social upheaval?

There are no present answers to these questions, and merely posing them has already brought the charge that ecology is being used as an argument in favor of slowing both population growth and development in the less-developed countries. Octavio Paz has said, "We Latin Americans are uninvited guests who have sneaked in through the West's back door, intruders who have arrived at the feast of modernity as the lights are about to be put out."[2] But the questions are good ones. They have to do with the life or death of what we call civilization on our planet and with the life or death of millions, or even billions, of the planet's inhabitants.

IV

LATIN AMERICA AND THE UNITED STATES

16
THE SPECIAL RELATIONSHIP

BY THE MID-1970s the United States had carried out in Latin America the most massive program of economic aid in history, and aid was continuing at a high level. But Cuba, which had been closer to the United States than any other Latin American country, had become a Communist state, and Chile, a favored recipient of aid, had narrowly escaped communization.

Latin America, of course, is a part of the world. Its problems have much in common with those of other areas, especially of the Third World with which it has chosen to identify, and the problems the United States encounters in its relations with the Latin American countries resemble in many ways those that arise in its relations with other Third World countries. But US–Latin American problems and differences take on an added dimension and provoke strong emotional reactions because of the special relationship that has existed among the American republics over the years.

The special relationship has derived from geography and from history. Latin Americans drew inspiration from the United States' war of independence, and Americans were pleased and encouraged that freedom and, apparently, democracy were coming to their neighbors to the south. Nevertheless close relations were slow in developing.

The First International Conference of American States, attended by the United States and all the Latin American countries except the Dominican Republic, was held in Washington at the invitation of the United States. It lasted from October 2, 1889, to April 19, 1890, and included a tour by special train of forty-one American cities.[1] Although the travel, the entertainment, and the speeches the delegates were compelled to listen to were fatiguing in the extreme, most of the Latin

Americans became more familiar with the geography of the United States than they were with that of their own countries.

The United States was interested in trade and was prepared to go a long way to obtain it. It proposed nothing less than a customs union among all the American states. But the Latin Americans courteously declined to go along. They had been privileged to view the enormous mills and factories in more than one American city and had no desire to be embraced by the industrial giant they were dealing with. The conference did agree, however, to establish the Commercial Bureau of the American Republics, charged principally with publishing statistics and other useful information on the trade of the member countries. The Commercial Bureau was not a very powerful tie among the American republics but it grew into the Pan American Union and, later, the Organization of American States (OAS). The OAS is the world's oldest regional organization; for years many persons judged it to be also the most successful.*

Latin America as well as the United States wanted good relations. But good relations between a confident, progressive and interventionist United States and its weak, politically unstable neighbors did not come easily. Both sides wanted security but they had different views of where the threat to security was to be found. For the United States the threat came from Europe, and it was the Monroe Doctrine that met it. But the Monroe Doctrine was a unilateral instrument. It was the United States that had proclaimed it and it was the United States that interpreted it and applied it. Its aim was principally to protect the United States; what protection it gave Latin America was secondary. And as the threat from Europe receded Latin Americans were less and less sure that it gave

*Of the twenty-eight members of the OAS one is the United States, twenty are Latin American states (Cuba, one of the twenty, is presently a nonparticipating member), and seven are small former European lands in the Caribbean that have only recently become independent. It is possible that by 1985 newly independent Caribbean countries, all of them non-Latin and with tiny populations, will number from fifteen to twenty-five out of a total of thirty-five to forty-five OAS members. That has implications most of which are not clear. A clear possibility, however, is that one or more of those ministates, many of which will have only nominal attributes of sovereignty, will fall under the control of international communism, or of narcotics smugglers, or of the Mafia, or of some combination of groups or individuals. The time is approaching when the one-nation–one-vote system of the OAS must be reappraised if the organization is to continue to have a useful role.

them any protection at all. Many of them considered that the United States itself was now the principal threat. They complained bitterly of United States "hegemony" over Latin America.

When the Sixth International Conference of American States met in Havana, in 1928, the United States' continuing interventions in Haiti and Nicaragua had led to increased anti-Americanism in the hemisphere. Former Secretary of State Charles Evans Hughes was chairman of the United States delegation. Intervention was warmly debated but although Mr. Hughes had brought an end to the intervention in the Dominican Republic and had taken the initial steps to terminate the other interventions, he was unwilling to agree to any limitations on United States rights.

"What are we going to do when government breaks down and American citizens are in danger of their lives? Are we to stand by and see them killed because a government in circumstances which it cannot control and for which it may not be responsible can no longer afford reasonable protection?" Hughes asked the Latin Americans. "Now it is a principle of international law," he continued, "that in such a case a government is fully justified in taking action—I would call it interposition of a temporary character—for the purpose of protecting the lives and property of its nationals."

Of course the United States, in its interventions, had gone far beyond protecting the lives and property of its nationals. Nevertheless Mr. Hughes, one of the most respected jurists in the hemisphere, convinced many Latin Americans that it had no aggressive intentions toward its neighbors. But the Latin Americans remained unreconciled. They opposed intervention in principle, whether it was called intervention or interposition.

President Franklin D. Roosevelt's Good Neighbor Policy, particularly his commitment to nonintervention, went far toward breaking down Latin America's distrust of United States intentions. It brought the American republics closer together than they ever had been. War in Europe also helped to bring them together. In 1947 they met at Rio de Janeiro and signed the Inter-American Treaty of Reciprocal Assistance. It provided that an armed attack against any American state should be considered an armed attack against all, whether it came from within the continent or from outside it, and that each state should assist in meeting the attack. The treaty tied the American republics together in a true defensive alliance. It seemed to many that the inter-American system had never been so solid. Nevertheless difficult times were in the offing.

The postwar period brought vexing economic and social problems to Latin America. President Truman's Point Four program was well received, but it was far from meeting Latin America's needs. Later the Alliance for Progress was welcomed enthusiastically. But it also gave rise to extravagant expectations on the part of Latin Americans. Since it was the promise of large-scale American support of the Alliance that had been principally responsible for those expectations, failure to meet them was judged to be a failure on the part of the United States. And not only was United States competence questioned; its intentions also were placed in doubt. Its aid program, put forward as a grand cooperative gesture, was labeled by some Latin American critics an instrument of American "imperialism."

When President Nixon, in an effort to restore a degree of dynamism to US–Latin American relations, asked the Latin Americans to list their aspirations, they responded with the Consensus of Viña del Mar which reiterated many of the demands UNCTAD and ECLA had been expressing. But the peremptory manner in which the Chilean minister of foreign affairs, flanked by all Latin America's ambassadors to the United States, presented the consensus to the president did little to raise hopes that the demands would soon be met.

Through the early 1970s Latin America made continued demands on the United States—for higher prices for its exports, for higher levels of aid, for preferential tariff treatment of manufactured products, and for other concessions. The steps required were not easy however. The Congress was slow in giving consideration to President Nixon's request that it authorize preferential tariff treatment to all the less-developed countries. Nor did Peru and Bolivia make the task of cooperating easier when they seized the properties of US petroleum companies, nor did Chile when it seized the properties of US copper companies.

When the Congress finally got round to approving a Trade Act that granted preferential tariff treatment to the less-developed countries it denied the preferences to Venezuela and Ecuador because of their membership in OPEC, which had raised petroleum prices some 500 percent. Not only those two but also the other Latin American countries, in a gesture of solidarity, protested this act of "discrimination" by the United States, and much of the good will the Trade Act was intended to create was lost in Latin America. The protesting countries included many that were suffering severe hardship as a result of the increased petroleum prices.*

In the mid-1960s, at a meeting of Western Hemisphere officials and scholars that I attended, a Canadian suggested that any special relationship the United States might have was with Western Europe, Japan, and of course Canada, rather than with Latin America. His remark aroused strong objection among the Latin Americans, for whom the special relationship with the United States was a fact not open to question. But a decade later many Latin Americans, and many Americans as well, had begun to suspect that the relationship was not firmly based.

The factors that initially tended to hold the republics together had eroded with time. America was no longer isolated physically from the rest of the world. The airplane, the radio, and of course television, had robbed distance of much of its meaning. The United States' deep involvement in world politics and all the American states' membership in the United Nations Organization meant that the hemisphere was not politically isolated either. Ideology was a less meaningful tie. Castro's success in communizing Cuba and converting it into a satellite of the Soviet Union had reduced the Monroe Doctrine to a faded scrap of paper. While the United States seemed to be effectively deterred from intervening militarily in Latin America, Castro's Cuba had embarked, with little protest from other Latin American countries, on military intervention in Africa. And the fact that the United States was not only Latin America's principal trading partner and source of outside capital, but also its leading aid donor, often proved to be an irritant rather than an emollient. Latin Americans complained increasingly of dependence on the United States. "Dependency" had replaced "hegemony" as a source of resentment against their northern neighbor.

BILATERAL AND MULTILATERAL RELATIONS

A distinction needs to be drawn at this point. International relations are conducted through the medium of diplomacy. Diplomacy, in turn, may be on a bilateral (nation-to-nation) basis, or it may be multilateral.

*The Trade Agreements Act of 1979, which President Carter signed on July 26, opened the door to the extension of preferential tariff treatment to both Venezuela and Ecuador.

In the latter case three, or a dozen or, in the case of the United Nations, some one hundred and fifty countries, may join in a discussion or a negotiation.

Bilateral diplomacy is usually quiet diplomacy, conducted far from the noise of the microphone and the intrusiveness of the television camera. It makes it possible for governments to talk to one another in confidence. It permits them to adjust their positions—to compromise, in other words—without being accused, publicly, of "caving in" to the other side. At any given time the governments of the world are conducting countless conversations on a bilateral basis. Bilateral diplomacy is the traditional device for bringing peoples together.

Multilateral diplomacy, on the other hand, is new in its present dimensions. One reason it is increasingly practiced is that more and more problems affect not only two countries, or a few at most, but many; some problems, indeed, affect all countries. But it is practiced also because weaker countries, especially those of the Third World, consider that bilateral diplomacy places them at a disadvantage in their relations with the more powerful ones. Multilateral diplomacy is a device through which weaker countries, by combining their strength, hope to place themselves in a better negotiating position vis à vis the more powerful countries.

But multilateral diplomacy gives rise to its own problems. In practice it is frequently public diplomacy, a diplomacy of long speeches, of "strong" positions openly taken, of language that is calculated to make headlines that will impress supporters at home. It could hardly be conducted without the microphone, and much of it takes place before the television camera.

In 1973 the United States and Panama were engaged in bilateral negotiations aimed at altering the status of the Panama Canal in ways that would be more acceptable to Panama. In an effort to bring multilateral pressure to bear on the United States, Panama arranged for the United Nations Security Council, under the presidency of the Panamanian delegate, to hold a week-long session in Panama. The United States vetoed a council resolution calling upon it to withdraw from the Canal Zone (it was only the third time it had exercised its veto power in the council), while the position of many Americans who opposed a new agreement with Panama hardened.

Panama solicited the support of the other Latin American countries in its conflict with the United States, and every one of them gave it public support. An efficiently operated canal has enormous importance to Latin America, especially to those countries bordering on the Pacific. But support of Panama had little to do with whether Panama's aims were compatible with those countries' interests (many Latin Americans in political life were frank in saying privately that they wished the United States could continue to operate the canal). It was an expression of Latin American solidarity, an example of multilateral diplomacy.

In the mid-1970s bilateral relations between the United States and most of the Latin American countries could be described as good. There were problems in those relations, as there were problems in relations among Latin American countries. But except in the case of Cuba few problems the United States had with its neighbors could be considered grave.* Cooperation, quiet cooperation that rarely made headlines but was as real as it was traditional, characterized bilateral relations.

Multilateral relations were quite another thing however. Inside the OAS (and the UN as well) differences among Latin American countries tended to be submerged while differences with the United States were stressed. The phenomenon had taken on added importance after Latin America was caught up in the "revolution of rising expectations," and saw the United States as its principal hope for meeting those expectations. The OAS had become less a forum for improving relations than one Latin Americans were using to exert public pressure on the United States, especially to make public demands for greater economic cooperation. The picture one often got was that of an omnipotent but unwilling United States dealing with an eager but largely helpless Latin America; of a United States untrammeled in its ability to help and a Latin America incapable of improvement through its own efforts.

Secretary of State Henry Kissinger was referring to this phenomenon when he said, at a symposium in Macuto, Venezuela, on February 17, 1976:

> The Latin American nations . . . seemed to think that the United States, with its great strengths and responsibilities, could act unilaterally to resolve all issues . . . ; that Latin America should propose and the United States should respond. . . . Latin America demanded quick results; each meeting became a deadline by which time the United States had to show "results" or be judged lacking. But as economic difficulties beset us all in a period of world recession, it became obvious that if

*One problem, derived from its human rights program, I shall discuss later.

> Latin American aspirations were expressed to the people of the United States in terms of categorical and propagandistic demands, they could not elicit a sufficiently positive response.[2]

In an effort to meet changing needs the OAS charter had been revised in 1967. In 1973, at Latin American insistence, another attempt to revise the charter was initiated. But the new effort held out little promise of improvement. Under the heading "Collective Economic Security" it was being proposed that a state taking measures that had negative effects on another state's economy would be considered to have committed "economic aggression" against that state; and that in such an event a tribunal of other states should sit in judgment and assess damages against the offending state. It was clear from the discussion that by "economic aggression" the Latin Americans had in mind such things as the requirement in US legislation that aid should be denied to countries that seized properties of American citizens without compensating their owners. The United States indicated that it would not join in creating a court, a judge, and a jury to try it for what it considered sovereign acts in defense of legitimate United States interests. It proposed that the OAS drop discussion of the new charter draft and start from the beginning again. Nevertheless the OAS Council approved the "collective economic security" concept in the face of continued United States objection.

There is no reason to believe that the council's action was helpful. Whether Latin America's economic failures are the fault of others, or whether they are the fault of Latin Americans (fault surely rests on both sides), the view assiduously pressed by Latin American political leaders and intellectuals that they are the fault of others is a grave impediment to the self-help that Latin America must increasingly practice if its needs are to be met. To the extent that the OAS reinforces the impression that fault lies with others, particularly the United States, it adds to that impediment.

The Latin American Economic System (SELA). While the Latin Americans were attempting to employ the OAS (and the UN) to extract economic concessions from the United States they continued to seek new ways of achieving greater cooperation among themselves. The Latin American Free Trade Area, which had been organized with enthusiasm, was languishing; the Central American Common Market was in trouble;

and the Andean Common Market was having difficulty getting off the ground. The device adopted was still another organization, the Latin American Economic System (usually known by its Spanish initials, SELA). The United States, of course, was not a member of SELA, but Cuba was.

Even before SELA's charter had been ratified by a majority of signatories, meetings were being held at the ministerial level. SELA supported an UNCTAD-inspired "new international economic order" under which the industrialized countries, by making radical and unilateral concessions to the less-developed countries (e.g., governments would have full right to expropriate foreign investments but no obligation to compensate their owners), would make it possible for those countries at last to achieve the economic gains they were seeking. One of the new international economic order's promoters had been Mexico's president, Luis Echevarría Alvarez. At Macuto Secretary Kissinger, while welcoming the formation of SELA, expressed the hope that it would not become a new instrument of confrontation with the United States.[3]

Peacekeeping and Elections. Meanwhile the Organization of American States itself continued to perform useful services. Its members had no Russian veto to contend with, as they had in the United Nations (OAS support of the United States during the 1962 missile crisis had been important to success). But the organization also had acquired a large and costly bureaucracy many of whose functions were redundant or largely irrelevant. In 1977 it appeared that it might have to curtail its activities when the United States insisted that its assessed contribution to the support of the 1,469-man organization be reduced from slightly less than two-thirds of the total to just under one-half. Its delegate to the OAS remarked that although the United States did not dominate the organization it sometimes appeared that it did, and that it was time that appearance gave way to reality. But Latin Americans were loath to agree: the OAS was a rich source of patronage for Latin American politicians and bureaucrats, and for some that was sufficient reality.

The OAS's most important role was peacekeeping. At the same time it was a limited role. The organization had long helped to maintain a precarious peace between Nicaragua and Costa Rica, for example, and it had restored a quasi-peace between El Salvador and Honduras. But despite the presence of troublesome boundary disputes and other differences, the greatest continuing threat to peace was internal, the inability of power groups in most of the countries to get along with one another. Even before Marxism became an important factor, disorderly politics had fostered interventions and even wars in Latin America. Cuba demonstrated that Marxists in power could greatly increase the threat to peace.

In Nicaragua and the Dominican Republic, where politics had been traditionally violent, the only free elections that were ever held had been supervised by the United States or by the OAS. United States supervision of three elections in Nicaragua, two presidential and one legislative, had not brought democracy to that country (although it had been followed by the longest period of relative peace and the most rapid economic development in the country's history). But the Dominicans had been more fortunate in that respect: their last four national elections had been freely conducted and had brought sixteen years of uninterrupted peace. The OAS had supervised or observed all of them.

The time for the United States alone to supervise elections in Latin America is past. I suggest, however, that if governments and political groups in countries that have been unable to achieve democracy or stability truly want the internal peace they say they want they will ask the OAS to supervise their elections. They will retain the OAS in this role over a long period of time, until the benefits of free elections and institutional government have become evident not only to Latin Americans as a whole but also to politicians who now claim, often falsely, to represent them.

Supervised, free elections might not only bring political peace; they might also increase the possibility that Latin Americans will achieve what they most hope for today: rapid economic development. The principal impediment to development, to higher living standards, to jobs for burgeoning populations that are spilling over national boundaries in desperate search of improvement, continues to be political. What Latin Americans most need in order to achieve satisfactory development are not higher commodity prices, lower foreign tariffs, or more effective aid, although those would be very helpful, but an end to disorderly and disruptive politics in their own countries. Happily in the OAS they have an instrument that, if they will improve it and use it (that is if the member countries will submit to electoral supervision by their peers when it is called for), offers some hope—the greatest hope perhaps—that the high political, economic, and social aims they proclaim will be achieved. Not all Latin American governments will agree that supervision is desirable, and no government should be obliged to accept supervision. But those who do accept it may take pride in their action.

Supervision can never be a cure-all of course. Democratically elected governments do not always act democratically. They can be as tyrannical as nonelected governments. And tyrannical elected governments can be reelected. A majority may continue to vote for a tyrant or a myth, as it did in Perón's Argentina. Or, if tyranny persists and chaos threatens, disaffected citizens or groups may conclude that they cannot wait for elections. When that occurs the OAS's peace-keeping role will be put to a severe test.

17
THE ISSUE OF DEMOCRACY

ON MARCH 6, 1866, Secretary of State William H. Seward, responding to a request from the United States minister to Peru that the United States extend recognition to a new government the military had set up, informed the minister that "the policy of the United States is settled upon the principle that revolutions in republican states ought not be accepted until the people have adopted them by organic law, with the solemnities which would seem sufficient to guarantee their stability and permanency." The minister replied that "should the United States wait until Peru is governed by organic law, in fact as well as in name . . . it will . . . be a far distant day before our country is represented at all in Peru." A week later the secretary, presumably after reflection, authorized the minister to extend recognition to the new government.[1]

Nevertheless political weakness and political failure in Latin America continued to create problems for the United States. They opened the door to mischief-making by extracontinental powers. They were a threat to the security of the Panama Canal. It was political failure that provoked the United States into intervening and cast it in the unwelcome role of international "strong man." Over the years a number of devices were tried in the hope of bringing about stable, democratic government, particularly in the turbulent Central American and Caribbean areas. Under pressure from the United States the Central American republics, first in 1907 and again in 1923, agreed to deny recognition to regimes that came into power in any of the five countries through a coup d'etat or revolution against a recognized government so long as the freely elected representatives of the people had not constitutionally reorganized the country. But the effort to promote democracy failed. It ended in 1936 when it became evident that its effect was less to reduce revolution than to prolong dictatorship.[2]

DEMOCRACY AND INTERVENTION

President Kennedy experimented with denying both recognition and aid to the military government that seized power in Peru in 1962, but he succeeded only in alienating the politically powerful armed forces in that country. In 1969, when Richard Nixon became president, most Latin American governments were dictatorships. In his report to the Congress of February 25, 1971, the president said:

> The United States has a strong political interest in maintaining cooperation with our neighbors regardless of their domestic viewpoints. We have a clear preference for free and democratic processes. But it is not our mission to try to provide—except by example—the answers to such questions for other sovereign nations. We deal with governments as they are. Our relations depend not on their internal structures or their social systems but on actions which affect us and the inter-American system.

What Mr. Nixon said sounded new to many persons, but in fact he was restating the policy that had guided the United States during most of its history. His position was consonant with the numerous commitments to nonintervention made by the United States and the other American republics. In pledging to leave Latin America's politics to the Latin Americans the United States was standing on principle. It also was trying to avoid the criticism that it always attracted when it intervened. But Mr. Nixon's statement revived criticism from those Americans who still thought the United States *should* intervene in Latin America, not with troops necessarily but in other ways that were open to it.

Some Americans thought the United States should deny recognition to governments that came into power by force (few of those persons were aware of the failure of that policy in Central America). Others thought the United States should maintain relations with such governments but that it should treat them differently from the way it treated democratic, constitutional governments; that it should embrace the constitutional president but offer only a handshake to the dictator. One problem with such a policy, of course, was that there were very few embraceable presidents left in Latin America. By embracing only them the United States would make enemies of all the rest.

Another problem was the difficulty of defining "democratic" and "constitutional." Was a president who gained office in a rigged election more democratic and constitutional than one who achieved power through the direct application of force? And how could the United States determine which elections were rigged? The charge that elections were rigged was made almost automatically in most Latin American countries; it was a normal part of the electoral process. In any event did the United States have the right to make such a determination, and if it did make it would it be doing the Latin Americans a favor? Wasn't democracy a home-grown plant, and wouldn't any attempt by a foreign government to implant it in Latin America do more harm than good? These were a few of the questions that arose in connection with any effort by the United States government to set itself up as judge of Latin America's politics.

When the United States began to extend large-scale aid to Latin America pressure on it to bring about political improvement in the area increased. The idea of granting aid to dictators was repugnant to many Americans. They regarded such aid as equivalent to "supporting" dictatorship. The fact that aid was directed at helping people and that people usually could be reached only through governments made little impression on such persons; unless Washington was "against" a dictator it was "for" him, they thought.

Among Washington's instruments for "promoting" democracy was the Central Intelligence Agency (CIA). When it became known, in 1954, that the CIA had helped to overthrow the procommunist Arbenz regime in Guatemala, Communists and other extreme leftists, and many moderates as well, criticized the operation, but on the whole criticism was subdued. Many persons in the United States and throughout the rest of the free world took pride in the success of the operation; many Latin Americans who criticized it publicly applauded it privately. After all it was well known that Communist countries intervened systematically, almost as a matter of right, in order to advance their interests. Why, such persons asked, should not the United States intervene as an act of self-defense?

The CIA's Bay of Pigs operation, aimed at overthrowing the Castro regime in Cuba, was a disastrous failure, and, in part for that reason, criticism of it also was comparatively moderate. In the mid-1970s, however, congressional investigations in the United States revealed, among other things, that CIA agents had been in contact with the persons who assassinated the dictator, Rafael Leonidas Trujillo, in the Dominican Republic; that they had plotted to assassinate Fidel Castro; and that they had tried to influence Chile's politics before and during the Allende administration. There was little reason to believe that the CIA's actions had been responsible for developments in any of the countries, but they were widely condemned, inside the United States as well as abroad, and they gave rise to a spate of charges that the agency had engaged in numerous other acts of intervention. United States prestige, and its ability to foster democracy or even to defend its own good name, declined precipitously.

In Latin America, meanwhile, there was no longer any pretense that most governments were democratic. Except in Cuba even the dictatorships continued to profess allegiance to the democratic ideal, but many of them were searching for new forms, and even new definitions of democracy. Within the OAS the democratic ideal had been subordinated to "a plurality of ideologies," which of course could open the door to inclusion of Castro's Marxism-Leninism. Within the United Nations Cuba had already been readmitted to the Latin American caucus.

HUMAN RIGHTS: RHETORIC AND REALITY

Democracy was no longer an issue in inter-American affairs. Replacing it was the broader issue of human rights. An odd feature of the new issue was the degree to which Communist and other Marxist governments throughout the world became leading proponents of human rights—not in their own countries of course, but in Latin America. Marxist interest became acute after the Chilean military forces had overthrown the Socialist-Communist government of Salvador Allende. The new Chilean regime became a principal target of the international Marxists—and also of the United States Congress.

Subversion in Chile. In 1970, when Allende became president, the Chilean military had one of the longest and best records of support of democratic government of Latin America's armed forces (I am omitting Mexico where the military are a powerful interest group within the country's essentially one-party political system). It was only after Allende had engaged in gross violations of civil rights of citizens and foreigners alike; after he had jettisoned the country's free economy; after the Supreme Court had announced that he had "destroyed Chile's juridical system" and the Chamber of Deputies had concluded that his regime had "tried to grasp total power with the evident intention of . . . setting up a totalitarian system," that the military overthrew him.

Although the armed forces had plainly decided to end the Socialist-Communist threat to Chile's political, social, and economic system, they were also acting in self-defense. Sergio Ramos, a member of the Technical Committee of the Chilean Communist Party and political advisor to President Allende, said in a paper, "Chile, an Economy of Transition?" published in March, 1972: "The conquest of political power is achieved necessarily through the destruction of the standing army and the police, as instruments of repression in the service of the bourgeoisie and against the proletariat."

Allende had set up a paramilitary system, a kind of parallel army under his personal control. It was supplied with arms brought in secretly from Cuba and stored in "safe houses" that ringed Santiago (some were stored in one of Allende's several residences). Some thousands of Cubans and other foreign leftists, many of them prepared to engage in guerrilla warfare if the need should arise, were in the country. The military moved quickly to dismantle this extralegal apparatus and their methods were far from gentle.

Following Allende's overthrow the OAS Commission on Human Rights, with the consent of the new regime, conducted an on-the-spot investigation of charges that government agents had engaged in torture and other violations of human rights. Hundreds of Chileans appeared before the commission and testified freely against the government and its agents. The commission, while recognizing the special circumstances that had existed, reached the conclusion that extremely serious violations of human rights had occurred. The international media gave wide publicity to the report. In contrast they gave little or no publicity to the report of the OAS Special Consultative Committee on Security, which documented many of the Allende regime's offenses.

Although it was clear from Allende's own words and acts that his purpose had been to destroy Chile's democracy, he was praised as a democratic martyr, while the armed forces, with an excellent record of support of democratic government, were condemned as enemies of democracy. The US Congress reacted by prohibiting military aid, and limiting economic aid, to Chile. But that was only the beginning of a larger effort by the Congress to withhold aid from governments which, in its view, had committed human rights violations. The case of Argentina became another cause célèbre.

Tyranny in Argentina. Salvador Allende, soon after his inauguration, had said, "I am not the president of all the Chileans." So far as we know Juan Domingo Perón never made a statement of that kind, but although he was elected to the presidency three times by a majority vote he clearly did not regard himself as president of all the Argentines. Allende failed in his effort to establish a tyranny of the minority in Chile. Perón succeeded in imposing a tyranny of the majority in Argentina. During his first presidency he packed the courts, closed non-Peronist newspapers, and persecuted politicians, intellectuals, students, and other non-Peronistas who had incurred his wrath. Perón set new records for corruption and reduced Argentina's economy to a shambles before he was ousted by the military in September 1955.

Perón died in July 1974 after having served less than a year of his third term. He was succeeded by his widow, María Estela Martinez de Perón, a former dancer who was also vice-president. Terrorism, which Perón had incited when he was out of office, had become endemic. After inflation had reached 1,000 percent, and effective government had ceased to exist, the armed forces, in March 1976, took over the government by force.

The new regime substantially reduced terrorism, but at the cost of some thousands of lives. Many of those lives had been taken by government agents or supporters. But they were taken in what had become an undeclared civil war. To place total blame on the new government was a vast oversimplification, and to punish it was an injustice to the Argentine people. Nevertheless the United States Congress did punish it as it had already punished the Chilean government.

Human Rights and President Carter. The Congress's action in punishing human rights violators and alleged violators had considerable popular support in the United States (what American does not favor promoting human rights?), and it became a crusade when President Jimmy Carter, soon after his inauguration, undertook his own campaign to enforce respect for human rights throughout the world. He signed the 1969 American Convention on Human Rights, which was broad enough to include not only such things as freedom from cruel, inhuman or degrading treatment but also freedom to take part in government—a freedom that was restricted, to say the least, by most Latin American governments, including many that had ratified the convention.

The Congress not only supported the president's campaign; it went far beyond his wishes. Legislators who were eager to punish human rights violators, or alleged violators, by cutting off aid, were joined by others who opposed aid in principle, or had become disillusioned with it in practice and were happy to see it reduced or even eliminated. The Congress threatened to withhold or oppose aid of all kinds, military and economic, bilateral and multilateral, to governments whose acts or failures to act in the rights field it did not approve, and it did withhold aid to a number of them. It became questionable that a significant foreign aid program could survive in the new moralistic atmosphere of Washington.

The Congress held public hearings in Washington and invited Latin American governments whose deportment it was investigating to send representatives to testify (the governments indignantly rejected the invitations). It required the administration to report to it on the status of human rights in the countries the administration wished to extend aid to, and then released the reports to the press. Countries complained bitterly of intervention in their internal affairs. Some target governments angrily renounced further aid from the United States. Brazil, whose soldiers had fought shoulder to shoulder with Americans in World War II, cancelled all five of its military agreements with the United States.*

It was not the loss of aid that the governments most resented; it was being labelled pariahs by a friend, or former friend, and ally. That was damaging not only to their pride and sense of fairness but also to their international credit.

*US naval and air bases in northern Brazil played an important part in the Allied invasion of North Africa. A Brazilian expeditionary force of 26,000 men joined Americans and British in the hard-fought Italian campaign; some 500 Brazilians died.

At the same time that President Carter and the Congress were denouncing human rights violations and alleged violations by authoritarian Latin American governments, they were also denouncing rights violations in totalitarian Soviet Russia. Latin Americans who were criticized quite naturally felt that they were being placed in the same category as that systematic rights violator. And the fact that the United States was exempting countries it considered were of "strategic importance" to it (Iran for example) from sanctions for human rights violations led Latin Americans to accuse it of hypocrisy. They considered it still another example of the little importance the United States gave to Latin America.

History and Human Rights. What surprised many observers was Washington's failure, in its judgments of Latin America, to take into account the historical factor or even to give evidence that it was aware of it. There were undoubtedly violations of human rights, many of them serious. There always had been violations, unfortunately, and there were probably more of them now. In the United States itself Senate investigators had revealed that many violations of human rights had occurred without the knowledge of citizens or of most government leaders. In Latin America protection of human rights was infinitely more difficult to achieve, in part for historical reasons.

One could not judge the Pinochet regime in Chile without taking into account the Allende regime that preceded it. The country's gravest problems were created by that regime. They were problems the United States had been largely spared, and was therefore ill fitted to appraise. Similarly one could not judge the Videla regime in Argentina without taking into account the problems it had inherited from the Perón regimes, or the problems of the Uruguayan government without recalling the infamous Tupamaros who had helped to undermine the country's democracy. The runaway inflation that had taken place in the three countries was quite enough to bring about political, economic, and social chaos, with their accompaniment of terrorism and other lawlessness, and it did help to bring them about. But Washington appeared to give no importance to those earlier factors. It was as though nothing had happened in the world before the United States discovered the human rights issue.

President Wilson had wanted not only to "teach Latin Americans to elect good men," but to make the whole world "safe for democracy."

Sixty years later there was less democracy in Latin America (and probably in the world) than there had been in Wilson's time, and now another American president, and an American Congress as well, were trying to change a large part of the world. They were accusing an increasing number of Latin American governments of violating a range of human rights so broad that it was difficult to know what the term excluded.

Ironically the principal targets of the American crusade were the very nations that were trying hardest to restore conditions favorable to respect for human rights. Persons who have worked in the international world know that only in capitalist countries are human rights respected and real democracy practiced, yet the governments against which the United States was discriminating included those of Chile, Argentina, and others that were making great efforts to rebuild free economies after anticapitalist regimes had brought the countries to political and economic chaos or near-chaos. At the same time, oddly enough, the United States was praising and continuing aid to may socialist countries throughout the world where violations of human rights had been institutionalized. And criticism of that notorious violator of human rights, Communist Cuba, with which the United States established informal but direct diplomatic relations on September 1, 1977, was for a long period strangely muted.

Some Latin Americans were suggesting that the United States had succeeded in doing what Bolívar had been unable to do: unite Latin America. The pity was that this new found unity was being directed against the United States. While the administration and the Congress basked in an aura of self-righteousness a majority of Latin American governments were developing an antagonism toward the United States and a conviction that the United States was an undependable helper and ally, that might take years of conventional diplomacy to overcome. Nor was it clear that the cause of human rights was being furthered.

The human rights program was an example less of diplomacy than of antidiplomacy; a continuation of domestic politics by other means. Latin American political leaders who sought and needed our friendship, and whose friendship we sought and needed, had long feared the United States less because they believed that we intended to do them harm—few believed that—than because they were aware of our enormous power to do them harm even though we wished not to. In the opinion of many leaders the human rights program amply justified such fears.

THE UNITED STATES AND THE BISHOPS

While the United States was accusing Latin American governments of violating human rights of their citizens, and was imposing sanctions on them for alleged violations, Latin America's Catholic bishops, with equally unhelpful results, were accusing the United States of violating the rights of those same citizens by impeding economic and social development in the area. Although Pope John Paul II had spoken to the 1979 Puebla meeting of bishops in unmistakably anti-Marxist terms, the bishops had barely ended their meeting when they addressed a message to the peoples of Latin America in which they said, among other things:

> The civilization of love rejects subjection to a dependence which is prejudicial to Latin America's dignity. We do not accept the condition of satellite of any country of the world, or of any ideology. We wish to live fraternally with all peoples, because we repudiate narrow nationalism. It is time for Latin America to warn the developed countries not to immobilize us, not to impede our progress, not to exploit us, but rather to help us with magnanimity to overcome the barriers of our underdevelopment, respecting our culture, our principles, our natural resources.

That is a political, not a religious statement. Most of it is directed against the United States, Latin America's closest and most powerful neighbor, and its principal trading partner. All of it conforms to Marxist doctrine.

Marxists and other "anti-imperialists" complain of what they refer to as Latin America's financial, technological, and—in general—economic "dependence" on the more-developed nations, of foreign control of Latin America's principal means of production, of Latin America's role as supplier of raw materials and as market for manufactured goods, of exploitation of Latin America by the "imperialistic" countries, of Latin America as a dependent element in the "imperialist" system. The bishops have joined them in their complaint.

No one would suspect from reading the bishops' message that whereas early Spanish and Portuguese imperialists did in effect rob their American colonies of precious metals, the American copper mining companies in Chile, before a Socialist-Communist regime confiscated their properties, had supplied that country with 60 percent of its foreign exchange and had paid as much as 80 percent of their earnings to the Chilean government in direct taxes. No one would suspect that the United Fruit Company had left seven new dollars in Latin America for every dollar it remitted abroad, or that Sears, Roebuck and Company had contributed much more to Latin America than it had taken out of it. Nor would one suspect that the United States government had carried out in Latin America the most extensive program of economic aid ever carried out by a government in any area of the world. A reading of the bishop's statement would not suggest that Latin American countries are so far from being satellites of the United States that while the United States itself is enjoined by treaties and public opinion (in the United States as well as in Latin America) from intervening in Latin America even in support of freedom, Cuba, a Latin American country, is free to intervene in countries and even in continents of its choosing in support of Russian imperialism.

Perhaps the bishops, or most of them, do not know those things. But if they are determined to make statements on nonreligious matters—statements that have great political and economic (and even military) significance to Latin America and to the rest of the world—it would be well that they learned these and many other things they give evidence of ignoring. Churchmen have an awesome power to destabilize Latin America. Unfortunately their power to restore or create stability and to promote prosperity is extremely limited. In Argentina the Catholic hierarchy supported the candidacy of Juan Domingo Perón, but as president Perón established new records for demagoguery and corruption. His followers burned Catholic churches in Buenos Aires, and Perón himself bequeathed political, economic, and social problems that have taken thousands of lives and will continue to plague the country for years to come. In Peru the military group that overthrew the freely elected government of Fernando Belaunde Terry in 1968, and promised to promote social justice in the country, had the Church's enthusiastic support. But eleven years later the military, although promising elections, were still in power, the country was in dire economic straits, there were more poor than there ever had been, and the Church was powerless to alter the situation.

CARTELS AND INTERDEPENDENCE

By the mid-1970s it was beginning to appear that any special relationship the Latin Americans now had was more with other countries of the Third World than with the United States, and that any special relationship the Latin American members of OPEC had was more with other members of OPEC than with the United States or even with other Latin American countries.

The world had changed remarkably in only a few years. The modern world had been molded by free peoples who worked within a competitive economic system. But it seemed to many that in the new world of OPEC freedom and competition were being cancelled; that compulsion and monopoly were taking their place.

The Arab countries' use of oil as a political as well as an economic weapon gave concern to many nations. The knowledge that governments now controlled the supply of oil to the free world, and were trying to gain control over supplies of other vital materials, took on new importance. When companies competed with one another results were apt to be lowered prices and improved products. Even when they joined together to establish cartels (a practice prohibited or restricted by the laws of the United States and some other countries), the worst that one might expect was somewhat higher prices and somewhat inferior products. When governments were the active parties, on the other hand, results could be quite different. Competition among governments for high economic stakes could lead to war among the competitors. Government price fixing—the kind of price fixing the OPEC countries had engaged in—could also lead to war, between exporters and importers in that case, or even between the superpowers.* Or it might lead to disruption so widespread that it would differ little from war in some of its effects.

*Secretary of State Kissinger, in reply to a question from a journalist concerning the Arab oil embargo, said, "It is one thing to use [force] in the case of a dispute over price, it's another where there's some actual strangulation of the industrialized world" (*Washington Post,* January 5, 1975, p. B5).

The Common Interest. The nineteenth-century imperialists believed that industrial countries should control their sources of raw materials. Short of a worldwide cataclysm it is unlikely that imperialism of that type can be revived today. What, then, is the alternative? How can *all* nations, industrialized or not, have access to adequate supplies of the food, the materials, and the services they require? That needs an answer. But the answer is elusive.

Yet it is clearer than ever that the world is interdependent. Even the United States, which has preached interdependence for many years, has failed to understand how nearly complete it is. It has taken OPEC, which Venezuela helped to form, to bring that out adequately. And Latin America has taken other initiatives that have had important effects—in supplying the Third World with an ideology, for instance, and in pressing for change in the law of the seas. And of course Fidel Castro's adventuring in Africa has made him a world actor. No wonder there is speculation concerning how far and in what new directions Latin Americans are going to lead.

The United States is far from approving all of Latin America's initiatives in the international field. But its ability, and frequently its will, to influence developments is limited. Nor is it clear how far Washington should go in urging its views. What is quite clear is that the United States and Latin America continue to be joined together not only by geography and history but, more importantly, by common interest. They have an experience of cooperation that both need to continue. Even past mistakes can be helpful. Most of those mistakes have been made not out of a desire to ignore or evade problems but in efforts to solve them, and they hold lessons that ought not to be lost. Cooperation may not be possible in all circumstances, and when practiced it may fail to bring about the results being sought. But it is evident to those who look beyond today's needs and desires that no other policy can succeed.

Epilogue: NICARAGUA

THE UNITED STATES AND THE SOMOZAS

THE SOMOZA dynasty in Nicaragua, which lasted forty-two years, has an important place in US–Latin American relations. It illustrates the kinds of problems Americans encounter, and indeed may help to create, when they try to alter institutions in other countries, or to create institutions where none have existed—that is, when they try to change people.

There is a saying in Nicaragua that no one leaves the country with his reputation improved. In 1927 the United States intervened in Nicaragua, and it was badly scarred in the process. It arranged a peace between warring factions and organized a "nonpartisan" *Guardia Nacional* that it hoped would maintain the peace after its forces had left. Forty-six years after the intervention had ended charges continued to be leveled at the United States. Nicaragua had lapsed into old habits but now it was the United States that was to blame. Or so the Somozas' critics, and much of the international media, claimed.

There were two principal charges: (1) The United States had put the first Somoza in power. The usual phrasing was "The marines put Somoza in power." Even the American press stated that repeatedly without contradiction. (2) The Americans had maintained the Somoza dynasty in power. Neither charge is true, although there is a shadow of truth in both of them. But it has no more substance than any shadow has.

Concerning the first charge, a problem that had to be faced in 1932, when the marines were preparing to evacuate Nicaragua, was how to select the Nicaraguans who would replace the American Guardia commander and other senior American officers following the marines' departure. The intervention had been relatively brief and no graduates of the fledgling military academy had attained field rank. Nicaragua's two political parties were barely on speaking terms. President Moncada, a Liberal, had threatened to shoot former president Emiliano Chamorro, who was now the Conservative vice-presidential candidate, on sight. The two finally met at an American Legation dinner especially arranged to bring about a reconciliation between them, but even that had its crisis, and in any case one dinner was far from making them friends. It fell to General Calvin B. Matthews, a marine officer of impeccable fairness who commanded the Guardia, to work out a procedure for selecting the new officers. The candidates endorsed the procedure prior to the elections and Anastasio ("Tacho") Somoza Garcia was selected Guardia commander under that procedure.

The candidates also promised to preserve the nonpartisan character of the Guardia, and they signed an agreement to that effect in the presence of the American minister, Matthew E. Hanna, who signed as witness.

Neither Matthews nor Hanna determined who the new Guardia commander was to be. Matthews was a mere technician in the process, Hanna no more than a witness in a different though related process.

Although the Americans had not placed Somoza in command of the Guardia I am not suggesting that they were not pleased at his appointment; they were. Tacho had had a long association with the United States. He had studied in Philadelphia. His English was colloquial, although his slang was a little out of date (he thought "twenty-three skidoo" was still the latest thing). He had served Henry L. Stimson, who in 1932 was secretary of state, as interpreter when Stimson, as President Coolidge's personal mediator, had visited Nicaragua and brought an end to the civil war. Mr. Stimson liked Tacho.

As undersecretary of foreign relations in President Moncada's government Tacho had been fair and friendly in his dealings with the United States. Minister Hanna was genuinely fond of him. He was pleased at Tacho's appointment.

Newly elected President Sacasa, on the other hand, although he knew Tacho well (Mrs. Somoza was Sacasa's neice), and had accepted him as Guardia commander, never quite trusted him. Nor would he probably have completely trusted any other person who was named. He was quite aware of the political power the Guardia would have with the Americans gone. In Nicaragua power had always come out of the muzzle of a gun, and now Tacho held the gun. The president also recognized that Somoza was an effective political leader. Sacasa himself, a medical doctor, had little taste for politics. He had become president out of a sense of duty and he was not happy in the role. Somoza, in contrast, had a passion for politics and a talent for it. Conflict between the two was in the cards. On June 6, 1936, after many months of dispute and confrontation with Somoza, Sacasa resigned his office. In December Tacho was elected president. The Somoza family were to hold power, in or out of the presidency, until 1979.

The second charge—that the United States kept the Somoza dynasty in power—is equally ill-founded, although some of the reasons for it are evident. It was not the United States but the supposedly nonpartisan Guardia that kept the Somozas in power, and the Somozas assured that it did by commanding it themselves. The United States gave assistance to the Guardia after the marines had left; but except when Nicaragua was supporting the Bay of Pigs operation against Castro's Cuba, it was the same kind of assistance it was giving to the armed forces of other Latin American countries. The assistance undoubtedly exceeded Nicaragua's needs. The nonpartisan police force that the Guardia was intended principally to be grew into a powerful and partisan army. But that was merely one more example of the tendency of United States programs (domestic as well as foreign) to go to extremes, with the result that effects might be quite different from the ones sought. There was no intention, no effort, to keep the Somoza dynasty in power, nor did the Somozas probably need US assistance to remain in power. Even without military assistance, or with a minimum of assistance, they probably could have maintained their authority. And naturally any effort by the United States to prevent their remaining in power would have been correctly criticized as United States intervention in Nicaragua's internal affairs.

There is no doubt, on the other hand, that the United States gave the impression, to many Nicaraguans as well as to the international media, that it was on the Somozas's side, not only because of the military assistance it gave them but by the ostentatious friendship of some of its ambassadors toward them. Representing the politically powerful US government in a dictator-ridden country is not an easy task of course. If the ambassador does not get along with the dictator he may be considered a failure. If he does get along with him he may be considered a "supporter," even an accomplice. Some of our ambassadors filled their posts admirably. Others, political appointees in every case, were regarded with some justice as Somoza toadies. It was hard at times to avoid the impression that the United States was supporting the Somozas even though in Washington's view it was treating Nicaragua no differently from the way it treated other friendly Latin American countries.

Tacho and Sandino. It is easy for me to be objective concerning such notorious dictators as Rafael Leonidas Trujillo and Juan Domingo Perón, whom I never knew. I never dealt with either of them as a young Foreign Service officer, as I did with Tacho when he was undersecretary of foreign affairs. I never entertained them in my home, as I did Luis, Tacho's son, the second of the dynasty who, it should be noted in passing, was no tyrant. Nor did I know either of them when he was a child as I knew Anastasio Somoza Debayle ("Tachito"), Tacho's second son and the last of the dynasty. Even now, when Tacho and Tachito are widely and justly condemned as greedy tyrants, it is difficult for me not to remember them as I knew them years ago. Of course even then I knew that Tacho was *mañoso*; that he was on the clever, even cunning, side. But let us be frank: in Nicaragua's society a degree of *maña* might be a requisite to survival. Nicaraguans were not Groton graduates, nor are they today. In the United States Tacho might have become a respected senator. More likely he would have become a wealthy businessman. In Nicaragua politics was the quickest road to wealth.

There are two principal characters in Nicaragua's modern tragedy. One is Tacho; the other is Augusto César Sandino. Both lost their lives by assassination. Sandino was assassinated by Guardia members at Somoza's order; Somoza was assassinated by Rigoberto Lopez Pérez, described by Father Miguel D'Escoto, who was to become Nicaragua's foreign minister in 1979, as "a patriotic young poet who attempted to liberate his country by a means which did violence to his sensitive soul and ensured his own death."[1] Sandino is a popular hero; he is all white. Tacho is a villain, all black. But history is rarely that simple.

Sandino, like Somoza, had formidable political talent. He aroused sympathy for his movement in Nicaragua and also abroad. It often occurred to me that there were more Sandino sympathizers in Argentina and the United States than in Nicaragua itself. Sandino was an originator of modern guerrilla warfare. He conducted it with consummate skill and demonstrated its usefulness against much larger forces. He never succeeded in holding much territory but he denied control of vast territories to the Nicaraguan government. Sandino also was an originator of modern terrorism. He terrorized the mountainous north until there was no employment for peasants, and then he recruited the peasants. One of his principal lieutenants, Pedrón Altamirano, had his own *corte de chaleco* (vest cut) which he applied to prisoners he wished to get rid of. It involved torturing the prisoner, then cutting off his arms and finally his head. Pedrón designed the *corte de chaleco* for use on marines and Guardia, but he did not hesitate to apply it to peasants who were not sufficiently respectful to him.

Only a few weeks after the marines had left Nicaragua and Tacho had become Guardia commander, Sandino agreed to lay down his arms, but not all of them. He was permitted to retain sufficient weapons to equip one hundred men who would preserve order in the Coco River Valley, far distant from Managua and difficult of access, where his followers could live on public lands and engage in agriculture. The government would pay the upkeep of the armed force for a year, after which its status would be reviewed. The "peace" he had signed had been wrung from a distraught president against the Guardia's wishes, and it was highly favorable to Sandino. It had given him a principality of his own, and an army of his own the size and armament of which the government was unable, and not even disposed, to monitor (no one believed he had turned in all his weapons).

Sandino's aim was not to get rid of the Americans; they had already departed. As it had been from the beginning it was to take over the Nicaraguan government. To do that he would have to destroy, neutralize, or take over command of the Guardia.

At the end of the first year, when the status of Sandino's armed force was to be reviewed, Sandino refused to give up any of his arms. On the contrary he offered to protect President Sacasa from the "unconstitutional" Guardia. The president, instead of forcing Sandino to disarm, invited him to come to Managua to parley. The agreement that was reached was decidedly in Sandino's favor. On February 21, 1934, minutes after Sandino had left the presidential palace, a Guardia patrol assassinated him.[2]

Without condoning assassination, there are strong reasons to believe that if Tacho had opposed eliminating Sandino he, Tacho, would have been in danger of assassination, as much by his own Guardia officers as by Sandino. Those officers, wise in Nicaragua's politics, indeed close to the heart of it although the Guardia was supposed to be nonpartisan, had ample reason to fear that the Guardia's survival, and perhaps their own, required Sandino's disappearance. If all this sounds like gangsterism, please remember that Nicaragua's politics bore a striking resemblance to gangsterism. And it will be a novelty in Nicaragua's history if it does not bear the same resemblance in the future.

Tachito. I served in Managua from 1929 to 1933. I next visited it in 1971. The only cities that had changed as much during my absence were Panama and Madrid. And all the changes one could see were good.

In addition to the primitive Gran Hotel that had somehow survived the 1931 earthquake, there was a new and modern hotel that would have graced any capital city in the world. Tall buildings were becoming common in the business section. The number of small, modern homes had increased noticeably. There was a new suburb with American-style houses that would have cost $50,000 or more in the United States (in 1971 dollars, that is).

There was no country club in Managua in 1933. There was a primitive golf course that a few Americans had hacked out on the side of La Loma, the hill on which the presidential mansion stands, and only a handful of us played on it. In 1971 I lunched at a country club on the edge of the city. The clubhouse was ample and elegant. The maître d'hôtel was an American; the food was excellent. The greens on the golf course were manicured. I was told that a share in the club cost $1,000 and that there were 1,200 members.

I drove to Casa Colorada, an old haunt of mine in the nearby mountains. The well-paved highway that led to it was lined with substantial homes. It was obvious that Managua's tiny middle class of 1933 had become sizable and affluent. A substantial middle class had not brought democracy to Nicaragua. Nevertheless it constituted an important step in that direction. Without a substantial middle class democracy could not exist.

Much of what I saw in Managua in 1971 was destroyed in the 1972 earthquake. Much of what was left was destroyed in the civil war of 1979. How much of the middle class would survive remained to be seen.

While I was in Managua I called on Tachito. I asked him how he reacted to the charge that he had used his office to enrich himself. He said he did not react; to react would be to give greater currency to the charge. He said the charge was being made by Communists (it was indeed being made by the international Communists; Castro, in particular, had never forgiven President Luis Somoza's cooperation with the CIA in the ill-fated Bay of Pigs venture; but the charge was being made correctly by others too). Tachito said the Somoza fortune was not his; it belonged to the Somoza family. Nor were the Somozas the richest family in Nicaragua; there were two or three richer families (he did not name them). He acknowledged that the Somozas owned many businesses, but he said that some of them were losing money and that all of them helped Nicaragua; many of them would not exist if the Somozas had not created them. (One of Tachito's critics whom I talked to later said that, indeed, some of Tachito's businesses lost money; that Tachito was not a very good manager. That was far from saying that he was in the business of losing money.)

Tachito maintained that there was freedom in Nicaragua; that the constitution was being respected (it had also been manipulated); that elections were fair (I did not ask him whether votes were honestly counted). He said the press was free; Pedro Joaquin Chamorro's *La Prensa* attacked him on a daily basis (a reading of *La Prensa* confirmed that; the same *La Prensa* had attacked the freely elected Moncada government on a daily basis when I was serving in Managua). He maintained, quite correctly, that attacks such as Chamorro's would have brought imprisonment in many Latin American countries (Chamorro's assassination in 1978 hastened Tachito's downfall). Tachito said that many Latin American governments throttled the press and still were immune from criticism in the United States (there was truth in that).

I asked Tachito how his relations with the United States were (the American ambassador at the time was being severely criticized, even by members of his staff, for being excessively intimate with Tachito). He said the trouble with the United States was that it applied American standards to Latin America. If Americans saw a peasant living in a thatched hut that cost him nothing, they wanted him to live in a cement house that the peasant could not afford and the economy could not provide. He said that Nicaragua, with a rapidly growing population, had been more or less forced into the modern world, and that there would be poverty until the country had a modern economy, which the Somoza family was helping to build (it owned a large portion of it as Tachito cheerfully admitted).

I asked Tachito if there could be a peaceful transition from the Somoza dynasty. He said there could be, but that the Somoza family would continue to be important (I understood him to mean that the Somozas would continue to be in charge).

We also talked of other things. Tachito was relaxed and communicative. But without laying claim to any special prevision I could not help wondering whether I was talking to the last of the dynasty. Tachito, still young, was nevertheless an anachronism. His kind of dictatorship was out of fashion. Not because it was harsh; other dictatorships in Latin America were equally harsh or harsher. It was vulnerable largely because the Somoza family had become immensely rich while in power, and it had been in power much too long.

And it had become rich not only by building factories that Nicaragua doubtless needed but also by acquiring lands that growing numbers of Nicaraguans needed and believed they had a right to possess. Under the Somoza dynasty a substantial middle class had developed, but the gap between the few who were increasingly rich and the masses who were impoverished, whose plight the "modern economy" often seemed to exacerbate, had grown. In that sense Managua was a microcosm of Latin America.

NICARAGUA AND THE UNITED STATES

If Latin America's hope for peace and democracy depended on an effective OAS there was little to encourage that hope in mid-1979. The Marxist-oriented Frente Sandinista de Liberación Nacional was leading a rebellion against Nicaragua's Somoza regime and had the support not only of the country's Marxists and a high percentage of its non-Marxists, but also of Fidel Castro's Cuba and Omar Torrijos's Panama and a few other Latin American governments as well (it had the support of the Palestine Liberation Organization too). Democratic Costa Rica was permitting its territory to be used as an anti-Somoza military base. Great numbers of men, equipped for battle, were filtering across the Costa Rican border into Nicaragua. No Central American government, subjected to such internal and external attack, could survive.

Those foreign interventions in Nicaragua's internal affairs were fraught with danger to peace and freedom in the hemisphere. The Somoza dictatorship had violated human rights; it had been a trying neighbor to Costa Rica; and it was generally repudiated not only by the international Marxists and the international media but also by leftist and some moderate regimes in Latin America. Nevertheless if Castro and Torrijos, dictators themselves, and the former a declared and effective enemy of freedom and democracy, could intervene in Nicaragua they could also intervene in other Latin American countries, including Costa Rica, their fortuitous ally. Years earlier Castro had intervened in Latin America, but with little success. As a surrogate for Soviet Russia, however, he had shown a disturbing ability to promote communism in Africa. If he were unchecked his power to influence events in Latin America might, it was evident, become very great. And the possibility that in Nicaragua itself Somoza's overthrow would lead to a Castro-like government was in the minds of many, including some who were helping to overthrow Somoza.

Still the OAS, whose members were pledged not to intervene in one another's internal affairs, was unable to deal effectively with the Nicaraguan crisis. It declined even to vote on President Somoza's request that, under the terms of the Inter-American Treaty of Reciprocal Assistance, it send military observers to the Nicaragua—Costa Rica border. It rejected a United States proposal that called for the cessation of arms shipments to Nicaragua, the formation of a government of national reconciliation, and the establishment of an inter-American peace presence (a euphemism for a military presence), if needed, to assist in maintaining order during the political crisis. Many members regarded the suggested peace presence as a new effort by the United States to intervene in Nicaragua's internal affairs. More accurately, perhaps, they feared the power of leftist groups within their countries who would inevitably charge that it represented such an effort.

Finally, on June 23, 1979, the OAS approved, by a minimal vote of seventeen members, a resolution that declared the solution of the Nicaraguan problem to be exclusively within the jurisdiction of the people of Nicaragua. After saying that, however, the resolution went on to call for the immediate and definitive replacement of the Somoza regime and the establishment of a truly democratic government (which Nicaragua, in its long history, had never been able to achieve). Reverting to its original position it then warned member states that they should scrupulously respect the principle of nonintervention in Nicaragua's internal affairs. States that were intervening approved the resolution more readily than some that were refraining from intervention.

This caricature of a resolution failed to indicate how the contradictory aims it proclaimed could be attained. The members of a divided and irresolute OAS remained divided, each on its own. The concept of collective security embodied in the OAS Charter and the Inter-American Treaty of Reciprocal Assistance, which in theory had replaced unilateral United States intervention, remained a concept. It was far from being a reality.

In those circumstances the United States, which for generations had borne the burden of maintaining peace in Central America, embarked on its own effort to prevent the Nicaraguan crisis from engulfing all the Central American countries, and perhaps others as well. With the cooperation of Nicaragua's neighbors and the Andean Pact countries it obtained President Somoza's agreement to relinquish power, and on July 19 Somoza fled to the United States. His Guardia Nacional was disbanded. Many of its members fled the country or found asylum in foreign embassies. Many others were imprisoned, to await investigation and possible trial as war criminals.

The Frente Sandinista de Liberación Nacional held total power in the new Government of National Reconciliation, and it could be counted on to retain it, at least until a permanent regime was set up, a process that Sandinista leaders indicated would take a number of years. And within the Frente Sandinista Marxist influence was powerful, and in all likelihood dominant. Nevertheless, it might not be as easy to impose Marxism in Nicaragua as it had been to impose communism in Cuba. In Cuba Castro was all-powerful. His victory had been a personal one. He owed nothing to any group. He delivered Cuba over to communism almost without resistance by Cubans. In Nicaragua, on the other hand, non-Marxists had played an important role in the revolution's success. They might have a voice in the country's future.

Sandinista leaders, including Marxists in high positions, said they wanted good relations with the United States (the new government already had close relations with Cuba, which was sending doctors and teachers, all of them doubtless practicing Communists, to Nicaragua). They even talked of securing arms in the United States. Whether that represented a policy or a tactic it was too early to know. There was no doubt that the United States, on its part, hoped for a Nicaragua with which it could live; a Nicaragua that would be a force for peace in Central America. The United States supplied Nicaragua with great quantities of food and other relief supplies; it was preparing to contribute to reconstruction in the country.

At the same time one could not ignore the danger that a Marxist dictatorship, by its very nature antifreedom and antidemocratic, would emerge. In the light of Nicaragua's history the alternative almost surely would be another non-Marxist dictatorship. But Marxists already occupied the key positions in the new government, and Marxists do not willingly give up power.

There was also a danger that Marxism would spread beyond Nicaragua. Given the weakness of most Latin American regimes, and the ease with which Marxists attract outside support that is denied to non-Marxists, that might readily occur. The destruction of the Guardia, on the pattern of Castro's destruction of the Cuban army, and the possibility that it would be replaced by a Marxist army, were causing acute concern in other Central American countries, particularly in El Salvador and Guatemala, which had long been under Marxist attack.

Marxism also threatened to spread in the Caribbean. Fidel Castro already exerted more influence over some newly independent Caribbean states than the United States did. A Marxist Caribbean plus a Marxist Central America would threaten not only the United States and the Panama Canal but also the continent as a whole. Before that could come about, OAS members would have another opportunity to close ranks and defend themselves; to make it impossible for Marxists and their sympathizers to pick countries off one by one without resistance from the hemisphere at large. And that kind of OAS might also be depended on to make a more positive contribution by supervising national elections when requested. Stable, democratic government still constituted the best guarantee of peace.

On the other hand, should the OAS fail to meet its obligations; should governments continue to violate their commitment not to intervene; should collective security prove to be just another hemispheric myth; then the United States would be freed of its own nonintervention commitment. It is not a corollary to nonintervention that others should be permitted to intervene freely. At a time when Argentina, Brazil, Uruguay, Chile, Bolivia, Peru, and Ecuador were struggling against great odds to restore democracy the hemisphere could ill afford to permit Marxism to be imposed in Central America or the Caribbean. The United States might find itself intervening, possibly in the company of like-minded Latin American governments, in the legitimate exercise of self-defense.

Joining with Latin American countries in such an enterprise would meet with strong criticism (and also with high praise) in the United States as well as in many other countries, not only because of doctrinaire opposition to American intervention but because, given the scarcity of practicing democracies in Latin America, some governments that might be willing to cooperate would already have been the objects of as much, and in some cases more, criticism for violations of human rights than the Somoza regime; and because some of them would have been subjected to United States sanctions for those violations or alleged volations. Nevertheless, the United States might decide that in the real world of which it is a part it had to work with the material at hand; that after all the bad, or what some had labeled bad, was preferable to the worse.

And there is another possibility; that the United States, after much soul-searching and with great reluctance, might intervene alone.

Then again, the American republics, the United States included, might decide to do nothing. That would be the most dangerous of all the possible courses.

Notes

CHAPTER 1

1. Miguel de Unamuno, *The Life of Don Quixote and Sancho*, trans. Homer P. Earle (New York: Alfred A. Knopf, 1927), p. 5.

2. *Encyclopedia Britannica* 1960, s. v. "Spain," p. 122.

3. Stanley J. and Barbara H. Stein, *The Colonial Heritage of Latin America* (New York: Oxford University Press, 1970), p. 32.

4. Ibid., p. 22.

5. Carl W. Degler, *Neither Black nor White* (New York: Macmillan, 1971), p. 138.

6. See especially Thomas E. Skidmore, *Black into White: Race and Nationality in Brazilian Thought* (New York: Oxford University Press, 1974), pp. 207–18.

7. Hubert Herring, *A History of Latin America from the Beginnings to the Present*, 3rd ed. (New York: Alfred A. Knopf, 1968), p. 96.

8. Preston E. James, *Latin America*, 4th ed. (Indianapolis: Odyssey Press, 1942), p. 709.

CHAPTER 2

1. Herring, *Latin America*, p. 214.

2. Stein and Stein, *The Colonial Heritage*, pp. 4–7.

3. Ibid., p. 9.

4. Ibid., p. 4.

5. Ibid., pp. 126–37.

6. Herring, *Latin America*, p. 277.

CHAPTER 3

1. Merle Kling, "Violence and Politics in Latin America," in *Conflict and Violence in Latin American Politics*, ed. Francisco José Moreno and Barbara Mitrani

(New York: Thomas Y. Crowell, 1971), pp. 221–22.

2. Kalman H. Silvert, *The Conflict Society* (New Orleans: Hauser Press, 1961), p. 20.

3. Eliseo Vivas, "The Spanish Heritage," in *Conflict and Violence*, ed. Moreno and Mitrani, pp. 8–9.

4. I was ambassador to Paraguay at the time and witnessed these events.

CHAPTER 4

1. U.S. Congress, Senate, Committee on Foreign Relations, *Hearings on Defense Department Sponsored Foreign Affairs Research*, 90th Cong., 2d sess., May 9, 1968, p. 34.

2. Ibid.

3. My comments on war colleges are based on experience as deputy commandant of the National War College, on reading, and on visits to several war colleges in Latin America and conversations with their administrators, faculties, and students.

CHAPTER 5

1. Geoffrey Barraclough, *An Introduction to Contemporary History* (New York: Basic Books, 1964), p. 47.

2. Ibid., p. 54.

3. Ibid., p. 155.

4. Herring, *Latin America*, pp. 904–5.

5. *Foreign Relations of the United States*, 1895 (Olney to Bayard, July 20, 1895).

6. Dana G. Munro, *Intervention and Dollar Diplomacy in the Caribbean, 1900–1921* (Princeton, NJ: Princeton University Press, 1964), pp. 43–60.

7. Quoted in Monro, *Intervention and Dollar Diplomacy*, p. 77.

8. Ibid., p. 110.

9. Thomas A. Bailey, *A Diplomatic History of the American People*, 8th ed. (New York: Appleton-Century-Crofts, 1969), p. 488.

10. *Papers Relating to the Foreign Relations of the United States, 1925*, vol. 2 (Washington, DC: US Government Printing Office, 1940), p. 337.

11. Ibid., *1935*, vol. 4, pp. 878–79.

12. Víctor Alba, *Nationalism Without Nations* (New York: Frederick A. Praeger, 1968), p. 86.

13. Bryce Wood, *The Making of the Good Neighbor Policy* (New York: Columbia University Press, 1961), p. 300.

CHAPTER 6

1. Hans Kohn, *Nationalism*, rev. ed. (Princeton: Van Nostrand, 1965), p. 9.
2. *Nationalism, a Religion* (New York: Macmillan, 1960), pp. 96–97.
3. Quoted in John J. Johnson, *Simón Bolívar and Spanish American Independence 1788–1830* (Princeton: Van Nostrand, 1968), pp. 137–39.
4. W. Raymond Duncan and James Nelson Goodsell, eds., *The Quest for Change in Latin America* (New York: Oxford University Press, 1970), p. 13.
5. Ibid., p. 15.
6. John J. Johnson, "The New Latin American Nationalism," in *Government and Politics in Latin America*, ed. Peter G. Snow, (New York: Holt, Rinehart and Winston, 1967), p. 454.

CHAPTER 7

1. Luis E. Aguilar, "Marx and Engels on Latin America," in *Marxism in Latin America*, ed. Luis E. Aguilar (New York: Alfred A. Knopf, 1968), pp. 64–67.
2. For an excellent discussion of this subject see John P. Powelson, *Latin America: Today's Economic and Social Revolution* (New York: McGraw-Hill, 1964), pp. 11–31.
3. "The Unofficial Russia," in *Encounter*, February 1974, p. 17.
4. Quoted in Gottfried Haberler, "Marxist Economics in Retrospect and Prospect," in *Marxist Ideology in the Contemporary World—Its Appeals, and Paradoxes*, ed. Milorad M. Drachkovitch, (New York: Frederick A. Praeger, 1966), p. 123.
5. Second General Conference of Latin American Bishops, *The Church in the Present-Day Transformation of Latin America in the Light of the Council, II. Conclusions* (Washington: US Catholic Conference, Division for Latin America, 1973), p. 45.
6. Ibid., p. 111.
7. Camilo Torres, *Revolutionary Writings* (New York: Herder and Herder, 1969), cited in *The Roman Catholic Church in Modern Latin America*, ed. Karl M. Schmitt (New York: Alfred A. Knopf, 1972), p. 142–43.
8. Helder Pessoa Cámara, "Is Violence the Only Option?" in *Models of Political Change in Latin America*, ed. Paul E. Sigmund (New York: Praeger, 1970), p. 150.
9. Ivan Illich, "The Seamy Side of Charity," ibid., p. 156. Originally published in *America*, January 21, 1967, pp. 88–91.
10. Introduction to Richard Millett, *Guardians of the Dynasty* (Maryknoll, NY: Orbis Books, 1977), p. 13.

CHAPTER 8

1. Preston E. James, *Latin America*, 4th ed. (Indianapolis: Odyssey Press, 1942), pp. 845–48.

2. Ibid., p. 851.

CHAPTER 9

1. Institute of Latin American Studies, *Development Problems in Latin America: An Analysis by the Economic Commission for Latin America*, with a foreword by Carlos Quintana (Austin, Texas: University of Texas Press, for the Institute, 1970).

2. John Pincus, *Trade, Aid and Development* (New York: McGraw-Hill, 1967), p. 164.

3. Ibid., pp. 132–33.

4. Ibid., p. 353.

CHAPTER 10

1. Lincoln Gordon, *A New Deal for Latin America: The Alliance for Progress* (Cambridge: Harvard University Press, 1963), p. 84.

2. Inter-American Development Bank, *Economic and Social Progress in Latin America: Annual Report 1975*, p. 108; ibid., 1976, p. 111.

3. Ibid., *Economic and Social Progress in Latin America*, 1976, p. 101.

4. Ibid., p. 108.

CHAPTER 11

1. For a detailed treatment of this subject see Rodolfo Stavenhagen, ed., *Agrarian Problems and Peasant Movements in Latin America* (Garden City: Anchor Books, Doubleday and Company, Inc., 1970), particularly Solon Barraclough and Arthur L. Domike, "Agrarian Structure in Seven Latin American Countries," pp. 41–94.

2. Frank Tannenbaum, "The Future of Democracy in Latin America," *Foreign Affairs*, April 1955, pp. 429–44.

3. Munro, *Intervention and Dollar Diplomacy*, p. 19.

4. Barraclough and Domike, "Agrarian Structure," p. 87.

CHAPTER 12

1. Wood, *Good Neighbor Policy*, p. 169.
2. Ibid., pp. 168–71.
3. Ibid., p. 178.
4. Ibid., p. 203.
5. Richard N. Goodwin, "Letter from Peru," *The New Yorker*, May 17, 1969, pp. 42–45.
6. Charles T. Goodsell, *American Corporations and Peruvian Politics* (Cambridge: Harvard University Press, 1974), p. 53.
7. Ibid., pp. 121–22.
8. Ibid., p. 143.
9. Ibid., pp. 143–44.
10. Powelson, *Latin America*, p. 153.
11. Wood, *Good Neighbor Policy*, pp. 262–63.
12. Ibid., pp. 277–78.
13. Rómulo Betancourt, "Recurso energetico que no tiene igual," *Vision* 40, no. 3 (February 12, 1972), pp. 22–31.

CHAPTER 13

1. *Chile Economic News* (New York), November 1975 (no. 56/D), p. 7.
2. Pincus, *Trade, Aid and Development*, pp. 342–43.
3. Stacy May and Galo Plaza, *The United Fruit Company in Latin America* National Planning Association Series on US Business Performance Abroad, no. 7 (n.p.: The Association, 1958), pp. 229–31.
4. Letter to author dated December 27, 1971, from office of Mr. Kenneth O. Page, Sears, Roebuck and Company, Skokie, Illinois.
5. Charles C. Cumberland, *Mexico: The Struggle for* Modernity (New York: Oxford University Press, 1968), pp. 141–42.
6. Goodsell, *American Corporations and Peruvian Politics*, pp. 49–50.
7. Barend A. de Vries, "Unemployment and Poverty—What Remedies Are Feasible?", *Finance and Development*, March 1972, p. 11.

CHAPTER 14

1. Theodore H. White, *In Search of History: A Personal Adventure* (New York: Harper and Row, 1978), p. 316.

2. For President Nixon's own version of the incidents see Richard M. Nixon, *Six Crises* (New York: Pyramid Books, 1968), pp. 195–252.

3. Douglass Cater, "The Lesson of Punta del Este," *The Reporter* (March 1962), p. 22.

4. *Inter-American Development Bank, Proceedings, Fourteenth Meeting of the Board of Governors* (Kingston, Jamaica: May 1973), p. 100.

CHAPTER 15

1. See, especially, Donella H. Meadows et al., *The Limits to Growth: A Report for The Club of Rome's Project on the Predicament of Mankind* (New York: Universe Books, 1972).

2. Octavio Paz, *The Other Mexico: Critique of the Pyramid,* trans. Lysander Kemp (New York: Grove Press, 1972).

CHAPTER 16

1. Bailey, *A Diplomatic History of the American People*, p. 408.

2. *The Department of State Bulletin* 74, no. 1916 (March 15, 1976), pp. 315–16.

3. Ibid., p. 314.

CHAPTER 17

1. *The Department of State Bulletin* 71, no. 1847 (November 18, 1974), p. 685.

2. Memorandum by the assistant chief of the Division of Latin American Affairs (Beaulac), 18 February 1936, "Recommendation That American Policy in Central America No Longer Be Affected by Any Provision of the Central American Treaty of Peace and Amity of 1923," *Foreign Relations of the United States, Diplomatic Papers, 1936*, vol. 5, *The American Republics* (Washington, DC: US Government Printing Office, 1954), p. 136.

EPILOGUE

1. Millett, *Guardians of the Dynasty*, p. 7.

2. Ibid., p. 260.

Glossary

Words translated are Spanish unless otherwise noted.

Altiplano	High plain
Bandeirantes (Port.)	Pioneers (lit., “flagbearers”)
Brazil (Port.)	Dyewood
Caballero	Knight or cavalier; gentleman
Cabildo	Municipal council
Cabildo abierto	Council meeting (i.e., of citizens and councillors)
Callampa	Shantytown
Caudillo	Boss, natural leader
Caudillismo	Bossism, leadership cult
Colonizador	Colonist
Comunidad	Commune (Indian)
Conquistador	Conqueror, empire builder
El deseado	The people’s choice (lit., “the desired one”)
Donatario	Rccipicnt of land grant
Ejido	Communal (Indian) village
Ejidatario	Inhabitant of an *ejido*
Encomienda	Patronage (over Indians); the colonist granted an *encomienda* had the right to tax certain Indians and the obligation to Christianize them
Favela (Port.)	Shantytown
Fazenda (Port.)	Plantation
Fazendeiro (Port.)	Planter, plantation owner

Hacienda	Large farm or ranch
Justicialismo	Ideology of the Justicialista Party (Argentina)
Latifundio	Large estate
Latifundista	Owner of large estate
Minifundio	Small estate
Minifundista	Owner of small estate, smallholder
Pampa	Prairie
Patrón	Protector, or "boss"
Peninsular	A Latin American born in peninsular Spain
Reducción	Mission village
Repartimiento	Forced labor
Villa miseria	Shantytown

Index

Latin America
MEXICO
GULF OF MEXICO
Rio Grande
Mexico City
Havana
CUBA
Cienfuegos
JAMAICA
Kingston
HAITI
Port-au-Prince
DOMINICAN REPUBLIC
Santo Domingo
Puerto Rico
CARIBBEAN SEA
NORTH ATLANTIC OCEAN
BR. HOND.
Belmopán
GUATEMALA
Guatemala City
HONDURAS
Tegucigalpa
San Salvador
EL SALVADOR
NICARAGUA
Managua
COSTA RICA
San José
Panamá
PANAMA
Caracas
VENEZUELA
Port-of-Spain
TRINIDAD & TOBAGO
GUYANA
Georgetown
SURINAM
Paramaribo
FRENCH GUIANA
Cayenne
Rio Orinoco
Bogotá
COLOMBIA
Quito
ECUADOR
GALÁPAGOS IS.
Manaus
Amazon
Belém
B R A Z I L
Recife
Rio São Francisco
Salvador
PERU
Lima
La Paz
BOLIVIA
Brasília
PACIFIC OCEAN
Antofagasta
PARAGUAY
Asunción
São Paulo
Rio de Janeiro
EASTER I.
ARGENTINA
Rio Paraná
Pôrto Alegre
Valparaiso
Santiago
Rosario
Buenos Aires
URUGUAY
Montevideo
CHILE
SOUTH ATLANTIC OCEAN
FALKLAND IS.
BOUNDARY REPRESENTATION IS NOT NECESSARILY AUTHORITATIVE
105
90
75
60
45
30
15
0

500334 4-71